THE DRAMATIC RADIANCE OF NUMBER

Selected Plays of Jay Wright, Volume 1

Kenning Editions / *Every house has a door* 2022

ISBN: 978-1-7343176-8-8
LCCN: 2021949778

Will Daddario, project editor

Cover design: Crisis
Interior design: Cory Rockliff

Cover art: Antelope dance headdress Chi Wara, male Minianka type, Bambara

Published in Chicago by Kenning Editions and *Every house has a door*

Distributed by Small Press Distribution in Berkeley, California: Spdbooks.org

This book was made possible in part by the subscribers and supporters of Kenning Editions.

Every house has a door gratefully acknowledges support for this publication by The MacArthur Funds for Art and Culture at the Richard H. Driehaus Foundation, and the generosity of individual donors.

Kenningeditions.com
Everyhousehasadoor.org

PASSAGE

CHARACTERS   Bursach

Chalana

Pierre ⟷ Francis ⟷ Malachi

Agnes ⟷ Margaret

[BURSACH, *a tall, indescribable man, wearing a tattered Breton red sweater, a gray poncho, thick winter trousers and boots, enters. He pulls a cigar, prepares it, lights up. He addresses his presumed audience.*]

BURSACH: January was too damned cold in Vermont. You couldn't smoke a cigar outside. Not that I'm complaining. But listen, do you know that you can't even bury people in January, in Vermont. I don't want to get started on the wrong foot. You see I'm in disguise. The fuckers can't get used to my accent. *Ni hablar.* This morning sits easy with me. I came upon this idea of the three-particle universe, where I had been searching that book of evidence I had been reading for the metaphysics of John the Scot. This all led me to that perfect understanding of how I came to be here without being referred to. Well, it was an extraordinary insight because it just went along with what I had been saying to Francisco Hernández.

[CHALANA, *a small beautiful woman, elegantly dressed in a cashmere pullover, turtleneck, gray woolen slacks and light boots, appears.*]

CHALANA: Another digression.

BURSACH: You didn't let me finish.

CHALANA: Go on.

BURSACH: Didn't I tell you the story of the time when Paco and I…?

CHALANA: I don't want to hear about that dog.

BURSACH: Well, I realize you don't like his poetry that much…

CHALANA: I didn't know he wrote poetry. Are we talking about our Paco?

BURSACH: Which one? I think you've got my Paco confused with the one we put down.

CHALANA: I didn't put him down. He went off to Canada. With his wife. The one who helped me to discover the scorpion in the kitchen in Xalapa.

BURSACH: That's not the Paco I'm talking about. I'm talking about the one who has proposed the solitude of the cube.

CHALANA: Yes.

BURSACH: I'm not getting it right. How shall I propose it now? "*Soledad al cubo.*" The guy didn't make it easy for us. This pissing about making a labyrinth for a cube. I get the resonance. But, *ya, hombre.*

CHALANA: You? Are complaining about someone making reading difficult? I think I'm going to have to lie down. This Paco has got you upset.

BURSACH: I don't mean that.

CHALANA: *Mais, tu as lu?*

BURSACH: That's not the point. It's the theory of it I'm dealing with now.

CHALANA: Ah, the theory. The one that rode over here with John.

BURSACH: Damn, I started off the day in good shape. But, hell, I don't even know if I want to finish this cigar.

CHALANA: I'll take it.

BURSACH: What?

CHALANA: The cigar. It's still winter in Vermont, Bursach. I can't have you filthying up your room.

BURSACH: Here. I've lost my appetite for it. Now, there's an interesting proposition. What if the universe were as expendable as that cigar?

CHALANA: You're talking nonsense. What, have you become one of our atelier versifiers, with your little gimmick—the universe as an expended, expendable, expansible cigar? Oh, I can see you'd get some heat out of that one. But it's heat we're talking about, aren't we? Or is that cat piss that has the room thirty degrees above normal?

BURSACH: You're talking about my profession, now.

CHALANA: What, neutering cats?

BURSACH: Can't I get up one day, and feel the celebratory power of poetry, without feeling foolish?

CHALANA: Wait, I have to check the clock. Today is today. And wasn't it yesterday—let's see, it must have been, was it nine?, yes, it was none...? What am I talking about? That was the day before, when you referred to your being referred to, and thereby repudiated poetry. You will have to explain to me how the physics of John Duns Scotus led you to this pass.

BURSACH: I will, you'll see. Give it up. I have given it up. I quit hanging out on 126th and Eighth Avenue a long time ago.

CHALANA: Judgment. That sounds like a judgment to me.

BURSACH: There was a German who preceded me.

CHALANA: So? In what?

BURSACH: I could go through the history of poetry...

CHALANA: Whose poetry? What would John the Scot say?

BURSACH: I thought you knew. You accused me of judgment, some assertion of truth. What would he say? "All the attributes of being are virtually included in being and in those things that come under being." How is that? I'm not losing everything. No, sir, I can remember some things, things that make sense.

CHALANA: Then maybe I can call upon you.

BURSACH: And...?

CHALANA: Don't worry. You won't have to cross the street.

BURSACH: Oh, my chorus master, everybody believes that I don't leave the room unless you hold my hand.

CHALANA: Forget that. This is serious business now. Wait. [*She goes out, comes back with a chair.*] Come over here. Do me a favor. I want you to sit here, and watch that house.

BURSACH: Watch the house?

CHALANA: I want you to watch the woman in that house, and tell me I see what I'm seeing.

BURSACH: What do you see?

CHALANA: I want you to see what you see.

BURSACH: I have to have some framework. All perception…

CHALANA: Another theory. If you had been watching just now, instead of contemplating your theory button, you'd have seen what I'm talking about. There it is again.

BURSACH: There's what again?

CHALANA: Sit down in the chair. Just lend me your eyes.

BURSACH: My eyes are yours.

CHALANA: I know.

BURSACH: If I'm to sit here, spying on people, shouldn't I be in disguise?

CHALANA: You are in disguise.

BURSACH: I mean to myself. Nobody out there can see me, so they can't know I'm in disguise. You say I'm in disguise. But I need a disguise that speaks to this new role I've taken on. Something that says I'm somebody else. You know what I mean?

CHALANA: Wait. [*She goes out, comes back with a long, bright red scarf.*] Here.

BURSACH: A red scarf? Who am I supposed to be?

CHALANA: If I told you that, where's the disguise?

BURSACH: All right, all right. I'm in the chair. I have on my red scarf. I'm watching the house. I have my instructions. No, I don't have my instructions. What are my instructions?

CHALANA: Watch the house. And tell me what you see.

BURSACH: Are you going to stand there?

CHALANA: No. It was just that the scarf reminded me of someone. The way you're wearing it.

BURSACH: A little unconscious borrowing. Who was it?

CHALANA: You didn't know this person.

BURSACH: I see.

CHALANA: Not at all. Because you didn't know this person.

BURSACH: I saw movement over there. You know, this reminds me of sitting on our porch in Albuquerque, New Mexico, watching the sun set and the pigeons coming to roost on the old Fred Harvey's at the train station. God help me, I feel guilty about it now. I took too much pleasure in those gardens. I never understood them. I never knew what they cost my life. This is silly. This red scarf. Sunsets. People who loved my wife, and disappeared. What were we talking about?

CHALANA: The garden.

BURSACH: That's right. The garden. I wish I had your care for gardens. I'm stupid. Inattentive, I can't remember what was there. Certainly, there were the willows, and juniper, and quaking aspen. They were the breeze; they were the shade. And there were lilacs and roses and rhododendron, and I'll swear there was birchleaf buckthorn and blue violet, and a strange little thing called a balloon flower. That might not be the garden I saw, but one I wanted. Did I say wanted? Hey, you don't think a little colored boy from the other side of the tracks could have anything to say about gardens in the great Fred Harvey's yard, do you? No, that's fantasy. I've just told you a lie.

CHALANA: Something new.

BURSACH: You've got used to me now.

CHALANA: Yes, I have.

BURSACH: Good. After all, you keep your little secrets.

CHALANA: I do not.

BURSACH: I remind you of the house across the street, and this little disguise.

CHALANA: Oh, don't be so theatrical.

BURSACH: Am I to take this seriously?

CHALANA: Give me the scarf. Get out of the chair.

BURSACH: I want to do this now.

CHALANA: Do what? You can't even make up your mind about what you want to do.

BURSACH: I see.

CHALANA: I didn't mean what you thought you heard. You know perfectly well what you want to do. But you are right. You have been inattentive. Or you would have noticed that I've sold our car.

BURSACH: That's impossible.

CHALANA: Where is it?

BURSACH: God, if I know.

CHALANA: Ah ha, you don't know.

BURSACH: All right, it's gone. Why?

CHALANA: We don't need it. It's just an expense.

BURSACH: I thought you liked the car.

CHALANA: I do.

BURSACH: You said it was easy to drive. You talked about the design.

CHALANA: I did.

BURSACH: Then why the hell did you sell it?

CHALANA: Let's not talk about it. Don't pretend that you care the car is gone.

BURSACH: No, I guess I won't pretend that I care the car is gone. It was yours. It never really involved me.

CHALANA: There you go. So now you'll forget it.

BURSACH: I feel sorry for you.

CHALANA: Why?

BURSACH: We're sitting here, and little by little the world is being taken away.

CHALANA: Nonsense. What makes you say that? I don't like to hear you talk this way. I got rid of a useless car. I sold a few dishes. Oh, I know you didn't notice. But we're comfortable now.

BURSACH: Comfortable. [*He sits in the chair.*] Give me the scarf. Leave me alone. Go. I'll do what you want. Watch the house.

CHALANA: Good. [*She starts to leave.*]

BURSACH: Don't you have anything else to tell me?

CHALANA: No. You will tell me what you see?

BURSACH: I will.

[CHALANA *leaves.*]

Have I lost everybody's trust?

[*A small, dapper man, wearing a homburg, enters with a small table and a stool.*]

PIERRE: I presume you could use some company.

BURSACH: You. You are not there. You are not going to disturb me. You see I'm on a mission.

PIERRE: A mission. What the fuck you mean, a mission?

BURSACH: Don't swear.

PIERRE: You? Telling me not to swear.

BURSACH: Show me some respect.

PIERRE: I do.

BURSACH: Do I know you?

PIERRE: If you're like the other motherfuckers, you think you do. Don't swear. I call myself Pierre. At least this time. At least for now.

BURSACH: You put it that way, it must mean you have a true name.

PIERRE: A real name. Like yours.

BURSACH: Well, yeah, like mine.

PIERRE: You've got a good woman.

BURSACH: Glad you approve. But there's still this little matter of your true name.

PIERRE: Pierre.

BURSACH: Okay. That'll do. You turn up here, looking right at home. No explanation. Got your little homburg on. You seem to know what I'm doing. But look at you. What am I to understand here, brother?

PIERRE: I could tell you why the car's gone.

BURSACH: Oh?

PIERRE: I could even tell you why you had to put the scarf on. But I don't concern myself with stating the obvious. How 'bout a hand of rummy? Hearts. Poker. Ever what suits you.

BURSACH: You said that like my father.

PIERRE: Just a mark of the times.

BURSACH: What times?

PIERRE: Times I knew your father.

BURSACH: You did not know my father.

PIERRE: Oh, I see. You figured me out. Only, if I take off my hat and you see my kinky head, what you go'n say?

BURSACH: Have some respect for yourself.

PIERRE: I do. So you see I give myself a new name, a new occupation, and set myself a good service I could perform for a soul in heat. Here. Let me set up here beside you. You can still keep your eye on the house, and we can have entertainment and some conversation.

BURSACH: You going to take off that hat?

PIERRE: Not yet. [*He deals the cards.*] You spent some time in Scotland. Right?

BURSACH: How do you know that?

PIERRE: Never mind. I remember it as a gray landscape, a whore house, with cats walking around with shaved heads and razors.

BURSACH: That's shit. That's got nothing to do with the place.

PIERRE: So you deny your eyes?

BURSACH: I deny having you tell me what I experienced.

PIERRE: The experience wasn't yours. You were a guest in the galaxy, a moon without an orbit.

BURSACH: Hey, listen…

PIERRE: Keep your eye on the house across the road. Do something for once that makes sense. Oh, he's offended. But keep your eyes on my hands. This situation is a bitch, ain't it? You got the house, you got me. You say the world is being taken away little by little. What does John the Scot say?

BURSACH: Get up. Get out. Who the fuck are you? Why do I have to suffer you?

PIERRE: Why not? I'm offering you consolation, my man. Don't you read me? Don't you see me? Look over there. Goddamn, you missed it. I'm disappointed in you, Bursach. You can't seem to hold things together. Where is your imagination?

BURSACH: Chalana!

PIERRE: She can't help you.

BURSACH: Chalana!

PIERRE: Stand up for yourself.

[CHALANA *enters.*]

CHALANA: I was just putting the spaghetti on. What's he doing here?

BURSACH: You know him?

CHALANA: Of course. Why shouldn't I? He still owes me for the fish heads. Is that why you're here, sir? To make restitution for the fish heads?

BURSACH: When was this?

CHALANA: You remember, we had just moved to Boston. A little place just off the South End. We'd have been better off in Roxbury, or Jamaica Plain. But, no, this little real estate broker told us we'd be murdered in our beds. So we ended up with the roaches and the noisy traffic down by South End.

BURSACH: I've never seen this guy.

CHALANA: What do you mean you've never seen him? How could you forget this dandy?

BURSACH: He claims to know me from Scotland.

CHALANA: That's possible.

BURSACH: Well, speak up, my man. Why do you keep following us around?

CHALANA: You won't get a thing out of him. Look at him. He won't speak. He does this. Give him a few minutes, he'll disappear. I hope, Bursach, you're not counting on him for anything.

BURSACH: He was helping me in my vigil.

CHALANA: You didn't tell him!

BURSACH: Tell him what? What you see is what you see. He walked in here as though he belonged here. He started reading me my life.

CHALANA: Yes. He'll talk to you. But since that time he hasn't spoken to me.

[PIERRE *begins to remove his clothes, to change his posture and attitude, until he is transformed into a more forlorn figure. He confronts* BURSACH.]

PIERRE: Surely, brother, you recognize me now. I am your happy self.

> *"Y era la muerte, al hombro la cuchilla,*
> *el paso largo, torva y esquelética."*

BURSACH: You. Was it you? There, in the Parque Alameda? There was a rambling bookstore right at the edge of the park, just before you stepped over to Bellas Artes. I had that book. It was evening. I had a lovely *comida corriente* at a small place on the corner of Juárez and Dr. Mora. The light was going, and I had just closed the book.

CHALANA: Oh, he's got you going.

BURSACH: Who? Who? We're not talking about the same man.

CHALANA: I don't believe you. Don't you see what he's doing?

BURSACH: This is my friend, Pierre. Aren't you my friend Pierre?

PIERRE: Who is this Pierre?

BURSACH: That's what I said before. I said, he's just testing me to see if

I recognize him. To see if I want to recognize him is what I should say. Sure, I understand that.

PIERRE: You fucker. I was cold and hungry. I was miserable. You had a book.

CHALANA: Where was I? Why were you alone?

BURSACH: You were in Oaxaca, or on your way. We had gone over the ground. I remember the singing frog. We were on the only bus there was, second class. The heat of the darkest night was as intense as midday. We sheltered each other through the high banana groves. The boatlike sway of the bus threw us closer together. It was lovely to hold your gentle head on my shoulder. I felt the peace in your body.

CHALANA: And after that, you exiled me to Oaxaca?

BURSACH: No, madame, I am devilishly confused. I was amiss in the city.

PIERRE: I tell you I was miserable.

BURSACH: Yes, you told me! I recognized you. Oh, now he will come on with his other name. His other disguise. You're right, Chalana. This man is untrustworthy.

PIERRE: Oh, what a pleasure of renunciation. Listen to him. Listen to the two of you. Why were you alone?, indeed. Exile, indeed. I lived during that disappearance. You follow me? Whatever you brought to the city disappeared with your inattention. You belong, my man, to stream beds, caves, to darkness and to certain stones. Do you want me here? I mean now. I came at your request.

CHALANA: You can't let him stay here, Bursach. He lies.

BURSACH: I tell you, he knew me. He knew...No, no, no. Hey, I get you now. You do this. You almost had me believing that I had been referred to. Slick. Sweet. I can't be humiliated anymore.

PIERRE: How extravagant. I? Humiliate you? Why should you use such a word? I get it. Your help cometh from the woman. Tell me your name again, sister.

CHALANA: *Mirabile dictu*. This idiot has addressed me. Do you want the name you abused when you robbed and abandoned us? You know my name.

PIERRE: Stop it. This assault. What am I, some bird pecking around your yard, looking for pig shit? I'm here now. I came because you wanted me. Do you have any use for me, sir? If not, send me home. I don't need to be here swimming in the rancid oil of your confusion.

CHALANA: Leave.

PIERRE: I want to hear it from him.

BURSACH: Bam! Damn. Yes. I'd let you go. But you owe me an explanation.

PIERRE: Please.

BURSACH: Ah, how delicate the man is. Beyond explanation. So right. Beyond justification. Absolutely. I'm foolish. Believe me, sir. I admit it. There I sat, wherever it was, reading misery, and I had the idea that the misery was my own. And here you are again, bearing gifts. Now I see that all along the way I missed my confirmation. Go. Go. What can I do for you?

PIERRE: I'll just take my things.

BURSACH: Don't you touch a thing.

PIERRE: Well. [*To* CHALANA.] Just family. Right, sister? All goodbyes ain't gone. [*He leaves.*]

CHALANA: Are you all right?

BURSACH: I feel like shit.

CHALANA: Why do you let this happen?

BURSACH: Let what happen? I don't know what you're talking about.

CHALANA: You're the one, you know. You have to be responsible for yourself. No, I put that the wrong way. You have to be responsible to yourself.

BURSACH: He just turned up.

CHALANA: He has nothing to do with you. You say you don't want this old gang around. You're finished. You owe your allegiance to John the Scot. I turn around, and there you are, playing cards, having a drink, a cigar, really carrying on.

BURSACH: It wasn't as elaborate as that.

CHALANA: You called me. Why?

BURSACH: I was cold and hungry.

[CHALANA *starts off.*]

Don't go. I was afraid. We were coming too near a celebration I thought I had put behind me. I wanted it to end. And then you came. It should have ended. But the festivity simply changed its clothes.

CHALANA: Do you want to stop?

BURSACH: Stop?

CHALANA: Being my eyes. I've seen enough to make me sure. There's no reason to get you agitated. If you want to stop...

BURSACH: I'm not agitated. I promised you I'd do this. I'll do it. I don't mind.

CHALANA: You're sure?

BURSACH: I haven't been at it for very long. Besides, I'm intrigued.

CHALANA: Well, you might not be so intrigued. But, if you don't mind, I'll leave you to your illumination. [*She leaves.*]

BURSACH: I know why she offered to release me. So I sit here, and wait for some moment to speak to me from across the way. Such faith. Why should anything arise there to astonish me? That can't be the point. I'm sitting here, in my disguise, waiting for something, someone, to come out of the long winter night and terrify me into some joy. Nay, nay. I am inattentive, but, no, I have not seen that unchained imagination Chalana has me spying on. I'll just sit here a while longer. Please her. I can sleep easier, knowing I've performed some little duty.

[*He sits, nods. A young woman, wearing a wedding gown, appears, pauses and disappears. A girl, wearing a light blue dress and carrying a small bouquet, appears and approaches* BURSACH.]

AGNES: She didn't tell you to sleep.

BURSACH: Who said I was sleeping?

AGNES: Then you must have seen the adorable one.

BURSACH: Who are you talking about? Who are you? What is this? Is my place the neighborhood staging area for saints and misfits? Was the door open?

AGNES: As a matter of fact, it was. That was a strange thing to say, about saints.

BURSACH: Don't you get wise about my trafficking in saints.

AGNES: I have no idea what you do with your time. Your scarf is an astonishing red. The color of fire. And speaking of saints, you know that it's the color of martyrs. But, of course, you know that.

BURSACH: Why, my little lady, I'm not sure I know anything that you don't know.

AGNES: You can see to the other side. You wouldn't miss much, if you were attentive. Are you attentive, Bursach?

BURSACH: You're about to tell me that you're my mother, that this is just a dream I've had, and that you don't normally speak this way to us old folk. Don't sustain this torture. Tell me your name.

AGNES: Would it make a difference?

BURSACH: Of course.

AGNES: Then give me one.

BURSACH: Nay, I'll only respond to the one you have taken.

AGNES: Then I'll call myself Agnes. For now.

BURSACH: I'll pretend you've told me the truth.

AGNES: Oh, Bursach. Shameful. You didn't ask me to tell you the truth. You asked for my name.

BURSACH: There you go. Every kid out here is a goddamned diplomat. Begging your pardon, your excellency. I don't know what my greatest offense is, letting my eyes tell me you're a child, or asking you to give up something that keeps your fires burning. So there, I'm finished. You move. I'm busy.

AGNES: They were right, weren't they?

BURSACH: What?

AGNES: They said that you were so unused to society that the only language you had developed was the language of insult.

BURSACH: What crow-gobbling bastard told you that worm-breeding horse draw?

AGNES: Does it matter?

BURSACH: Keep on with this chicken plucking catechism. Hear? You take a look in my eyes. Do I look like the disoriented innocent they, whoever they are, sent you to torture? The adorable one. I'm 'on have to get into that bouquet you're carrying. Chewing or snuffling, it has got to be communicating something very special. Sit down.

AGNES: Make up your mind.

BURSACH: No, you make up your mind. Who is this adorable one? Why does my wife have me here waiting for a fucking visitation?

AGNES: Ask your wife.

BURSACH: No, I want to ask you. You're here.

AGNES: Of course.

BURSACH: There's nothing of course about it. You're here. Answer that. Agnes, I have forgotten who you are. Let's start all over. Shall I introduce myself?

AGNES: If it pleases you.

BURSACH: Well, yes, by god, it will please me, because it will give me a chance to lie. Oh, they didn't tell you that about me? Ha, Agnes, I can see you're a woman after my own heart. You believe that I am always capable of the truth. Notice my delicacy. If I have to call attention to it myself.

AGNES: These moments rarely come, you know. I have to tell you that, when I came in and saw you dozing there, I was disgusted. What *if* there were nothing to see? It wouldn't excuse your behavior. You sat there, becoming a little too comfortable in your duty. Where is the exhilaration? Where is the ecstasy? This is the poet? Oh, god, I had to laugh.

BURSACH: You and the others.

AGNES: Well. I guess I touched a nerve.

BURSACH: I'm a network of injury. This catechism I accused you of, does it matter? There is the injury. You'll have to tell me the names of the flowers in your bouquet.

AGNES: You don't fool me, Bursach. You don't ask questions you haven't already answered.

BURSACH: That's impossible. That attitude—let's not call it thinking—is a thorough misunderstanding of my work.

AGNES: Oh, Bursach. Stand out of the way. There. That's good. I'm calm. I felt a new rhythm taking my body. Oh? You didn't notice?

BURSACH: I see they've prepared you well. They sent you to uncover the joke of my inattention. At some point, they'd say I had turned your blue dress to yellow. I suppose that whatever face I gave you would have been one you had long ago outgrown. Well, I am committed to the attention I have been asked to give. Will you wait here with me? I wonder, though, if I have anything to share.

[PIERRE *and* CHALANA *ride on in a toy engine car and caboose.* PIERRE *has now changed his name to* FRANCIS.]

FRANCIS: You got to get out of the way, or suffer the disruption of your bones.

BURSACH: Pierre, my friend, do you…?

FRANCIS: There's no Pierre here.

CHALANA: Bursach, how could you forget someone who meant so much to you?

BURSACH: Who is this?

FRANCIS: Francis. Who do you think? And I don't submit to Frank, Frankie, Fran, *algo así.* There is a formality in my being that I will damn blue sugar respect. You hear me now.

CHALANA: Tell him, Francis.

FRANCIS: [*Indicating* AGNES.] And this is?

AGNES: [*To* BURSACH.] You didn't tell me the train passed right under this window.

BURSACH: What difference does it make?

FRANCIS: Whoa, that's an ungainly attitude. There is, I acknowledge, a time for skepticism, for an egregious withholding. I've been caught in such a tangle myself. But let us be fair. This is not that time.

AGNES: Oh, he's restoring your powers, Bursach.

FRANCIS: Discerning. *Wie heissen Sie, junges Mädchen?*

AGNES: Agnes.

BURSACH: You did no better than I did, Francis.

FRANCIS: What do you mean?

BURSACH: Her name's not Agnes.

FRANCIS: Well, why not Agnes? Or Hannah? Camilla? Faith? But of course this is Agnes. I recognize her. [*To* AGNES.] Am I not as sharp as I said I was gonna be? Look. I am the soul of generosity. Don't contradict me, sir. We've been in transit for some time now, and we have observed the diminishment of courtesy. But I say, not me. Therefore, I offer you the service of this magnificent engine. Don't be shy, Bursach. Wouldn't you love to get your handles on these handles, and go spooking down the night? Take Agnes. Go. Chalana and I will wait here. You'll have the refreshment of the journey, and we'll have the refreshment of this pause.

BURSACH: You're a joke. What's the matter with you, Chalana? Am I so feeble that I have to believe in this idiot? And this penny machine you've knocked up, all frazzled wires to a past that never happened?

CHALANA: I think you should climb up there, and take off.

BURSACH: What about my duties here?

CHALANA: I'll hold the fort until you get back.

BURSACH: I see. You want to get rid of me.

CHALANA: Yes.

BURSACH: You probably hope I don't come back.

CHALANA: You *could* get lost.

BURSACH: [*Indicating* FRANCIS.] This one would certainly be happy.

FRANCIS: Bursach. The machine is like a heifer. It knows the way home. No more argument, sir. Climb up there. Come on. You, too, Agnes. Make yourself comfortable here. Hold on, I'm about to fire it up.

BURSACH: Ridiculous.

CHALANA: Oh, Bursach, say that it's marvelous. I want you to be happy.

FRANCIS: Boy, the engine has taken to you, Bursach. It's already rolling. Let me get out of the way. Hold your head up, Agnes. You're shining.

[BURSACH *and* AGNES *ride off.*]

I never knew Bursach was so diffident.

CHALANA: There's something I want to take up with you.

FRANCIS: Yes. But first show me the house you talked about.

CHALANA: You know the house. It hasn't changed since you were here.

FRANCIS: That is impossible. Why, I can see already that this window has a different shape. The light enters on a different plane. No, my dear. We have to pin it down. No more speculation. Is that the habitation that concerns you?

CHALANA: [*Sings.*] "I've grown accustomed to your face." Bursach will never recognize you. Pierre. Francis. Different light.

FRANCIS: My mother called me Malachi.

CHALANA: I'm sure.

FRANCIS: Oh. You don't believe me.

CHALANA: I do. Do you believe in Borges?

FRANCIS: I sense a speculative moment arriving by moonlight. Who, or what, is this Borges?

CHALANA: A face on a book. There it is, a twenty-year-old face. His lovers and disinterested enemies could tell you, would tell you, that it is the same blind face of his old age. I wonder what the man who spent so much of his life engaged with mirrors would say. But why shouldn't he acknowledge his infant self? The seed of his being? You're too innocent for me, Malachi. I renounce you. Come back to me when you understand how those random patches in the fabric of space became the face we see. Or how your name modulates into all names. But, no, hold still. I'm not through with you. Why do you torture Bursach with this gauzy thread of your being? Such fucking arrogance. Generosity, indeed. You'll help me, won't you?

FRANCIS: My, my. This is absolutely delicious. First, you kick me in the balls. Then, you claw my reputation, and take away my eyes, disembowel my name, and then mewlingly petition my aid. Damn me, if I use the word pride. Don't pretend I can serve you. But what is it?

CHALANA: There, across the way. Don't tell me you were blind to it. I know what you're saying. You picture me fastened to the wall, watching that shadow. You think I don't sleep, or that my sleep is what I see. No, I am certain that there is a miraculous expression of love that comes, lingers, and asks to be taken in.

FRANCIS: You can see that from here?

CHALANA: Absolutely.

FRANCIS: What has this got to do with Bursach?

CHALANA: Everything.

FRANCIS: Then why am I helping you?

CHALANA: Step by step.

FRANCIS: To where?

CHALANA: So you're like the others. Stand here. But then don't. There it is, the white wedding dress. Well, turn around, Malachi. The dress is made for a maiden. But look at her. I've seen her coming and going. I ask myself, why is she preparing? Then, he shows up. I say to myself, this is not true. I say to myself, we need a garden. We need church bells. What does this mistake mean? There is nothing there that is the case. Do you see what I'm getting at? There is no seed. You say, there's the woman. That other shadow you see is an indubitable relation, a companion to a perfect movement. But why there? Is there some silent third flowing through, or with, the movement? You see I need you, Francis. Your gift for evasion will tutor me.

FRANCIS: Well, that's a compliment. You're living with the most assiduous shape shifter in existence. The man is Gemini, isn't he? But go on. Say. What does my caution teach you?

CHALANA: You call it caution, do you? Yes, well, maybe that's what she calls her rambling. I know. You'd take her side. After all, what is my perspective? But, if you had to watch her, day-by-day, you'd go crazy. Nothing she does adds up. Every little gesture seems so indecisive. I imagine her turning around the same point. She knows I'm here; she has to know. Will she look this way? Oh, no. I know what you're thinking. Give it up. What's she to Hecuba? No, Francis, there is a resolution devoutly to be wished, and I refuse to be deprived of my contemplation.

FRANCIS: My god, I think Chalana thinks she can design her own entrapment. Where the hell is Bursach?

CHALANA: Do I frighten you, Malachi?

FRANCIS: Stop pretending you have the key to me.

CHALANA: I know better.

FRANCIS: Don't think I showed up just to indulge you.

CHALANA: I'd never.

FRANCIS: You know, all things are not true or false.

CHALANA: I did my logic in the south.

FRANCIS: Insult won't advance you. You hear?

CHALANA: Bursach says there are perhaps a half dozen radiant moments in existence. We have to be prepared for them, though there is nothing we can do to induce them. I'll bet you half of yours have slipped away.

FRANCIS: That shows you how much you know. I'm disappointed in you. You rode to this summit with me.

CHALANA: No, you traveled with *me*. Your presence was only probable.

Like hers. Damn it, do you understand the script, sir? I mean the con-figuration of your bones.

FRANCIS: Don't play with me.

CHALANA: There is the play. [*She points to the young woman in the wedding gown who has appeared.*]

FRANCIS: I didn't believe you.

[*The young woman disappears.*]

God help me, she's radiant. I should have known you'd hold something back.

CHALANA: Fuck you. Get out of the window.

FRANCIS: I've seen her.

CHALANA: Hurrah for you.

FRANCIS: What about the old man?

CHALANA: Who told you about any old man?

FRANCIS: You did. Goddamn it, Chalana, this is unruly business now.

CHALANA: Watch your language.

FRANCIS: You know what I mean.

CHALANA: You said, I believe you. What was it you believed?

FRANCIS: You won't put me off.

CHALANA: What a way to talk.

FRANCIS: I see what you're doing. You're trying to close me out. You called me for a witness. And now you don't trust yourself.

CHALANA: Exactly.

FRANCIS: I don't want you to agree with me.

CHALANA: I don't agree with you.

FRANCIS: Call her back. Call her back!

CHALANA: Malachi, Malachi. Where's the message?

[BURSACH *and* AGNES *come zooming back.*]

BURSACH: Well, here we are. You counted on my being stupid about machines.

CHALANA: You made it, Bursach.

FRANCIS: I've got to check my 'chine. I can see the wear and tear from here.

BURSACH: Don't be foolish. I know these valleys. Once we got into them, it was just a question of being a patient guide. Damn, Francis...

CHALANA: Malachi.

BURSACH: What?

CHALANA: Francis is dead, and we have baptized Malachi.

BURSACH: Now, that's a hell of a thing, because Agnes has a statement to make.

AGNES: I was so ashamed. Bursach took me with him, just like that. I gave him no reason to trust me. But he never faltered, and he was as courteous as could be. I couldn't go on with my disguise. So, in a quiet moment, I told him my real name.

FRANCIS: Which is?

AGNES: Margaret.

CHALANA: No. I refuse to accept that.

AGNES: It's not up to you to accept...

BURSACH: Let's vote. Either way, we'll have purity.

CHALANA: You shouldn't say that.

AGNES: You can't vote on my name.

BURSACH: No, I suppose we can't. Maybe I was asking for a vote of confidence, a belief in us.

CHALANA: That, of course, doesn't apply to Francis.

FRANCIS: Bursach, I pity you.

BURSACH: Why?

FRANCIS: I can't say. Why would I say? You see, I've spent an extraordinary time, while you were gone, being introduced to ghosts. No, no, no. I meant to say, to fugitive constellations without a galaxy. But you are an adept, aren't you, Bursach? You like to live that way. Unbound. Without realizing that it can't be done. Hey, I get it. You left me here so Chalana could intimidate me, bring me into line.

BURSACH: Nonsense.

FRANCIS: Man tried to run the Murphy game on me. See that, Agnes. Bursach spent a day in the city, and picked up all kinds of bad habits. So now he and I go off together, and he fleeces me. Or he leaves you here with me because I trusted you to get here. Methodology. But what does he want?

BURSACH: I'll have a martini.

CHALANA: That's not nice, Bursach. Malachi has serious concerns.

BURSACH: Wait a minute now. Malachi, or Francis, or Pierre, says I'm a con man, and that you're a temple whore. I warrant you, madame, that I am most biblical, but I refuse to be the *terminus a quo* for the man's paranoia. And who sent me down the valley with Agnes? Why didn't he send me with you?

CHALANA: Bursach, did you really want to go down the valley with me?

BURSACH: Lady, it would renew my spirit.

CHALANA: Well, then. [*She sits in the caboose.*] Let's go.

BURSACH: Agnes, you bathe this boy before we get back.

FRANCIS: I didn't say you could…

AGNES: Relax, Francis.

BURSACH: [*To* CHALANA.] Come on up here in the engine room, baby. We're gone.

[*They go.*]

FRANCIS: Well, Margaret. Agnes. Whoever you are. What do you have to say for yourself?

AGNES: Am I on trial?

FRANCIS: Well, don't you think you owe me some explanation? You ride away with a madman, and come back as an innocent who thinks nothing of giving away my machine. How do I know that that idiot will even come back?

AGNES: Where would they go?

FRANCIS: To hell, if they take a notion. Don't think I haven't been concerned about these two. But, discretion. I savor discretion. What do you think they're doing? There's that big roomy caboose, if you know what I mean.

AGNES: The light has been disturbed here. Here, at the window. You've seen her, of course.

FRANCIS: Why do you ask?

AGNES: Why didn't you say you had?

FRANCIS: It was my moment, wasn't it?

AGNES: You were alone here then?

FRANCIS: No, of course not. You saw her here with me.

AGNES: Who? Chalana?

FRANCIS: What are you getting at? Yes, Chalana was with me. The bride was over there on her own ground. Nothing special happened.

AGNES: But you spoke of radiance.

FRANCIS: What if goddamn I did? How do you know? You weren't here. Hey, you've been too close to these people.

AGNES: You didn't see the old man?

FRANCIS: Old man. What old man? Don't you play with me now. You told me there was no old man. You told me…

AGNES: Go on.

FRANCIS: Ho ho ho. [*In a narrative tone.*] We met on a street in Brooklyn.

AGNES: That was a morning sun.

FRANCIS: I can't remember.

AGNES: What do you mean you can't remember? You recognized me.

FRANCIS: You were a dream, Chalana.

AGNES: No, you won't escape that way. Tell me what you first noticed about me.

FRANCIS: That you weren't you.

AGNES: And you weren't you. How difficult it must have been to imagine yourself in love, Bursach.

FRANCIS: Oh, yes. You laugh at Bursach now. You see him wasting away in Albuquerque, dressing himself to appear in a little New England village.

AGNES: No, now. Keep to the logic of it.

FRANCIS: I am.

AGNES: Stop it, Malachi. You're nothing but imagination.

FRANCIS: *I'm* telling this story.

AGNES: [*Sings.*] "*Cuando se duerme Guadalajara…*"

FRANCIS: I'm sure I won't get it right. So, go on. Sing. You're the singer, I'm not. I'm just a fuzzy bird who has to live with his exact incomprehension.

AGNES: All right. I'll tell you about the *chipichipi* in Xalapa.

FRANCIS: There. All right. I feel the vessel flowing back toward love. So, look here. I'm buoyant again. I'm even prepared to wait to see that figment of my imagination, the old man.

AGNES: Then, look. [*She points at a young man, dressed as an estudiantil and carrying a small string instrument, advancing upstage.*]

FRANCIS: No. That can't be the man.

AGNES: Who else? You haven't given him a chance.

[*The figure turns upon them, silently displays his disgust, and walks away.*]

FRANCIS: Well, damn the man. Goddamn you, sir! Goddamn you! Who does he think he is?

AGNES: I'm not sure, but I wonder who he thinks you are.

FRANCIS: I don't care what he thinks.

AGNES: You should. But, most of all, you should care what Chalana thinks.

FRANCIS: Damn her, too.

AGNES: Oh, my. Damn her, damn me, damn the man, damn the universe. But consider this. That is Chalana's domain. And these people are her people. They come, they go. She has been patient. She leaves you here. The lover appears, sees you and retreats. One only has to remember his attitude when he left to know that he might not return. So what do we have, Francis? A broken connection. And who broke it? Why, my dynamic and disastrously enthusiastic Francis.

FRANCIS: You've got the same bug-infested bird's nest for a brain that those two have.

AGNES: Don't think Bursach will defend you.

FRANCIS: Defend me! Against what?

AGNES: What we have here is a failure in imagination. I see I can't make you ashamed.

FRANCIS: Shame, is it?

AGNES: Sacred.

FRANCIS: Sacred?

AGNES: You wouldn't understand. I'm surprised by you, Francis. You show what you can never become. The time has passed when I could have instructed you.

FRANCIS: Oh, you're good. Turn the tap. We'll see what happens when they come back. If you have to tell. We can be quiet about some things, can't we? I mean, damn, things are just the same as when they left. Look around you. Would any normal human being notice the flug on the floor?

AGNES: I won't say a word.

FRANCIS: Good.

AGNES: I won't have to.

[*A bell music sounds.* BURSACH *and* CHALANA *drive on.* CHALANA *wears a flowing robe and a black student's cap.* BURSACH *carries a small string instrument. There is a large canvas bag in the caboose.*]

BURSACH: Here we are again. Did you miss us?

AGNES: You were never out of our minds.

CHALANA: Nonsense. The place looks like you held a public dance in it. That table wasn't like that when I left. And what did you do, breathe on the windows? Look at the streaks. We weren't gone that long.

FRANCIS: Long enough. You were in my 'chine.

CHALANA: Don't get aggressive with me, Francis. You must be hiding something.

BURSACH: Confess, Agnes.

AGNES: My sins are small. Look at the two of you.

BURSACH: Ha. You noticed. We were only a little way down river when we…

FRANCIS: Down river?

BURSACH: Yes.

FRANCIS: You were supposed to be in my train.

BURSACH: We were in your train.

FRANCIS: How the fuck could you be on the river in my train?

BURSACH: Why not? Listen, Francis, do you know anything about your 'chine?

FRANCIS: I've got to sit down.

CHALANA: Do. Because I've got to make an inspection around here before you leave.

AGNES: Leave him to himself. I want to hear the tale that goes with that cape.

BURSACH: I thought you would. As I say, we were only a little way down river when we ran into a chorus of scholars, wearing that cape. They were on their way to deliver a serenade, you see. Ah, I had forgotten the charm of it. But there they were, and there they were enraptured by Chalana.

They put the cap on her, and they sang. And later, they enfolded her in that robe. I was on the point of being jealous. They told me they dressed her out of respect for her sumptuous presence, and because they could see in my eyes my love for her and, in her posture, her love for me. So they, dear friends, enrobed our love, there on the river. You can imagine I started to sing some of my verses, those I could remember. But, no, they continued with their embarrassment of riches. They filled this bag with the treasures of the land around them. Yuca. Ñame. Papaya. Mangoes. Bananas. Tobacco. And the royal *cacahuatl*. And for you, good friends all, chocolate. There you have it. How could the starry heavens have been kinder to our hearts?

AGNES: Stand there, Chalana, let me look at you. I feel frenzied.

CHALANA: Goodness, Agnes. No pipe and sweet chocolate for you this evening.

BURSACH: What say, Malachi, shall we finish our game? I know I have to get back to the vigil.

CHALANA: You've got time. Right, Malachi?

FRANCIS: I see what you're doing. Definition. Methodology. Trying to bind me to a path I might not want to take. I came to help you, you know.

BURSACH: Pierre came to help me.

FRANCIS: Pierre was uninformed.

CHALANA: Definition.

FRANCIS: Well, if you really want to have someone around while you wait, I can spare some time.

CHALANA: Agnes, help me with this bag. Bursach would probably drop it again.

FRANCIS: I say, Bursach, you ought to start preparing yourself. I should be moving along.

BURSACH: You just got here.

FRANCIS: Well, I can see you don't need me.

BURSACH: Hey, Malachi…

FRANCIS: Francis. Not Malachi. Not now.

BURSACH: That's my problem. Obviously, I've done something that has offended you, hurt you.

FRANCIS: Don't be silly. Hurt me? You? Ask Agnes. What am I? Just your fucking imagination. Do I care that you're going to hell in a hand basket, spying on innocents?

BURSACH: Where's my editor? I'm deleting that last sentence. Francis, haven't I given you more resources than that? You embarrass me, brother.

FRANCIS: Then cut me loose.

BURSACH: Sit down. We'll smoke a pipe. Damn, Francis, we've got a feast in that bag. We brought back joy. What more do you want? Agnes, set us up.

AGNES: Do I look like your mule?

BURSACH: Mercy. Chalana, you see what you've done.

CHALANA: You've got hands.

FRANCIS: Forget it, Bursach. I appreciate your attempt at courtesy. But I have my pride.

AGNES: Pride, is it?

FRANCIS: Don't you start. We agreed…

CHALANA: What did you agree? Go on. Tell me. I've noticed that there is a weary stillness across the way. Have I missed something, Agnes?

AGNES: Ah, if only I'd been down river with you. You'll have to draw us a map to that place that suddenly flowered.

CHALANA: Bursach, I sense an accusation. They think we've conjured a place that doesn't exist.

BURSACH: No, Chalana. They're mistaken. *This* place doesn't exist. You see how clever they are? They've caught us out. Chalana. Bursach. A couple of innocents too dumb to understand the claims upon them.

FRANCIS: And here, church, he starts the false confession that relieves him of responsibility.

BURSACH: "Tell me, if you have understanding."

FRANCIS: Who "laid the foundation of the earth?" Not you, Bursach. Don't pretend. With all your talk of joy.

BURSACH: Will you take that away from me, too?

AGNES: I say, let's open the feast.

BURSACH: Chalana. Stop them from talking.

AGNES: Well, that's some pass. I was trying to let you know that I had forgiven you.

BURSACH: My god, she has forgiven me. Yes, I guess that's really appropriate. You must have heard that I no longer submit myself to the mathematical act of measuring, counting, balancing. Something about the spirit made that improbable. But, Agnes, why elevate this failure, and forgive me?

CHALANA: I'm hungry.

BURSACH: Indulge me.

CHALANA: Don't talk about failure.

BURSACH: It was Agnes...

AGNES: Never.

FRANCIS: Come on, Agnes. I said I'd take care of you. We're gone. I mean now.

AGNES: Mangoes! I have a memory of the taste of the sweetest mangoes ever. You wouldn't believe that I was sitting in Sardinia. Early morning. The cold turned my shoes a bright blue. Oh, I had been huddled in a boat all night. But there was coffee. And those mangoes.

FRANCIS: Agnes? Come to yourself. I said, it's time to shake the dust off our feet.

BURSACH: Biblical.

FRANCIS: I'll bible your crow-eating face. You can call your haggis snappers, and hold a picnic of funky-mouthed idiots. But you can't fool me. No, sir.

What was that river you was up, boy? Hold it. You ain't man enough to correct my grammar. You ain't conscious enough to see that I'm through with you.

BURSACH: I had seen that coming.

FRANCIS: Damn straight. Why would anybody want to get tied up with a man whose mind is nothing but a grave?

CHALANA: Oh, Francis, you didn't tell me you were a conjure man.

FRANCIS: I'm talking about him.

CHALANA: Yes, yes. We understand. We heard that on your river. We felt it as we hurried back here with our gifts. Or your gifts. God, Malachi, you have me confused.

AGNES: Sit down, Chalana. I'll stir us all up some chocolate. Sit Bursach. Sit Francis.

FRANCIS: Not with him.

BURSACH: If that's the case. [*He draws a torch from the engine.*] Let's just burn these goodies.

FRANCIS: What the fuck are you doing?

BURSACH: Your service.

FRANCIS: This is an insult, sir.

BURSACH: Make up your mind.

FRANCIS: My mind's made up. You don't have a clue. Oh, yeah, here, you're gonna burn up something people gave you. Because it suits you. That's you. You don't think about me.

BURSACH: I don't believe this.

FRANCIS: Believe it. Believe it. I'll be standing here 'til my dying breath to keep you from making a fool of yourself. Goddamn it, I deserve my chocolate now.

BURSACH: You deserve nothing but what I give you.

FRANCIS: So that's what it's come to. Bursach is God!

AGNES: Oh, no. That's a pain to endure much beyond Bursach. I thought we had an understanding about that, Malachi.

CHALANA: Delicious hours. Time passes. Don't you see, Bursach? Who has to work for understanding? Ask Agnes. But what would we ask Agnes? What is the question? Ah, yes, chocolate.

FRANCIS: I don't have to take this.

[*A bell music starts from across the way.*]

CHALANA: Strange they should begin the night that way. I don't recognize the tune.

AGNES: Have they done this before?

CHALANA: No.

AGNES: Then what's the point?

CHALANA: Maybe they're tolling an absence.

FRANCIS: I was here, Chalana. Don't talk to me about something missing.

CHALANA: I said nothing about anything being missing.

FRANCIS: Do I have ears?

BURSACH: As well as eyes.

FRANCIS: I'm going to leave you to your contemplation, Chalana. And you to your many misconceptions, Bursach. You called me. Remember you called me. And then you took away the reason for my being here. Now, Agnes, pull yourself up. We've got to go.

AGNES: We have a confession to make.

FRANCIS: We have no confession to make.

AGNES: I'll make it on my own.

CHALANA: I have made an inventory, Agnes. You have nothing to declare.

AGNES: As you wish. Goodbye.

[AGNES *and* FRANCIS *get in the train, and ride off.*]

BURSACH: I missed the exhilaration in their departure.

CHALANA: That sometimes is the way it is, Bursach.

[*The music stops.*]

BURSACH: You know, I've always thought that you would make a wonderful writer.

CHALANA: What makes you say that?

BURSACH: Well, perhaps, I should say, an artist. I've told you that story about, oh, you know who I mean. It doesn't matter who. The point is that art resides in the body prepared for it. And it will live, even in silence.

CHALANA: No, no, no, Bursach. This is cowardly evasion.

BURSACH: Tell me why you've put me on this vigil.

CHALANA: Oh ho. Is Francis right? Vigil. Grave.

BURSACH: You said you wanted me to confirm something.

CHALANA: I wanted you to join me in my contemplation. Perhaps, Francis was right to distrust a resolution that owes so much to absence.

BURSACH: You don't pay any attention to Francis, do you?

CHALANA: That's not the question.

BURSACH: What is the question?

CHALANA: Bursach, go to bed. Thank you for your help. But you don't have to do this. I can take care of it now.

BURSACH: Can't you tell me what you're waiting for? What was I supposed to see?

CHALANA: What you saw.

BURSACH: I didn't see anything.

CHALANA: There you go.

BURSACH: I'm sorry, Chalana. I never seem to help you much. I get tied up in my own little storms. Listen, I'm not tired. I want to do this.

CHALANA: You've done enough. Now, go.

BURSACH: All right. If you think I'm in the way.

CHALANA: Bursach. Before you go, I've been meaning to ask you. Would John the Scot have known Houston House?

BURSACH: God, the place is not that old.

CHALANA: But, if it were, would he recognize the peacocks and burgundy you gave to it? I only mean, would he have been happy upon those grounds and in that instant as we were?

BURSACH: I don't know. But I've grown used to a certain austerity, and, if he turns up in my dreams this evening, I'll ask him.

CHALANA: Do. Good night.

BURSACH: Good night.

[*He goes.* CHALANA *goes to the window. The bell music briefly sounds. The woman from across the way enters. She wears a white dress, white scarf, no shoes. She carries a small red traveling bag.*]

FIGURE: Are you ready for me?

CHALANA: Yes. Come in.

[*They clear the table, move the bag of gifts. The figure draws from the bag a white tablecloth, which they spread over the table. They place a small pot, a small basket, a gold necklace, a bell, a book, a single red feather and an ancient bottle of gin from the figure's bag and the bag of gifts on the cloth.*]

FIGURE: Shall we close it away?

CHALANA: No. Not yet.

FIGURE: I hope that our music didn't disturb you.

CHALANA: It *was* unexpected.

FIGURE: We noticed that you had gone down river, and we weren't sure when you'd return.

CHALANA: So you composed the music.

FIGURE: No, the music was always with us. We just never had an occasion to use it.

CHALANA: Then thank you for the homecoming.

FIGURE: Mine? Or yours?

CHALANA: Or theirs?

[*She points across the way where* FRANCIS *and* AGNES *now appear, looking toward* CHALANA *and the figure.*]

FIGURE: I expected them to have abandoned you by now.

CHALANA: We can't read too much into their appearance.

FIGURE: Certainly. But they are there.

CHALANA: And we are here. And you seem as free as a bird.

FIGURE: Ask them. [BURSACH *appears.*]

BURSACH: I'm sorry, Chalana. There was such a special darkness I woke up.

CHALANA: You can see that we're swimming in light.

BURSACH: Yes. I recognize the tokens.

CHALANA: No, Bursach, this is your moment. Speak simply.

BURSACH: I do. I will. I know, you expect me to ask for an explanation. But, no, you are Chalana. You have always known my secret life. And even there you will find the love I have always carried for you. I love you, Chalana.

CHALANA: I love you, Bursach.

BURSACH: And so it was written, and the book was closed.

[*A flood of the brightest light, then darkness.*]

THE HUNT AND
DOUBLE NIGHT OF THE WOOD

CHARACTERS   Frank Fawcett

Len Hope

Robert MacIntyre King (Bob King)

Jeffrey Peters

Vernon Sawyer

PLACE   The Sandia Mountains near Albuquerque, New Mexico

[*A sprawl of green and brown. The disorder of abandoned mining equipment, shading into the disorder of communications equipment. A red, laserlike light sweeps the area. A swirling fog follows it. On raised lines strung around the perimeter of the area, undulating light flows in one direction, reverses direction, comes to a high intensity and hovers.* LEN HOPE, *disheveled in buckskin, holding a rifle, moves through the area while looking cautiously all around. He disappears. The sound of two vehicles struggling, coming closer. One motor dies. Loud, inarticulate swearing and accompanying laughter. After several attempts to start the motor, it catches; the vehicles continue their struggle, until they come to rest amidst laughter, shouts and missing engines. Four men, carrying various bags and packs, enter.* KING *and* PETERS *have guns slung over their backs.*]

SAWYER: Sandia! Here we are! Aheeyah!

PETERS: God, give us a break, Sawyer. King, you better get that fixed before we come up here again. I do not intend to spend winter on the Watermelon.

KING: That's a perfectly good truck. I had it tuned day 'fore yesterday. I swear and be damned I'll have me some butt when I get back. That curly wolf must have been roostered when he did the job.

PETERS: Well, you had to be booze blind to give him the job.

KING: Don't you accuse me of gettin' into that Kansas sheep dip. Not that early. 'Sides, I owe his dad a blessing.

PETERS: Don't get started.

KING: Hell, an old fire escape like you, you're ready to forgive everybody. But not me. Not old Robert MacIntyre King.

SAWYER: Hear, hear.

PETERS: Excuse me, Sawyer. You don't even know the man.

SAWYER: Which one? Dad? Or the sheep dipper?

KING: Where you from, Sawyer?

SAWYER: Arizona.

KING: Not likely.

SAWYER: I assure you, sir. Originally. With time out back east while I helped to educate them.

KING: Yes. Frankie!

FAWCETT: I hear you.

KING: Hear me, but let me see you. We got to get this stuff off the truck before it rots.

FAWCETT: Leave me with it, I'll take care of it. I can do better without you.

PETERS: [Searching around him.] Where are my papers?

FAWCETT: Wherever you left them.

PETERS: Let's not get cute. I do not intend to do without my papers. I put 'em all in a pile in the same place. If somebody put his fleaflickin' fingers on my material, I'm going to bed him down.

KING: [To SAWYER.] Ain't this some way for a bible puncher to talk? Pay it no mind. The reverend has a good heart.

PETERS: And a need to keep other people's hands off his newspapers. Thank god, here they are.

SAWYER: Why do you need so many, when we're out here to hunt?

PETERS: Why do you need that computer you're holding?

SAWYER: I feel naked without it.

PETERS: Now, that's interesting. Since we're still hunting, I presume. I mean, what do you intend to do? Track the deer on your program?

SAWYER: I could.

KING: Ridiculous.

SAWYER: By no means, Doctor King. Much of what we know about the world can be discovered, and then addressed, right here.

KING: Look around you. Who was addressing this?

SAWYER: This?

KING: This. This. Didn't you pay attention when you came up? Look at this mountain. Look at the devastation. A wreck, this world is a wreck.

SAWYER: Perhaps, if people had been more attentive, to what the more technically adept had been telling them.

KING: Who are you blaming, Sawyer?

SAWYER: Why, no one. I don't see any reason for blame.

PETERS: Good. Good. Can we get ourselves organized?

FAWCETT: I do need some help.

PETERS: It's obvious you're above your bend.

FAWCETT: You really don't know me, do you, Mr. Peters?

PETERS: Why is it, Frankie, you have never called me Reverend Peters?

FAWCETT: Why have you never called me Mister Fawcett?

PETERS: Why, I think it would be inappropriate, given the circumstances.

FAWCETT: And what are those, Mister Peters?

PETERS: Perhaps we should get that stuff off the truck.

SAWYER: I can help out.

KING: Well, thank you, sah.

[*They go.*]

PETERS: Let me detain you a minute, Frankie. There's a little thing you do that obviously bears some significance. I hope you don't mind if I ask.

These matters fascinate me, as you can imagine. Tell me why everything you do is done in fours, as it were. You lay out four bowls on four boards, though you never eat with us. You call us to the table four times. Other things have caught my attention. Is there some magic in four?

FAWCETT: Why do you ask?

PETERS: As I say, I'm fascinated, by certain expressions of order, and I find it useful to take things apart and understand them.

FAWCETT: I wasn't aware that I was married to the number four.

PETERS: That's your answer?

FAWCETT: I can't see that your question deserves another.

PETERS: Frankie, Frankie. I'm not about to feed off my range. At least not in the way some would, if they were more attentive. I must say, though, that I don't appreciate your hostility.

FAWCETT: I don't appreciate your disrespect.

PETERS: Disrespect!?

FAWCETT: Disrespect. What are you trying to do? Wash me out with Doctor King?

PETERS: You'd do that on your own.

FAWCETT: Oh, would I now? How is that?

PETERS: There isn't room here for someone who needs to sit in judgment. Understand me.

FAWCETT: Nothing you do up here ever leaves here.

PETERS: I'm sure you're very discreet. That's not what I meant. I feel undressed when you're around.

FAWCETT: Undressed.

PETERS: Yes. I don't know what you see, Frankie. Things that seem innocent to me and Doctor King seem to offend you.

KING: Are you two helpin' or not?

PETERS: I'm on the way.

KING: We'd better get the tents up. It looks like rain.

FAWCETT: Are you setting that pup tent out there for me?

KING: That's what we had in mind.

FAWCETT: I had in mind throwing my sleeping bag in the back of the truck. The wet ground pains my joints.

KING: Suit yourself, but I didn't go out of my way to get this tent to have you spit on it. You got the best tent I could get, for the price. Of course, if you don't want to sleep in it, there ain't nothin' I can do about that.

FAWCETT: I appreciate your effort…

KING: Ha! Hear this. He appreciates my effort.

PETERS: What Frankie wants is to sleep in the same tent with us. That way he could keep an eye on us. Right, Frankie?

FAWCETT: I don't need to.

PETERS: Keep an eye on us?

FAWCETT: Share your comfort. I can make myself comfortable in the truck. You will have noticed, Mister Peters, that I keep my place quite tidy.

KING: Let's knock off the arguing, and do what needs to be done. Have a face lickin' time. Get us some deer. Get us some bear. Have a restful hunting trip, and go on home, relaxed and refreshed. What are you doin', Sawyer?

SAWYER: Checking my e-mail.

KING: Why don't you just set up an office? Where's my deacon seat? Set it up here for this boy. Do a little research. Right, Sawyer?

SAWYER: Sorry. Didn't mean to be intrusive with this.

KING: It's just that every goddamned thing is in the wrong place. I don't know about you, but I'm in the Sandia Mountains. Today. Know what I mean? It's twilight. That is juniper, and that is Ponderosa pine. That's chamina. There's an animal out here somewhere that needs my special care. I'm about to eat, and lie down. I'm among friends. I tell you, brothers, I have just described a sensuous event, and, goddamn it, that's what I need, that's what I want, and, believe me, that's what I'm going to have.

PETERS: You've got a faraway look in your eye, Sawyer.

SAWYER: It's just that I have to get used to certain misconceptions. No offense.

PETERS: Misconceptions. Tell.

SAWYER: I was looking around as we came up. A lot of abandoned mining equipment lying around. I'm sure you could tell me why. You know the area. But this seems out of place. It's not the heart of it.

KING: Of what?

SAWYER: Of mining.

KING: Depends on the kind of mining you're talking about.

SAWYER: The state's strengths. Uranium, coal, oil.

KING: You don't know what you're talking about.

SAWYER: I guess I'm talking about investments that have gone dead.

KING: What do you mean?

SAWYER: That I am not a man given to nostalgia.

PETERS: Well, we all have our misconceptions.

SAWYER: Meaning?

PETERS: That you would have any feeling...

SAWYER: For an Old Placers mine near Cerrillos, or the dead uranium pits around Grants.

PETERS: You seem well-versed in deaths, Mister Sawyer.

SAWYER: On the contrary, I've just been made conscious of other possibilities.

KING: Where was it again you went to school?

SAWYER: Dartmouth. A...

PETERS: ...small private school but very fine academically.

SAWYER: I see my reputation has preceded me.

PETERS: No. It was just that we cowboys expect a certain level of finesse from you Yankee-educated folk.

SAWYER: I wouldn't call it finesse

KING: What would you call it?

SAWYER: I'd call it a willingness to explore beyond the given.

KING: Leave home, then?

SAWYER: I came back.

KING: This is not home.

PETERS: You might have been gone too long, Mister Sawyer.

SAWYER: Can we drop the Mister Sawyer? I'm beginning to feel like a stranger.

PETERS: Well, you are, Mister…It's Vernon, isn't it?

SAWYER: Yes, Vernon. I was away, but I did my graduate work out west, Stanford. Why do you call me a stranger? I'm from right next door. These places practically grew up together.

KING: There are great differences. I used to traipse around Flagstaff, get down to Tempe, Tucson. Spent a good bit of time in Bisbee and Douglas, places you probably never bothered about.

SAWYER: Mining towns.

KING: Yes, mining towns.

PETERS: Like this, in your eyes, devastated.

SAWYER: I didn't say that. I have a special love for these places.

KING: Bullshit.

[*Thunder.*]

I said we ought to get set up.

[*They prepare.* SAWYER *brings his two hunting guns.*]

FAWCETT: Here, Vernon, I'll take one of those.

SAWYER: It's Mister Sawyer.

FAWCETT: Mister Sawyer.

SAWYER: That won't help you to get your hands on these guns. One thing I learned. Never let another man touch your woman or your gun.

FAWCETT: I just thought I'd lighten your burden.

SAWYER: Oh, now. That is the most sophisticated invitation I've had since I left the east.

FAWCETT: I was talking about the guns.

SAWYER: The guns. Sure. A brand new one I'm trying. Big game gun, Frankie. A magnum. Smooth bolt got double locking lugs. You got a pistol grip cap. See this? A hinged steel floor plate. That's to let you unload by just pressing this button. You following this?

FAWCETT: As far as you want to take me.

SAWYER: Three position safety. It's a little heavier than this one, though it's not any longer, overall, or in the barrel. Hey, make no mistake. That thirty ought six is a nice gun, but this one is made to pull the biggest bear to earth.

FAWCETT: Why do you keep the other one?

SAWYER: For deer. Rabbits. People who annoy me. Besides, I inherited that one. Family, Frankie. Right?

FAWCETT: Well, you've got yourself a fire-breathing one now.

SAWYER: What do you mean?

FAWCETT: What do I mean. No, young man, what do you mean? You're out here with a couple of boys who like to hear the owl hoot. Oh, please, Mr. Sawyer, don't tell me I'm out of line. See that ridge? You think you're capable of memorizing it? If I blindfolded you, and took you down then brought you back up here and turned you loose, do you think you could find your way back to just that ridge? And know where you were?

SAWYER: An engineering problem.

FAWCETT: You might say. I prefer to think of it as a metaphysical problem.

SAWYER: Jesus, my first night out, and I run into a lizard scorcher with a conscience, or a soul, or a…what do you call it, Frankie? This thing you're trying to impress upon me.

FAWCETT: I have no interest in you, Mr. Sawyer.

SAWYER: But you've been so enlightening, Frankie, that I've become more than a little interested in you.

FAWCETT: That's the best you can do? A little. If I had time, I'd tell you a little story. Family, Mr. Sawyer. Soften up this rough ground you're about to sleep on. The circle is much wider than you think it is.

SAWYER: What the fuck are you talking about?

FAWCETT: Do you know this ground? Talk to me when you do. I think they're waiting on you. I've got work. If you will excuse me. [*He walks away.*]

SAWYER: Hey, wait a minute.

[PETERS *slowly appears.*]

PETERS: Let him go. His pride rides him hard. He stews. He blames others for his misfortune, or for his mistakes, decisions he made. There are times I can't deal with him. What surprises you more, Vernon, that I can't or that I would even want to? He owes King. He owes me. Listen, be not disturbed. This is where we are. Perk up, Vernon. You know there is a passage in Duns Scotus that has disturbed me. The man is impossible. I read him, and I feel I'm barking at a knot. You needn't care. Hey, do you care, Vernon? The Scotus tells us it is not fitting to confine the intellect to sensible things. You understand that, don't you, Vernon? This seductive night that's just beginning. The blood smell of that animal that's waiting for the death with which you will honor it. Frankie's biscuits. The fucking sun that will shadow you all day, tomorrow, and the next, until you let it go. It is all necessary. Put the guns away. Let's get set up. We'll be eating soon. You'll have to make me an adept on the computer before we leave here.

[*They finish their preparations. They arrange themselves for the meal* FAWCETT *will serve. The laser light sweeps the stage.* KING *sits on a split log as though he sat on a throne.* SAWYER *fiddles with his computer.*]

KING: I see you've met Frankie.

SAWYER: I have.

KING: What do you think?

SAWYER: An interesting man.

KING: Come on, Sawyer. Give me some paper I can read. I'll swear the man gets worse by the day. Last year, two days after we got here, I had to send a jeep down to pick him up in Albuquerque. He'd run out of wine already and he'd hitched down with some bootlegger. This business with the gun has him mighty upset.

SAWYER: He told you about that?

KING: No.

SAWYER: I didn't encourage him.

KING: Surely. Just keep your guns with you, and out of his sight. When Frankie takes a notion, well, I don't have to tell you, he's a man of strong will. Physically, he's weak. I suspect first stages of cirrhosis, some hormonal imbalance. I doubt that he can get it up anymore. But he's a man of demon will. A great rage in him.

[FAWCETT *appears with the food.*]

FAWCETT: I hear the deer flapping in the leaves. You won't be disappointed.

PETERS: Thanks for the blessing, Frankie.

FAWCETT: Why are you looking at me like that?

PETERS: No offense, padre. I was simply counting. I had it down last year, and the count seemed to coincide with the one from the year before. But, damn me, I lost the paper. So, in a sense, I'm starting all over.

KING: You want to enlighten us, Jeff?

PETERS: I want to get Sawyer involved in this. We'll need that computer. You see, I've been watching Frankie, and measuring this strange and rich mathematical world he inhabits. Every step is measured. I kid you not. Maybe it's his being a technician. His whole body is programmed to move by the numbers, My god, I just had the thought that what we see standing there before us as Frank Huey Fawcett is not Frankie at all but a concatenation of zeros and ones, or an infinite string of digits that he himself composed. Think on that, Sawyer. Frank Huey Fawcett is no more substantial than the yucca branches we tore down getting up here.

FAWCETT: My middle name is not Huey.

PETERS: Sorry. What is it?

FAWCETT: I'll leave that for you to divine.

PETERS: Oh, well put. Notice the subtlety.

KING: Leave it, Jeff.

SAWYER: You want to talk about numbers. Look what a little surfing will do. Do you know that in 1880, in this great state you inhabit, twenty families owned three-quarters of the sheep. And we're talking, like, four million sheep.

KING: I didn't need a computer to tell me the world has gone to hell.

SAWYER: Well, I'm not sure that the engine said anything like that.

PETERS: It's an interesting proposition that it can say anything at all. But it does bear witness, doesn't it, Sawyer?

SAWYER: It keeps the faith.

KING: Does it bear witness to the people who turned these valleys into God's very own promise? Forget that. God. Whatever comes with it. That's Jeff's design. God help me, I'll be good and gone. Gone.

FAWCETT: I want to know, Mr. Sawyer, can your little instrument keep a secret?

SAWYER: What do you mean?

FAWCETT: Oh, just the little lies some people tell to keep themselves going. Secrets about numbers, about land, about certain relationships.

SAWYER: Those little lies, as you call them, might sit there undisturbed, but they might come tumbling out at the right touch.

FAWCETT: Do you have the touch, Mr. Sawyer?

SAWYER: My secret, Mr. Fawcett.

KING: I left this conversation at home. Feed me. Sit down, Sawyer. Jeff. You need anything, Frankie?

FAWCETT: At the moment, no. A few minutes of your time before we leave.

KING: I think I can spare that.

FAWCETT: Good. If you need me. [*He leaves.*]

KING: I wish that boy wouldn't always coyote around the rim.

PETERS: You don't ever give Frankie credit for the extraordinary delicacy he displays.

KING: You defending him?

PETERS: What's to defend?

KING: I need a drink. I don't want to get up. Jeff, look there in the bottom of that canvas bag there, the long one. That's it. Ought to be a couple of bottles.

[PETERS *produces a bottle.*]

Sit back, gentlemen. Pull that crate box over here, Sawyer. I used to have this old canvas back chair my wife would send out here every year. My Hollywood director's chair, she calls it. Women. I ain't been to Hollywood and I ain't seen a movie since I married her.

PETERS: Or been without that cane.

KING: God, yes. The bitch has had me on the cane since I married her.

[PETERS *serves.*]

PETERS: There you are, Dr. King. Mr. Sawyer. How will you have yours? Neat, I suppose.

SAWYER: Neat's fine.

PETERS: I'll mix mine with a little water.

KING: What do you think of it, Sawyer? Meet specifications? Tickle the buds? Man could load some grain behind that.

SAWYER: Righteous.

PETERS: Sacramental. I couldn't resist. You seemed out of your depth.

KING: Sawyer's a man of the world. I wouldn't have asked him up here, if I didn't think so. He ain't gonna be shocked by my telling him that you are a nooky loving son-of-a-bitch.

PETERS: No. But he might think there's something between us.

KING: Queer? You mean he might think we're queer? Impossible.

PETERS: It is possible, isn't it, Sawyer. Isn't that the first thought that came into your head?

SAWYER: As a matter of fact, no.

PETERS: Oh, come on. Be honest. You can be honest with us. Tell.

SAWYER: No. Really. I didn't think anything at all.

PETERS: You mean it just passed right over your head.

SAWYER: Yes.

KING: That's bad. Shouldn't nothing pass over your head. You can't tell when you can use it. You ought to realize that. You're in business.

SAWYER: Oh, well, now, if you're talking business.

KING: Yes, Sawyer. That's right. We're talking business. Funny you discovered those four million sheep. You practically wrote me out of the picture. I'm a man who treasures memory, Sawyer. Why do you think I put up with an old bible puncher like Peters?

PETERS: You've lost the point, Bob.

KING: Don't tell me about the point. John Chisum was the point.

PETERS: Dead.

KING: Charlie Goodnight was the point.

PETERS: Dead.

KING: Absolutely. The fucking valley died. The grass all over the damned state was ripped up. The water was poison.

PETERS: Who *did* that?

KING: Don't talk to me about blame. It's a heart-sucking pattern. Who can live with it? What does your machine say about that?

SAWYER: My machine, as you put it, is a rational being. I understand. You meant no harm. It's not the first time I've heard a certain memory called into question.

KING: Why, the man is playing with me, Peters.

SAWYER: No, sir. I was simply defending the integrity of that land you abandoned.

KING: You'd better ride over that trail again. You're just about to put me in a sod-pawing mood.

SAWYER: I ask you to look around, sir. You can't go twenty miles without seeing the carcass of some ingenious instrument, rotting, sinking into the ground. The air is filled with the voices of villages that ripened and then wilted. Was there a flaw in that heart you mentioned? I don't know. I look at the old mines. Dead. Where was the flaw?

PETERS: Surely, Sawyer, you're not accusing us…?

SAWYER: Of anything. I'm simply finding my way.

PETERS: Well, now. What do you want from us?

SAWYER: I see the evening's getting out of hand. You know me, Dr. King. Just a young man who likes to tinker with metallic things, and run his abacus over things that no one wants to calculate. You might say I have nothing in mind.

KING: Ridiculous. You sound like that fool hen, Len Hope. Out here among the willows.

SAWYER: I don't know this Len Hope.

KING: Good for you. I rescued his ass. I held a note on his business. I had to sign it away to let him get rid of it. In exchange for other compensation. Did he thank me? Oh, no. He put it around he always paid his debts, even when they were imposed upon him. It means nothing to you. Until someone tells you that he set fire to the locked cabin his drunken uncle was sleeping in. Thank god, he's not one of us.

SAWYER: Of us?

PETERS: These matters are too complicated for a night before hunting. We can rest.

KING: Rest. Never. Get this garbage out of my face. I'm too agitated to digest it. Why don't you come up with a passion, Sawyer?

SAWYER: Oh, I could go deep within the earth, Dr. King. I have an affinity for buried things, and for the instruments that bring them to life so they can be measured and, lord help me, used.

KING: A clever proposition, Sawyer. Don't let it lead you astray. Good night.

SAWYER: Good night.

KING: I trust you to clear this up, Jeff.

PETERS: Done.

[*They part. Pause.* FAWCETT *appears, wearing an old blanket.* HOPE *appears, approaches.*]

FAWCETT: You know Dr. King closed this area to you.

HOPE: Closed? What kind of nonsense is that? You've got a senile old man, if he thinks he can close a mountain to me. Take the blanket off, nigger. Stop pretending.

FAWCETT: Well, now, who's pretending? You're out here hunting. Hunting what? Hunting who? You haven't got over it. You haven't got the strength to insist on your right to use this mountain.

HOPE: Don't go on with your nonsense.

FAWCETT: You know, I take no delight in seeing you like this. You used to think you were a river in a desert. Soft words drove you crazy. I couldn't do enough for you. No, sir, you thought the wind was your chariot, and Dr. King your horse. Why are you out here?

HOPE: You and I have business. Don't deny it.

FAWCETT: There was the little business with the acequia.

HOPE: That's it. Let's go over old hurts. Don't you keep this shit in a book, Frankie? Someplace handy. Then we could go over it item by item until you filled your shit-filled gullet with the taste of my humiliation. Perfect. I'm with you.

FAWCETT: I don't humiliate my own.

HOPE: Frankie! You love me again. But you're being unfaithful to the doctor and the turd singing bird. Aren't you ashamed? Well, at least frightened. [HOPE *produces a pouch.*] Take this.

FAWCETT: There's nothing you have I want.

HOPE: No, no, no. Say it properly, Frank. There is nothing I have you think you couldn't get from him. He owns your house.

FAWCETT: I know that. So?

HOPE: It's the other land. You want to play with that ambiguity. Oh, you're a great one for ambiguity, Frank. Look at you. Part me. Part some hidden bone of King, perhaps.

FAWCETT: Nonsense. Romanticism.

HOPE: Romanticism, he calls it. He's learned to sing in a church. Big words. Who's running you, Frank? Peters? Why don't they tell you what they know about you?

FAWCETT: Maybe they have failed to understand me, Lenny.

HOPE: Don't believe it. Your body is transparent to them.

FAWCETT: My body!? Who gives a fuck about my body? That's your problem.

HOPE: No, that's your problem. You think there is no place for your body.

FAWCETT: You see me here?

HOPE: I see you.

FAWCETT: Good. I thought you'd gone blind.

HOPE: I wish I had. I wouldn't have to see you tomming.

FAWCETT: Tomming. Well, now, lay that out for me. What is this tomming?

HOPE: I passed your shack, down by the ditch. Pitiful. I went by there with Lucy Maahu. She couldn't believe that anyone could live with such humiliation. "Where is the pride?" You think I could tell her? You think I wanted to explain you?

FAWCETT: Why didn't you burn me out?

HOPE: Fire would do you no good, Frank. So you've bought that story they tell.

FAWCETT: Is it true?

HOPE: My god, he's worried about my soul. I'm not going to forgive you for taking such an interest in my soul. You have to remember. You took my ass up to Madrid, for a little business. What was it? Something about wood? I trusted you, Frank. I thought, damn, surely, Frank knows how to deal with carpet-baggers and sheep diddlers. We *had* to make money. We ended up walking around a little village, where nobody recognized us, nobody knew our names. I counted on your anger. But, no, you took me out along some back road, scorched earth. You picked out this bush. You started singing, man. I didn't know you. You kept saying, you don't understand, but it will all come clear. "Help me to understand!" I thought you would abandon me. When I pulled you up, just to hold onto you, you said, I will be responsible for you, Len Hope. And I believed you. [*He gestures toward* FAWCETT.] But such is the case.

FAWCETT: So what have you come to do?

HOPE: To keep you from falling.

FAWCETT: What makes you think I might?

HOPE: You want to speak to Bob King.

FAWCETT: You seem to know more than you should.

HOPE: I know you want that plot of land on the other side of the river. The Napoleon's land.

FAWCETT: I'd have to steal it from them.

HOPE: You would.

FAWCETT: Why would I do that?

HOPE: You want to read the book again.

FAWCETT: The book, the book. You and your damned book.

HOPE: You know, of course, Napoleon's other name.

FAWCETT: How do I know what that geechee calls himself?

HOPE: What is this I hear?

FAWCETT: Napoleon is misguided.

HOPE: Not about his name. Which is Miguel Valdivielso or Lucius Napoleon, under the proper dispensation.

FAWCETT: And what is that?

HOPE: You mean to play with me, don't you? Leave that aside. Look at me. You baptized me in Madrid, Frank. You took me in.

FAWCETT: Not there.

HOPE: Then some other place. Or am I mistaken?

FAWCETT: You are mistaken.

HOPE: What was it you were singing that night?

FAWCETT: Hope, I've got a long day ahead of me. You're trespassing.

HOPE: Trespassing.

FAWCETT: Yes, trespassing. I don't remember being in the bush near Madrid.

HOPE: Funny you say it that way. Being in the bush. When you used to talk to me, Frank, you were quite eloquent about the bush.

FAWCETT: Night has come.
All men have their eyes on you.
The women have run into their houses.
You must set out,
You must return to your canyon of stone.
Night has come.

Are you any wiser?

HOPE: No, that's not the song. I would recognize that rhythm.

FAWCETT: How would you, if you had never heard it before?

HOPE: How do you know I haven't? You know, Frank, you're like a new bride who has entered a new home, and she shuts her eyes to the old one. It is a necessary death.

FAWCETT: Napoleon. Yes, Clinton Napoleon. Thank you for reminding me. And this Miguel Valdivielso, is it?, was the man we were going to see in Madrid. It was spiritual business, not wood, Len. Now that I think of it, I wonder why I asked you to come along. You would have been so inappropriate. You'd be out of place now. But that was my compassionate period. I could read the faces of people who had been hurt. I knew you were an injured bird, and I must have asked you to come along. Isn't that the way you remember it?

HOPE: It's your story.

FAWCETT: It is my story. Think of what it took to get you to shake it out of me.

HOPE: Don't go on. I get the point.

FAWCETT: No, Len Hope, you do not get the point. I haven't come to the point. You see, we had to go up a road that had been traveled by people who were intent on divesting me.

HOPE: Shame ought to hold your tongue.

FAWCETT: Why should I feel ashamed? I was established here.

HOPE: You!?

FAWCETT: Yes, I. Oh, he's scandalized. But I haven't taken you anywhere. Think of the road up to Madrid. But there is the road down. And there is traveling along that road, and only my voice brings it to light. Now I know why I took you with me. You had to witness to my encounter with this Miguel Valdivielso, or Clinton Napoleon, whichever is which.

HOPE: Are you finished?

FAWCETT: No. I must remind you of the fruits of our visit.

HOPE: Stop it.

FAWCETT: You ought to recognize this as the form of our kinship, Len Hope. You. Me. Bob King. Miguel Valdivielso. Lucius Napoleon. You ought to see why I want to speak to Bob King, or to any shadow he sends to the house.

HOPE: I resent that you find me so vulnerable to your lies.

FAWCETT: I never lie. Look at me. I'm never astonished by anything that happens. You come through that wash, at night, when the air closes down on a silence, and, suddenly, you're there. That is, here, engaging me in a conversation that doesn't explain why you've come armed and speaking a language I've never heard, or have left behind. You argue with the way I'm dressed. You pretend that you have come to save me. I know better. Why don't you leave me now, Len Hope? The night is too far gone.

HOPE: I remember the words.

> Tears run.
> The hoe is broken.
> The hoe is broken.
> The axe is broken.
> He has taken the goatskin.

FAWCETT: Amazing. You remember. And you weren't even there.

HOPE: Maybe that's the point of it. This child's play. I thank you, Frank. And I do pay my debts.

FAWCETT: Leave me your gun.

[HOPE hands FAWCETT a pistol.]

HOPE: Maybe I did make you understand.

FAWCETT: Time will tell.

[HOPE goes. FAWCETT turns in. PETERS does martial arts maneuvers with a long knife. SAWYER appears.]

SAWYER: I see you don't need much sleep.

PETERS: Not true. I need oceans of sleep. Oh, my, bad metaphor that, or whatever it is. But that's why I no longer practice the craft of poetry. What about you?

SAWYER: I've never written.

PETERS: I was referring to sleep.

SAWYER: Sleep. Yes, I visit it occasionally.

PETERS: Wired.

SAWYER: Twice over.

PETERS: I still turn pages. My commitment to the smallest unit of meaning costs me the night's compassionate embrace. But that is fuel for another fireside. You had something in mind.

SAWYER: No. I heard you moving around here. I take it you follow the ancient arts.

PETERS: I do. This is only one of them. I tell you I seriously disturb Frank Fawcett. You see, I have sometimes stalked a deer, using only this, killed it and dressed it, ceremoniously. Frank thinks I have no right to that ceremony. You must have noticed, Frank has a gift for ceremony, and I believe he has assigned me my place, out of which I seem to have slipped. I should have said that he has a gift for contingency. He denies me my mental rectitude. He doesn't see that I have no need for a special light. Are you Avicennian or Scotist, Sawyer?

SAWYER: Pardon?

PETERS: Never mind. We were talking about Frank. Weren't we? It's obvious that he has a bug up his ass, which will come crawling out in time to ruin this hunting trip. Some business with the Napoleon's land.

SAWYER: Napoleon?

PETERS: Yes. River people of some strangely configured heritage. They have the river bank covered with graves.

SAWYER: Napoleon, you say.

PETERS: Yes. You know them?

SAWYER: I guess it's a common enough name. I did know a Clinton Napoleon, back home in Arizona. Talented. He could carve just about anything you wanted to see. Back out my house, we could go right up into the mountains. He had me out there every day, looking for cottonwood, ash, walnut, cherry, anything he could get his hands into. I told him I'd give him more than a nickel, if he ever put his hands into some cactus and came up with something I could recognize. He just laughed. I kept some of his things until I left Arizona. The friendship had died anyway. Hey, no more of this. Graves follow me everywhere.

PETERS: Sounds interesting. This story of the grave.

SAWYER: Heady air up here. I shouldn't be telling you any of this.

PETERS: My, it seems to have turned into a confession.

SAWYER: Mine or yours?

PETERS: You left me dangling over this Napoleon grave.

SAWYER: I said nothing about a grave. Well, it was Clint's grandfather. Lived to be a hundred and five, died just about the time Clint came into his sixteenth year. Being one of Clint's best friends, I felt bound to go to the funeral and be around when they celebrated. I tried to talk to Clint, cheer him up. He wouldn't be cheered, got more sullen, distant. It all came to a head when we went out to the grave. They put a plastic bucket on his coffin, just before they lowered it, and the people passed by, one by one, and dropped money into it. When I asked Clint about it, he lashed out at me, almost on top of the grave, and the others chased me off. I have never been back.

PETERS: What happened to the carvings?

SAWYER: I gave them away, buried them. I don't know.

PETERS: Not your craft. Just wood fibers and vessels slowly sinking into the earth.

SAWYER: That's a way of putting it.

PETERS: No offense. But I think he was after your soul. Don't laugh. Pity me. I'm after Len Hope's soul. I've given up on Frank. Bob is another proposition.

SAWYER: Keeps you on the straight and narrow.

PETERS: You might put it that way.

[*A rhythmic ringing of bells in the distance.*]

SAWYER: What was that?

PETERS: I didn't hear anything.

[*Repeat.*]

SAWYER: The bells.

PETERS: I'm sorry. I'm no use to you. I've been here so often and for so long that every instance of being is so familiar to me that I'm at sea in sensation. Perhaps that's why you carry your little instrument everywhere you go. To arrest these moments.

SAWYER: Misapprehension. This little instrument is very much alive.

PETERS: Forgive me. I was merely commenting upon experience.

SAWYER: Surely. But then there was the ringing of those bells.

PETERS: Look at how the light folds back across the landscape. It seems to mirror the land.

SAWYER: Maybe the magmatic waters affect them, too.

PETERS: Buried things, again.

SAWYER: Yes. Buried things.

PETERS: Ah, this is my magic hour. I was about to put this thing down and take a walk.

SAWYER: In the dark?

PETERS: It is not dark, Sawyer. Some of my colleagues, true, do expand upon the distinction between darkness and the absence of light. I'm not one of those. My mind is set on other dangers, some occasion for knowledge. And, in that light, what is darkness upon this desert?

SAWYER: This isn't a desert.

PETERS: Oh, exactitude.

SAWYER: But stop me before I tell you about the metals in the earth's crust.

PETERS: And you must stop me before my winged sermon on understanding.

[*The sound of a racing horse and buggy, the image of a driver. Distant, then closer. The light is a turbulence.*]

SAWYER: That was Bob King.

PETERS: No.

SAWYER: I swear it was. He almost ran us down.

PETERS: Sawyer, Sawyer. You and I are the only ones awake. Look at me now. We were talking about a metalliferous mineral.

SAWYER: Why are you screwing with my mind? What have I done to you?

PETERS: What kind of question is that? Pull yourself together. We were having a lovely conversation about Old Placers, mining camps in the mountains. You were extremely eloquent about the pit at Cerillos, about gold, silver and lead.

SAWYER: You did not learn this from me.

PETERS: Then from who? Let me restructure that. From whom?

SAWYER: This is not a fucking exercise in grammar. Come here. [*He grabs* PETERS.] I had to be certain you were here. This dangerous way you have of drawing me out. I can't be sure of what you hear.

PETERS: I hear you, Vernon Sawyer.

SAWYER: Frankie!

PETERS: Absent.

SAWYER: Frankie! Frankie!

PETERS: Sawyer, I think you have need of that special light.

[SAWYER *takes* PETERS' *knife.*]

SAWYER: I'll take this.

PETERS: Oh, certainly. Take the knife. Take the light. Take those bells you seem to hear. Take that bush in the distance. Take the fucking mountain. This necessary event can't be deduced from these things. Ah. Did I put that right? No. This contingent event can't be deduced from any necessity. Oh, put it any way you like.

[*The sound of digging.*]

Is that you, Sawyer? Burying something?

[*The beep beep of an absent machine.*]

Are you going, Sawyer? Take me with you. I don't want to drown in this desert.

[SAWYER *walks quickly away.* PETERS *finds* KING *and* FAWCETT, *standing on opposite sides and watching him.*]

Let's just say he belongs to you.

[PETERS *and* KING *disappear.*]

FAWCETT: If I thought you were capable of this mountain, I'd rein it in and hand it to you. [*He produces the pouch.*] Let's see what we have. I don't trust the man. What he returns, he returns in such a niggardly fashion I'm embarrassed for him. Everyone around me goes in disguise. [*He holds up the pouch's contents.*] Nothing but tokens, tokens of what the earth throws up. Len Hope thinks it can unseal my heart, or seal it. I don't know which he intends. Fact is, I have grown wary of intentions. I ought to take this up with Peters. Mr. Peters. A contradiction.

[KING, *dressed in gaucho clothes, pulls* SAWYER, *wearing a pith helmet, khaki shorts and shirt, into* FAWCETT's *sight.* SAWYER *is bound.* KING *carries a shotgun. The three act as though they were in another narrative.*]

KING: I caught him mining, which is to say I caught him thieving. Well, what do you say about that?

FAWCETT: Why bring him to me?

KING: He gave me your name. You want to vouch for him?

FAWCETT: Do I know this man?

KING: Point is, he knows you. Second point, he doesn't belong here. Third point, he was engaged in activity that, given the circumstances, is strictly illegal.

FAWCETT: What are the circumstances?

KING: He didn't clear it with me. I mean, take a look at it. This joker comes in, sets up, starts exploring, raping the land. And he doesn't have the decency to get the proper papers. And, too besides, he seems to have something to do with you, who have been a hive on my behind. I'm talking serious business.

FAWCETT: What is it you want?

KING: I want you to understand what's at stake here. This boy's about to go up Green River, and he's gonna take you along. Unless you're careful. Unless you want to assure me that I've got the right and only man. Is that the way you see it?

FAWCETT: Mining? What have I got to do with mining?

SAWYER: You lying old whoremaster. It was you. It was you. I had my work. Would I be here, if you hadn't stirred me up about the richest silver ore bodies you'd ever seen?

FAWCETT: [*To* KING.] There you go. You've got a madman here. Go on, boy. What else did I tell you?

KING: I'll ask the questions. I've put it to this gentleman that we're on, that is to say, he's on, sovereign ground. He keeps going over the same ground. He babbles. Something about Turquoise Mountain, Shakespeare and some woman named Magdalena, or Kelly. He claims he's gone up the road with you to Madrid.

FAWCETT: The man is living in the past.

KING: Oh? Well, I think I've got me a live animal bound up right here. And, before I brought him before your honor, he filled me with the living word. I don't know why he's here. I don't know what he knows. I know his presence makes me uneasy because he appears to have some design upon this land that escapes me. And furthermore, deacon, he seems to have a clear idea of how this world, my world, is disappearing. Being taken away, he says. And he knows you, and claims to have a written invitation from your very own hand.

FAWCETT: I've never seen him before.

KING: So you repudiate this man?

FAWCETT: Repudiate. Why use words like that? They don't go with what you have before you. This man has just worked up old dreams.

KING: Like yours.

FAWCETT: What?

KING: You don't dream any longer, Frankie? You don't have your eye on that little plot of land that's going to flower into true love and riches?

FAWCETT: You called me Frankie.

KING: Did I?

FAWCETT: Do I know you? I thought there was supposed to be some distance between us. I don't know you. You've kicked up some intimacy between us so that you can sit in judgment of my dreams. Is that it?

KING: Is what it?

FAWCETT: This thief you have here. This idiot who claims to know me.

KING: Why, he speaks your language. He had me going about fissures, fractures, erosion, destruction, all those things that seem to concern you.

FAWCETT: It's common enough.

KING: But this man has turned them into accusations. So I've got him here, your disciple, to help you to explain to me how I'm responsible for the ordinary failings of the world.

FAWCETT: I ask you again. Who are you?

KING: Irrelevant.

FAWCETT: What do you want from me?

KING: I've got this guy here, who wants to help you to explore the world you claim no longer exists. Or that exists, but is not the world you thought you were inhabiting. Hey, now, you can be perfectly happy turning up the imperfections that keep things honest. *¿Verdad?* All you need is drainage, ventilation and the right instruments.

SAWYER: Trivial. Wake up.

KING: You talking to me, boy? Or your traveling companion?

FAWCETT: Leave him with me.

KING: I thought you'd get the point. Now, shouldn't we be talking about a little compensation?

FAWCETT: You mean a ransom.

KING: Call it whatever you want.

FAWCETT: What would you take?

KING: Your unredeemed black ass. [*Laughing, he walks away.*]

SAWYER: What did you expect?

FAWCETT: That he would at least take off his disguise.

SAWYER: Undo me.

[FAWCETT *starts to do that.*]

FAWCETT: Don't pretend to know me.

SAWYER: Wake up. Wake up. Wake up. Wake up.

[FAWCETT *does.* SAWYER *disappears.* FAWCETT *plays with the pouch.*]

FAWCETT: Tokens. Nothing but tokens. This is how he pays me. We'll see.

[PETERS, *dressed in a cassock, pulls* KING, *bundled in a blanket and lying on a travois, into sight.*]

PETERS: Thank god, I've run up on a human face. I tell you, it is nothing I want to be doing until the bell is tolled up yonder. Hello, I say, you must see how it stands with us. Could you give me some help?

FAWCETT: Where did you come from?

PETERS: What's that got to do with anything? I have a sick, exhausted man on my hands, as anyone who isn't blind can see. Oh, I'm sorry. Forgive this little show of impatience. Can you get your ass over here? Is there no charity in you?

FAWCETT: Where did you come from? Who are you?

PETERS: Oh, god. They warned me. I wouldn't listen. I left all that sustained me for the possibility in these fucking mountains, and here I stand, subject to the caprice of a nigger's charity.

FAWCETT: Lift him, and get him out of here.

PETERS: What is this, a test?

FAWCETT: No, father, not a test. A recommendation.

PETERS: Curious that you invoke my profession. If that were, in fact, my profession. Or if my profession could be invoked for its function here. If such a profession had a function that could be invoked. But your confusion ends in your curiosity, or I should say, in the curiosity that invokes my profession. My brother is very sick, and I am just about in a rage.

FAWCETT: So?

PETERS: So what do you want from me?

FAWCETT: Take him away. He contaminates the place.

PETERS: I think you'll have to move me.

FAWCETT: So this is the test.

PETERS: A recommendation. Or an invocation. Perhaps you can tell me what that figure represents on the outcropping we passed on our way to here.

FAWCETT: Where? There at the point of this road?

PETERS: Yes.

FAWCETT: There are no figures on those rocks. It must be your eyes.

PETERS: My eyes. Yes. You seem to have buried yourself from sight back here. No one would notice that there is any sign of life back here.

FAWCETT: Why are you traveling this way?

PETERS: You assume we're traveling. Perhaps we're coming home.

FAWCETT: Don't be vulgar.

PETERS: Tell me how I've offended you.

FAWCETT: Why are you traveling this way?

PETERS: What?

FAWCETT: Like this. Half-eaten by hunger. Raggedy. Moaning and begging. You shame me.

PETERS: Do I now? I've heard you people are tight-assed, slaves to decorum. Spontaneity? Oh, no. You're like those others. They got exercised because we had adapted this buggy to get us from place to place.

FAWCETT: I don't know who those others are. But, of course, they have a right to ask your purpose.

PETERS: My purpose. The idiots couldn't seem to abide my garment, though its purpose ought to be perfectly clear.

FAWCETT: You're playing with me. Don't you think I recognize you?

PETERS: Bully for you. Tell me who I am.

FAWCETT: You're the same fucking trickster who passed through here before, trying to sell me damaged goods. I've got news for you. That nigger you imposed upon me escaped. Satisfied? Shall we start all over?

PETERS: Start over. We're starting now. None of what you tell me ever happened. You see me? You see that man lying there? We're all you could possibly have seen. We're the only ones with courage enough to come up that road.

FAWCETT: I see.

PETERS: Wipe that smile off your face. I refuse to be insulted by someone who is so ahistorical, so bereft of experience. I know what you think. They're suffering, you say. Yes, suffering. But I'll tell you what suffering is. Suffering is finding you here, with no idea of why that figure has appeared on that rock.

FAWCETT: Can he walk?

PETERS: What? Why, of course, he can walk.

FAWCETT: Good. I'm glad, because I'm relieving you of your buggy.

PETERS: You know what this will cost you.

FAWCETT: Get him out of my buggy. Indecent. You have no purpose. You can't get the names right. You've mistaken me for a Christian. And you expect to walk away, with my money in your pocket, my blessing on your head. What kind of man would I be, if I didn't strip you of your disguise? Up. Up. Out. Get down the road. Get out of my sight. Sell your story to someone who has experienced your suffering. [*He has them on their way.*]

PETERS: We're peaceful people. You're lucky we don't believe in violence. You think we didn't know what you were like? We'll see if you can hold on to your fucking balls.

FAWCETT: You will find me here.

[PETERS *and* KING *go.* FAWCETT *tests the travois, pulls it off.* HOPE *enters, wearing a poncho. He addresses the audience.*]

HOPE: Long night. I put myself in the way of meeting my old antagonist, who thinks of himself as my savior. Doctor Bob King. Doctor King. Or Doctor Bob, as some folk call him. Say, I've seen him myself on the water. He has a healing touch. We've still got some unfinished business.

[KING *appears above, talking as though casually to someone not there.* HOPE *continues in his own domain.*]

KING: This Len Hope. The man has just let himself go. One setback and he gives up. When he came here, I thought he was a man of spunk, of initiative. Times I thought of him as my own son. I took him under my wing, advised him, helped him. I was wrong. He didn't have it.

HOPE: He always treated me like an orphan. He pretended I turned up from somewhere else, not that I had roots deeper than his in the place. I could never get to that, why he wanted to deny me my heritage in this place.

KING: He's got no right to let himself go. I protected him. We have an obligation to protect each other. We have an obligation to be strong.

HOPE: They say he had a special affection for my mother. Say, don't think I accuse my mother of any weakness. She could not have asked for a better captain to see her daughter home from madness. He's like that, Doctor Bob, a shelter in the time of a storm.

KING: He fiddled with my strength. He took my good name and rolled it in the pig filth of his incompetence. I won't forgive him for it.

HOPE: He doesn't know how far I've moved since the time he tried to ruin me. You'll hear it. The death of my feed and grain. I used to ship it in boxcars. It was cheap enough. Until. Say, I lost my wheels so simply. King sent his men to load the boxcars with other things. I had to find another way. It cost me. This is not what I want to tell you. I have become a man of vision. Frank Fawcett is part of my vision. He loves to see himself approved in little tokens. But he needs me. I have begun to measure the available water. More important, I have begun to measure the spirit of the people to whom the water belongs. And this Sawyer has a funny bug about mines.

[KING *disappears.* PETERS, *dressed for the hunt, appears.*]

PETERS: What are you doing out here?

HOPE: A hell of a way to greet an old associate.

PETERS: So now we're associates.

HOPE: Unless I'm too disreputable for you to acknowledge. You're quite a distance from the camp. But I remember you. You were the one who rambled at night. Never got lost. Showed no fear. Amazing. I was in awe.

PETERS: Impossible, Len Hope. No power can receive what by nature it is unsuited to receive.

HOPE: Sounds as though somebody's putting words in your mouth.

PETERS: We've had this lesson before. I once had you near the gate of William of Ware. Certainly, I confused you with all the refutations and modifications, the thrilling discriminations, the distinctions that would honor a certain Scot. But, now that I have you here, I don't want to obscure your presence again, Len Hope. Tell me that I needn't any longer confuse you with Frank Fawcett.

HOPE: I'm slow, Mr. Peters. I miss those subtleties that tell me I'm just another nigger.

PETERS: Misprision. I accused you of no failing, except the one of being entirely inscrutable to yourself.

HOPE: Big words.

PETERS: True words.

HOPE: Whose truth?

PETERS: Yours. From the evidence.

HOPE: If I didn't know your habits, I'd say you were suffering the effects of a Kentucky breakfast.

PETERS: That's the one with three large whiskeys and a chaw.

HOPE: Mm hum. Local color. Folklore. Legend. The thing that's not you, but that you understand perhaps too well. We're rambling. The question involved something about truth.

PETERS: I admire you, Lenny. You stick to the point. Or to the question, at least. You seem to have been disconcerted by my tugging at your disguise.

HOPE: You didn't look me up to get into a discussion of disguises.

PETERS: I? Looked you up?

HOPE: Don't play me.

PETERS: Don't be absurd. How the hell would I know where to find you out here on the Watermelon?

HOPE: You followed me once, when I walked away from camp.

PETERS: I stumbled upon you once, when you walked away.

HOPE: No. I still see you. You were tracking me the way you would a deer. I sensed you, and I began to backtrack and to disappear into the brush on either side of the path. You were scrupulous.

PETERS: What were you doing?

HOPE: Testing the trapper's art.

PETERS: There were no trappers in these mountains.

HOPE: Did I say there were?

PETERS: Then what was the point?

HOPE: It was an exploration.

PETERS: Nonsense. The time had passed.

HOPE: Ah, yes. It's just another instance of a certain naiveté. Probably borrowed from those *norteamericanos*, but most probably the truth of being unsuited by nature.

PETERS: I never know how to take you, Hope.

HOPE: Good, good. Take hope.

PETERS: Go trapping.

[FAWCETT *suddenly enters, pulling* KING *on the travois.*]

FAWCETT: Not a bad idea. [*To* HOPE.] *Bonjour, mon cher.*

HOPE: I thought I'd seen the last of you, on your way to Chihuahua.

FAWCETT: I have no commerce with Chihuahua. There's too much innocence in these valleys, here around the Pecos, the Rio Grande. Besides, I don't enjoy having to ask other people for permission to freeze my balls off for the little drabs of bad coin circulating in these mountains.

HOPE: Haven't you got things a little backwards? What's he doing in the buggy? He should be pulling you.

FAWCETT: What an idea. Why?

HOPE: Obviously, you've just come down from up north. You and I understand that trade. And it looks rather suspicious that you seem to be in control.

FAWCETT: I am that I am. Hey, my brothers at Abiquiu put up the money and the sweat to get me to Ute country.

HOPE: I'm not questioning your ability to move your legs. It's a question of demand and control.

FAWCETT: You seem concerned. Why embarrass me before these others? Look at this man here. He can't make sense of me. God, what can I say?

PETERS: You might start by explaining yourself. And that man, I think I know. He looks devastated by the weather. What have you done to him?

FAWCETT: What have I done to him? I rescued his fucking ass. He was lounging in Taos, steamed up on that Taos Lightning. If you don't think I have a redemptive touch, take a look at the man in front of you. He snuck up from the Paso del Norte. He had no goal in mind. Where was he going, the upper Missouri, the Platte? He would have starved to death. But you see me, *yo*, Jean Baptiste...

HOPE: Is *that* the name you're using now?

FAWCETT: Well, no. Here, I am Juan Bautista. But the point is, I knew the business. I knew the business of business, the politics of business. I could take him into my art. I could make him an interpreter. I could teach him how to ride the waters.

PETERS: I'm not concerned with your genius. [PETERS *goes to* KING.] Are you all right? Don't be intimidated. I can handle either one, or both, of those two. Do you remember me? What's wrong here? Why doesn't he speak?

FAWCETT: Maybe he has nothing to say.

PETERS: Impossible. This is a man of experience.

HOPE: Experience, you say. Well, whose?

PETERS: Don't get cute. I have no patience with your beaver bushiness.

HOPE: Beaver bushiness. You've got everything by the tail.

FAWCETT: Or by the head. Let go. You see how this man gave in to my ministrations.

PETERS: I am prepared…

[KING *puts his hand on* PETERS' *arm.*]

KING: Did I tell you what I saw last winter? Up there, where I camped. Old furnaces, broken bits of pottery, "many small stone houses, some of which have one story beneath the surface of the earth." A true life. Gone now. I am now in this man's care.

PETERS: Do you want to be?

KING: God, what a question. Look at the energy.

PETERS: [*To* FAWCETT.] I don't know what you've done to him. But he is an old friend.

KING: I've never seen you in my life.

PETERS: He is an old friend, whose family bound me to his care. Even you would have to see that it makes sense for you to transfer his care to me.

FAWCETT: Why?

PETERS: Goddamn it, there's such a thing as decorum.

HOPE: Decorum.

FAWCETT: Let's talk business. Here we are…

PETERS: This is not business.

FAWCETT: Then what is it?

PETERS: It's a question of form, of the proper measure of things.

[SAWYER *is suddenly there with surveying instruments.*]

SAWYER: How true. Good. I see you understand. I am not violating any boundaries, any laws, any unspoken agreements, any trust. This is an objective service.

FAWCETT: [*To* HOPE.] You fucked around until you let this guy catch up to us.

HOPE: I'm not the one dragging dead baggage.

FAWCETT: Let's not argue in front of them.

HOPE: There is no argument. Not after that first understanding.

FAWCETT: Right.

SAWYER: Well, are you going to keep me waiting? Or can I just go about my work?

KING: Get on with it. Just don't trouble me with your difficulties.

SAWYER: This is not an easy measure to take. You see, I have to take all of you into consideration. It would be better if there were nothing here. That is to say, if there were no one here. Christ, I'm putting this badly. I mean this was here before any of you, and you, as it were, contaminate the measurement.

HOPE: Do you even know what the fuck you're measuring?

SAWYER: I warrant that any explanation would be beyond you.

PETERS: [*To* SAWYER.] Do you know these people?

SAWYER: We might have met.

PETERS: You can see how things stand. I'm trying to put things in some kind of order. My companion and I need to proceed undisturbed, and then we can see about these other matters.

SAWYER: Are you trying to distract me from my job?

PETERS: Not at all. I'm trying to help you.

SAWYER: In what way?

PETERS: I'm trying to get us out of the way.

SAWYER: That would be a start. What about these others?

PETERS: I leave them to you.

SAWYER: Oh, I see. It's my problem. Thank you very much. What do you want me to do for you?

PETERS: Just go about your work. Insist upon your authority. Open the way.

SAWYER: You are in the way. All of you.

HOPE: Don't you recognize me? We measured this land together.

SAWYER: This land?

HOPE: Not here exactly. That hidden valley. I had my authority from the same place. Why do you think I'm here?

PETERS: This idiot was exploring the remains of a trapping life.

HOPE: It's true. I can't shake you. Over years, I have had you in mind. I have had you within me.

PETERS: Within you.

HOPE: The fucking life that you scout up, every time you ascend. Do I need you? Out of that buggy! Off this mountain! Out of my life!

PETERS: Hope?

HOPE: On your knees.

[PETERS *drops to his knees.* HOPE *addresses the others.*]

Get out of here. He belongs to me. Go. I'm going to sacrifice this man.

[*The others scurry away.*]

PETERS: Hope, is this all I mean to you?

HOPE: We won't discuss it.

PETERS: Hope, I've always meant to ask you. Are you Avicennian or Scotist?

HOPE: Good night, Mr. Peters. I have a date with a certain power.

[*He goes. Pause.* PETERS *goes, leaving the travois. The five reenter, and arrange themselves around the area.*]

SAWYER: [*Indicating the travois.*] Evidence. Evidence. Things like this tell me I'm right.

KING: You go on about this evidence.

PETERS: And about being right.

SAWYER: I believe in the material existence of things.

KING: He believes. Oh, lord. He believes.

FAWCETT: Time was, I would have believed in him.

PETERS: And now?

FAWCETT: Irrelevant. I don't consider him part of the equation.

[HOPE *goes to the travois, pulls up a buckskin shirt.*]

HOPE: Look at this. It reminds me of my better days.

PETERS: Tell us about it.

HOPE: I will. You others listen. This man has no ears. I've heard his stories. You've seen the tortoise making his way across a mudbank?

FAWCETT: Be careful.

HOPE: I understand. I violate no boundaries, no laws, no unspoken agreements, no trust.

SAWYER: Are you finished?

HOPE: When I finish, you can sing.

SAWYER: Go on, then.

HOPE: I was there when they built the first locomotive. I named it. You don't believe me. I consulted with Cyrus Holliday in Kansas, when there was hope of cinching the country. You don't believe me.

PETERS: I won't stand for this.

HOPE: It's my story.

SAWYER: But there are rules. We're all agreed.

HOPE: Shall I start again?

PETERS: You must.

HOPE: The only necessity I know is the one that ties my heart to the place where I found the woman I love.

PETERS: A love story, then.

HOPE: That would please you more than the ones that show my power.

KING: Nonsense. Your power.

FAWCETT: You're not being fair to the man. Let him continue.

HOPE: Thank you. My father was a small man, brick red, of fiery temper. He loved the roads, and he loved the freight yards. His father had worked on the trains, and had taken him down to the shunting yards to give him a lesson in organization and design.

KING: Is this about your father, or about you?

HOPE: It's about patience.

SAWYER: You're a dreamer. Dreams have nothing to do with stories. Can I get a judgment? Is this man finished?

HOPE: I've only started.

SAWYER: Go on, then.

HOPE: I come again. I was there when the first cathedral was raised. And I knew its beauty was not in the wood and mud that held it up, but in the question that was in my heart when I saw it finished. I sat by the river with a child's slate learning to figure my body's necessities.

PETERS: And that was love?

HOPE: I need some patience here.

SAWYER: All we've got is a small man, who's an engineer or an architect, perhaps a divine with mathematical talent. This doesn't add up.

HOPE: This is the shirt I wore when I crossed the border. I knew I had come into a place where the water would be scarce, and where death would be as quick as love. You deny me? Good. So we start with essential things. Albuquerque is a fragile flower. It fades. You think I want to remember the names of the dead? I'm sorry. The love story is over. Take over from me in passionate song.

SAWYER: Not hard. There was a little black boy, and here he lowers his eyes for the arrogance of the expression, who had been raised with a delicacy that made him, if not clever, at least desirable. He lived with an older couple, who might have been his grandparents, his guardians, people who might have simply taken him in. The little town he inhabited showed no pity on one hand, showing him the backs of buildings, the poor cuts of the hog, the unrepaired drainpipe, but on the other hand a compassion in the commerce with numbers, the radiance of the things that were made around him. Teachers courted his facility. He nipped at numerical tricks like a puppy after dog biscuits. He had a natural way with the proper configuration of words, that is, he could spell his name. His hands, though, remained clumsy, even though he never stumbled over himself at games. There were those who cautioned him and his grandparents-guardians-rescuers-jailers against aiming too high. What could he say? He had plans. He had dreams. Well, to make an unfortunate story short, there came an opportunity for the little fellow to display himself and to aggrandize his supporters among the population at large. A contest. In reading maps. Now, our man had been fervently attached to the map room at school and in the public library. He had been taken on drives through various parts of the city and the state. He was acquainted with coordinates, and shape, and distances. He should have been able to identify a misplaced rock. Did I say that the task included a global perspective? One would have to identify Afghanistan. Well, the day dawned. The contest proceeded. Our scholar's turn came. They threw him a fish. And he drowned. He was asked to identify a neighborhood in central Albuquerque, one that he had traversed day after day, and he couldn't say where he was.

FAWCETT: What's the point of this story?

SAWYER: I'm not a moralist.

HOPE: It was a goddamned trick. All those inner city grids look alike.

SAWYER: Do they now?

PETERS: Listen. What is this? It's just a story. Well, a report.

FAWCETT: I see. Just a report. Insignificant.

PETERS: I didn't say *that*.

KING: Damn, you oughtta. Yeah. It was a significant occasion. I'd like to hear what the little bugger said.

HOPE: So would I.

SAWYER: Well, nothing. There was no malignity in it. He had been undone by human failings, by the way that things are. Say, it was the judges who cried.

HOPE: You broke the rule. I asked you to give us passion.

SAWYER: What do you want from me? I told you the fucking story. Am I responsible for this little idiot's pretension?

PETERS: It's over.

HOPE: Judgment. I come again.

KING: You're finished. You had your chance.

SAWYER: We're all full of stories.

HOPE: I don't believe you.

KING: Bless you, then.

FAWCETT: You've fallen apart.

PETERS: He said trust.

HOPE: That word was never uttered.

KING: That's a lie.

SAWYER: Please, can we get back…

FAWCETT: You belong to me.

HOPE: You failed me.

KING: You don't know how to understand…

HOPE: *"Lleno de mi, sitiado en mi epidermis
    por un dios inasible que me ahoga…"*

PETERS: *"Einmal,
    da horte ich ihn,
    da wusch er die Welt…"*

FAWCETT: *"Yo he pretendido odiar…
    lo he pretendido…"*

SAWYER: "*…de no saber nombrar*
               lo que no existe…"

KING: "*…un splendor mi squarcio 'l velo*
              del sonno, e un chiamar: Surgi: che fai?"

HOPE: "*Niemand…*"

PETERS: "*zeugt…*"

FAWCETT: "*für…*"

SAWYER: "*den…*"

KING: "*Zeugen.*"

[*They weave a counterpoint and aria from these expressions. They begin to speak in tongues. They modulate into singing hymns, each one singing a different hymn, while they ravage the travois for garments they display, put on and wave like flags. They reach a high pitch, pick up the travois and rush off. Two childlike figures—* ONE, *female;* TWO, *male—have established themselves upstage. They wear white shirts and pants, and are barefoot. The male whirls through a series of balletic poses. The female sits on a box, observing the dancer.*]

ONE: You shouldn't pretend. Look at the trouble it brings.

TWO: No trouble to me.

ONE: How can you say that? Look at our situation. Days without food. Not even a wolfberry with maggots.

TWO: What an imagination. Besides, that was in another place.

ONE: What other place? They're all the same. Nothing but suffering. I think it's these white clothes.

TWO: No. It's that box you carry. Your grasses and creosote bush, your scorpions and spiders, cicadas, dragonflies and ants. And that one lonely candle. Haven't I been with you? Does your solitude need these things?

ONE: Go on with your pirouettes and periphrases.

TWO: You disgust me.

ONE: How so?

TWO: You make me seem unruly.

ONE: Unruly.

TWO: Yes, unruled by rule.

ONE: Is *that* what it means?

TWO: Didn't you know?

ONE: I don't have your genius.

TWO: That is the begging bottom truth. So what do you say about that?

ONE: I say we've lost our way. I wouldn't be so offended, if I could be sure that the mountain is there.

TWO: Waiting for us.

ONE: Exactly.

TWO: Absurd. We're on a mountain. And it would take very little to assure us that we were on *the* mountain. Except, of course, this mountain might not be that mountain because it is only that mountain that resembles this.

ONE: I know what you're doing.

TWO: Oh?

ONE: You're trying to swim away from this entanglement.

TWO: Swim? What has swimming got to do with it? Don't mix your metaphors.

ONE: So the other place has followed us?

TWO: Don't confuse me.

ONE: I love your dance. It belongs to the place.

TWO: It belongs to me.

ONE: I've just noticed. We're dressed alike.

TWO: Don't try to make yourself strange. Oh, no. You want to make me strange. Then I go into your box. Clever.

ONE: Unruly. Like that escarpment which turns a different face to the same star. Your dance has its reasons. The rhythm veils a disappearance.

TWO: It's time to get rid of your box. [*He starts to do that.*]

ONE: Don't you touch my box.

TWO: It's time you stopped digging around and digging up these skeletons.

ONE: Listen.

[*They stop.*]

Water. Get these clothes off. My, my, it sounds like a flood. We'll be able to wash everything clean.

TWO: I don't believe it. This is not happening. Definition. We were lonely enough without this bitching water.

[*The first figure picks up the box and runs.*]

ONE: Hurry. We might be too late.

TWO: Definition. Definition. Don't let me see any of this. There is something malign about a force that would interrupt my dance.

[*The first figure returns, disconsolate.*]

ONE: Well, it's gone. Or was never there. Are you satisfied? Bastard. You preferred your pirouettes and periphrases to being in touch with living water.

TWO: If it disappeared like that, it was never there. I meant to take it up with you, how you're always holding me to account for these natural failings.

ONE: Who else should I blame, if not you?

TWO: No one.

ONE: Ah, no one. I sense the beginning of something fortuitous.

TWO: Forestalling.

ONE: Foreordained.

TWO: Never.

ONE: Shall we start again?

TWO: It wouldn't do any good.

ONE: Precisely. So we'll let it go as it is.

TWO: Precisely. No more blame?

ONE: I've buried it with the sound of the water.

TWO: Good. You know. I've just noticed. We're dressed exactly alike.

ONE: Imagine that.

TWO: It is the beginning of all our imagination.

[*The first figure sits on the box to contemplate the second figure, who turns through a series of balletic poses. They disappear.* KING, *in a drover's shirt, is downstage, shoveling.* PETERS *approaches.*]

PETERS: What in the world are you doing?

KING: What in the fuck have you been doing?

PETERS: Whoa. Did I miss dinner?

KING: You could have.

PETERS: I didn't. And though my presence might have been wanted, I can't see that you would have been enhanced by it. Again. What are you doing?

KING: Trying to solve a mystery, buddy.

PETERS: A buried body.

KING: Maybe. You might not have paid attention. But old Bob King has not been asleep. Frankie spends a lot of time out here. I heard him digging more than once. Look at the ground. It's freshly dug. Now, what is old Frank Huey Fawcett burying?

PETERS: His name's not Huey.

KING: Damn his name. I know his damned name. What I don't know is what he's up to, or how that affects me. The man hasn't spent twenty minutes in twenty years talking to me. Now, he wants to talk to me. Why?

PETERS: I thought you knew why.

KING: I know what you tell me.

PETERS: Did I tell you to come out here and dig up the mountain, to uncover Frankie's secret?

KING: You seem damned happy to keep his secret.

PETERS: If he has one.

KING: Tell me, Jeff. Who are you working for? Me? Or him?

PETERS: Don't be ridiculous.

KING: No, sir. I can't count on you anymore. Good god, I can't count on anybody anymore. People you think would understand what it costs me to put things in place. Who is this goddamned Sawyer? A little buford, nuzzling up to me for protection. I don't like the look in his eyes. The man will run, I tell you, the man will run.

PETERS: Give me the shovel.

KING: I'm not finished.

PETERS: I'll help you.

KING: I don't need your help.

PETERS: Maybe you ought to get some sleep, Bob.

KING: Don't tell me what to do.

PETERS: Don't let me interrupt.

KING: That's right. Don't interrupt. Well? Don't you have anything to say? Doesn't the Scotus have something to make this pain any easier?

PETERS: I think I understand why you have to insult me. You have this idea of my special needs. You see an old man pushing further into doubt. Hold still a moment, Bob. I'll come up with something from scripture that ought to soothe us.

KING: I'm busy here, reverend. [*He shovels, and turns up a tattered garment.*] What the hell is this? What is this? He buried this here. Look at it. What does this mean? What is this nigger trying to do?

PETERS: Calm down. What is it? What makes you think it means anything?

KING: Am I blind, Peters? [*He shovels again, hits a box.*] Ah ha!

PETERS: Leave it.

KING: Your ass. [*He starts to open the box.*] .

PETERS: It's none of your business, Bob.

KING: Well, now, tell me just what is my business, Jeffrey Peters.

PETERS: This is not your domain.

KING: I thought so. You're nothing but a camp inspector. I put my trust in you. But what do *you* want? [*He opens the box, which displays some beads, jewels, papers.*] Let's see what we have here. Let's see if old Frankie Fawcett has a secret worth telling.

PETERS: This is pure innocence. These are things Frankie wants to discard. What better place? I'm ashamed, Bob. You've never violated his privacy before.

[KING *hastily reads the papers, thrusts them at* PETERS.]

I won't touch them.

KING: Suit yourself.

PETERS: How remarkable. The way you've forced me into this corner, pretending a vulnerability you don't feel. I resent this lacerating squeamishness you display because it diminished me, it makes my love for you just a game that any child can play. So you drum up this charade of mysterious, dangerous Frank Fawcett.

KING: I heard you talking to him.

PETERS: That was soul inquiry, Bob. This is murder.

KING: Distinction.

PETERS: I'll take the box. And the garment.

KING: You want to challenge me for them.

PETERS: Put it that way.

KING: Rescue Frankie from the old redneck doctor.

PETERS: Put it that way.

KING: How would you put it?

PETERS: That I believe you. These things belong to Frank Fawcett. He had a reason to bury them here. I respect his reasons.

KING: He doesn't respect you.

PETERS: That may be.

KING: Doesn't it disturb you?

PETERS: Of course.

KING: It disturbs me. And you'll just walk in and hand him back his garbage.

PETERS: Please. I didn't say that.

KING: Well, now. You're tougher than I thought. But isn't it up to me to say what's to be done? To destroy this filth?

PETERS: Don't go on.

KING: I swear I don't know what's happening to me. Pity me, Peters. I have to live with your contradictions.

PETERS: Glory, glory. I thought I had failed you.

[KING *hands* PETERS *the box, throws the garment at him.*]

KING: Get these things out of my face. [KING *takes his shovel, and starts to leave.*]

PETERS: Is this all?

KING: Isn't it enough?

[*They go separate ways.* FAWCETT *and* SAWYER *appear.* SAWYER *seems still to be dressing. He carries a mail pouch over his shoulder.*]

FAWCETT: Now, you know I shouldn't be doing this. But I thought you ought to meet someone who has special knowledge about these mountains. It's rare, as you well know, to find anybody who knows how things came to be as they are. And it is rare, indeed, to find someone like yourself who has any interest in the way things are.

SAWYER: Len Hope is a geologist?

FAWCETT: Len Hope is a guide.

SAWYER: I got the impression that you and he don't, or didn't, get along.

FAWCETT: Gossip. It's the way some folk want it to be.

SAWYER: Then you are close. Family.

FAWCETT: We're all family, Mr. Sawyer.

SAWYER: Why are you giving me this special tour, Frankie?

FAWCETT: I'm not fooled by appearances.

SAWYER: Oh? You see through my disguise, assuming I have a disguise.

FAWCETT: You may very well have a disguise. That's not my concern. I was addressing the appearance of belonging.

SAWYER: Belonging. Longing. Hey, this is getting deep. Do you mean I belong to you?

FAWCETT: I see I'm making you uncomfortable.

SAWYER: You have a surprising delicacy, Mr. Fawcett.

FAWCETT: It's just down this way.

SAWYER: I will be pleased to come this way when the sun shines.

FAWCETT: With your other obligations, you'll just have to make a special effort. And bring another set of eyes.

SAWYER: For?

FAWCETT: The deep waters. Rocks that might seem a little bilious.

SAWYER: You spend a good bit of time up here, then.

FAWCETT: Not here. Further north, by the peak. These folk don't want to be too far from Tijeras.

SAWYER: Keep in touch with the source.

FAWCETT: Could be. Be near the springs.

SAWYER: Springs keep you healthy.

FAWCETT: That's what I like about you, Mr. Sawyer. You move easy. We get into a conversation about springs, and you're ready to draw me a map of the soul.

SAWYER: Funny. How high up are we? I'm beginning to feel a little disoriented. I thought I was talking to the master of springs. Suddenly, I find myself with a master at my feet.

FAWCETT: I'm not easily offended, sir.

SAWYER: What are we waiting for? Why did we come here?

FAWCETT: To hunt.

SAWYER: I mean this instant. This excursion at the end of a very long day. Why are you letting me in on your secrets, Frankie?

FAWCETT: All the wrong questions.

SAWYER: I'll see you in the morning.

[HOPE appears.]

HOPE: Patience, Vernon Sawyer. Let's do away with this formality. Formality belongs to the earth. To the Sandia. To those stars that present themselves in our hemisphere. All things in due course, and on course.

SAWYER: Who are you?

HOPE: Hope.

[He and FAWCETT laugh.]

SAWYER: Glad I could make you boys laugh.

FAWCETT: Let's do away with the boy.

SAWYER: That's a start, isn't it, Frank? Toward that rediscovered family. How can I help you? You didn't bring me out here to talk about the Precambrian crystalline rocks on the western side of these mountains.

HOPE: Listen to him, Frank. A schoolboy. You're right, Mr. Sawyer. We couldn't count on your knowing anything about where you stand.

SAWYER: What do you mean? Why, anyone out here on the Watermelon can know where he stands. Even you. Tell me about it.

HOPE: [To FAWCETT.] This is the opportunity you thought we should take?

SAWYER: Frankie said you were an expert. So, of course, you can tell me the dimensions of this uplift and how it stands to Albuquerque, and how it merges with the Hagan basin, and ends up down there several miles south of the Tijeras Canyon.

HOPE: Are you finished?

SAWYER: Finished!? I could sing forever about the sedimentary and volcanic deposits that began two billion years ago. But, of course, you can't know this. Weren't you supposed to tell me about how we got here? How we're looking at the roots of ancient mountains and shallow seas. How this little mountain we're standing on was once much higher.

HOPE: So you've done your homework. What do we have for Mr. Sawyer, Frank? A gold star? A ribbon?

SAWYER: So you want to talk about some esoteric knowledge that has escaped us.

HOPE: Escaped you. You're a miner, Sawyer...

SAWYER: I make no claims...

HOPE: Tell me about your failures.

SAWYER: Who am I talking to? What is this shit about failure?

HOPE: Let's go back to those shallow seas. You have a very agile mind. So good that it remains undisturbed by the rumor of things that never happened, by the evidence of many a great absence. You're a subtle man, *compadre*. The old lands you conjure don't really concern you. You're a courageous man, brother. You look at these bones, and you accept the death that their birth obscures. It's all right, isn't it? This movement you can't really understand, these hidden creative moments that leave something for you to ride in and make your own. Magic. [HOPE *asks for* FAWCETT's *pouch, opens it.*] Like these tokens.

SAWYER: What are they?

HOPE: Examine them.

SAWYER: Little bits of mineral. What are these, coins? Medals? What's the point?

HOPE: The point is there is no point.

SAWYER: Say, I'm a little bit on the other side of weary. I don't have time for these games.

HOPE: Tell me about Old Placers.

SAWYER: What about it?

FAWCETT: The Real de Dolores. Dolores. Suffering, Mr. Sawyer. It didn't help that you gave the land the Virgin's name.

SAWYER: It must be these premature wrinkles. Vernon Sawyer wasn't there.

FAWCETT: Family, Vernon Sawyer.

HOPE: And I *was* there. No place could have been more miserable, even when the father of light came to pursue the gold.

SAWYER: These things are dead.

HOPE: We hear you.

SAWYER: I mean the things you have in your hand.

FAWCETT: No quarrel.

SAWYER: That can't be the point.

HOPE: Frank, the man is a great logician.

FAWCETT: Indisputably.

HOPE: He sees us standing here, moving these memories around.

FAWCETT: He becomes fascinated.

HOPE: He doesn't have to get involved in any kind of family quarrel. He doesn't even have to pretend to be interested.

FAWCETT: So when my brother hands me a pouch with every token of my own dissolution, he can look the other way.

HOPE: And pretend that nothing that has been said concerns him.

FAWCETT: Certainly.

HOPE: I do detect a slight breathlessness.

FAWCETT: I knew you would notice.

HOPE: I count on you to put your finger on it.

FAWCETT: I think he thinks he might betray himself.

HOPE: Cut the wrong figure.

FAWCETT: Or none at all. After all, he has the machine.

HOPE: Ah, yes. That was my mistake.

FAWCETT: You tried to take away the formality of the machine.

HOPE: Exactly.

FAWCETT: Do you feel abandoned, Sawyer?

SAWYER: You know, of course, how ridiculous this minstrel show is. Don't bother. I can find my way back. I would have thought, hey, shit, Frankie wants to hook me in some of this mysterious shit he's cooking. Okay. A fall night in the mountains. Storytelling time. A little frivolous uneasiness. But, god, you didn't even offer a little homey drunkenness. I was better off in the tent, and the misapprehension of Bob King. That's what I get for following my intuition.

HOPE: Don't think you can just walk away from us.

SAWYER: Is there a problem?

[HOPE and FAWCETT laugh. FAWCETT twists SAWYER's arm.]

FAWCETT: Is there a problem, he says.

HOPE: Not at all. These mountains are an eastward-tilted fault block that shows large spectacular outcrops of Precambrian crystalline rocks exposed along the steeper western side. The deer are sleeping, or standing in pools in the moonlight. The man who has you in his embrace has over thirty years of service in the hospitality arts. And I have given up all hope of being true to my singular self.

SAWYER: What do you want?

HOPE: A witness.

SAWYER: To what?

HOPE: To us.

SAWYER: That means nothing to me.

HOPE: What do you mean? You were in our company. You talked with us. Isn't that enough? No? No, he's right, Frank. It isn't enough. He has to go back, and tell Bob King that he touched upon our ambition, and felt ashamed that he never noticed it before.

SAWYER: You haven't told me a fucking thing.

HOPE: Listen to the man. Sly. He cuts right through our reticence, gets us babbling about the coursing of the universe, and then he goes mute. Grows senseless. Can't remember why he came here. Do you know why you came here, my man? Let me tell you again. You were on your way into the recognition of a life you had forgotten. Look around you. [*He indicates the abandoned machinery.*] These are your orphans. Let him go, Frank. Let him go tell Bob King how senseless he's been.

SAWYER: You're lucky I'm a decent man. We'll forget about this. Nothing happened. I took a walk. I saw no one. Is that the way you see it?

FAWCETT: You're asking me to lie.

SAWYER: Only if he asks you.

FAWCETT: If who asks me?

SAWYER: King. When you talk to him.

FAWCETT: When I talk to him, I won't have to tell him anything about you.

SAWYER: I can make it back without you.

FAWCETT: We know you can, Mr. Sawyer. And, oh. [*He shows the pistol.*] I have no designs on your guns. Goodnight, Mr. Sawyer.

[SAWYER *leaves.* HOPE *refills the pouch, closes it and tosses it to* FAWCETT.]

HOPE: Why do we keep this around?

FAWCETT: It makes you seem ancient.

HOPE: I have the idea that you feel I'm no longer worthy of your deception, Frank. We have to get back on track, or the others will come between us.

FAWCETT: I was about to point this out to you.

HOPE: You knew you could count on my intuition.

FAWCETT: And your malice.

HOPE: Good. I was afraid I was losing my touch.

FAWCETT: Impossible.

HOPE: And what about you?

FAWCETT: I'm happy to say my skills have not deserted me. You know, Len Hope, I won't rest until I've uncovered every injury that keeps them tethered to their failings.

HOPE: And for me?

FAWCETT: There's hope.

HOPE: I annoy you.

FAWCETT: You let Sawyer off too lightly. We had agreed…

HOPE: Agreed what?

FAWCETT: I was ready to put the fire to him.

HOPE: I don't love you, Frank. I don't love this righteousness.

FAWCETT: Ho, god. Listen to him. No. Let him listen to himself. I heard you. You borrowed my words. You used them as though they belonged to you.

HOPE: Ridiculous.

FAWCETT: No. I let you go on. I said to myself, Hope has put his hand on my spirit. He's come home.

HOPE: I'm not putting up with this abuse again.

FAWCETT: Hey, now, that's a hell of a way to talk about our connection, Len. It makes our agreement a mistake.

HOPE: There seems to be a misunderstanding here.

FAWCETT: Why'd you give me the gun?

HOPE: To liberate you.

FAWCETT: You know, I'm beginning to worry about you. You come to me with these little pouches, a pistol, a strategy, some twisted explanation for why I find you out here chasing your tail. But you have this habit of losing things. Or forgetting what they were for. Why is that?

HOPE: Let's just write this off as a bad night.

FAWCETT: No. I want an answer to my question.

HOPE: Which one?

FAWCETT: Why you are trying to borrow my spirit, if all you mean to do is liberate me.

HOPE: It was a manner of speaking.

FAWCETT: And what about you, Len Hope? Haven't you thought about being free?

[HOPE *begins to dance around.*]

HOPE: Now, I get it. What's your woman's name? Pansy? Lilac? Some ethereal bloom. You wanted me in your church, didn't you?

FAWCETT: You finished?

HOPE: That's the point of this, isn't it? Anger.

FAWCETT: I thought there was no point. That's what you told the white man.

HOPE: I am the white man.

FAWCETT: I see I have to do away with you.

HOPE: Exactly right, Frankie. Do away with me. With Sawyer. With Bob King. That way all this rejoicing, all this ceremonial bullshit will make sense. The point will be that you have solved the puzzle of the universe.

FAWCETT: Why didn't you say that to him?

HOPE: To who?

FAWCETT: To the man I put in your hands. To Bob King.

HOPE: You didn't put Bob King...I spoke honestly to Vernon Sawyer.

FAWCETT: Did you now? [FAWCETT tosses the pouch into the dark.]

HOPE: An offering to the night.

FAWCETT: Don't get cute. [He unloads the pistol, pockets the bullets, tosses the pistol into the dark.]

HOPE: What the fuck are you doing?

[He starts for the pistol. FAWCETT wrestles him to the ground.]

FAWCETT: Who loves you, Len Hope? I know it's true now. They tell me. I tell myself. And I know it's true. You are a contradiction.

HOPE: Like you, Frank Fawcett.

FAWCETT: Let's agree upon one thing. That no one can leave this mountain tonight without being purified.

HOPE: Did you make the same agreement with them?

FAWCETT: They have read my manner.

HOPE: When do we start, Frankie?

FAWCETT: Why, god, man, we've already started. Didn't you lie to Vernon Sawyer? Weren't we just out in a boat on those shallow seas? Perk up, Len Hope, only the pure can be sacrificed.

[HOPE *struggles free, runs.*]

I'll arrange an interview with our little council. You should be welcome.

[*He listens for a moment, touches one of the abandoned machines, leaves.* KING *sits on his logseat. He holds his cane; the shovel is at his feet.*]

KING: Am I a redneck? A bigot? A scourger of niggers and other inferior beings? Not if I'm my mother's son. I'm not. She wouldn't let me be. Okay. You've heard this. The racist's evolutionary training in decency, which inexplicably decamps upon the first encounter with the unfamiliar. So I say in my gruffest benevolent curmudgeon's voice, hey, boy, I'm not like that. Start again. Am I a redneck? A bigot? A scourger of niggers and other inferior beings? Forget it. I don't have to justify myself, or apologize. This business with my bean master, Frankie, has me in a horn-tossing mood, though I acknowledge it saddens me. What's this goddamned mystery? Who's fooling, hiding some worthless papers and a garment that wouldn't cover a moth out in the fucking mountains? And he had to wait until he came up here with me. I'm going to become some kind of coconspirator because this belly cheater wants to appropriate the Watermelon. I read the papers. It's nobody's business what they said. If he wants to tell, he'll tell. Makes no difference to me. You'd think I owed him a living. He owes his life to me. Okay. You've heard that before. But I can tell you the day I took him, and his family, into my heart. He had a brother, who was as dark as Frankie is fair, and as full as Frankie is nimble. A churndash calf who thought of himself as a salty bronc, always in trouble. One winter evening, he leaned against a bullet going by, and Frankie had lost a brother. I had nothing to do with that. It was cleaned up, cleared before anybody thought to call me. But Frank wouldn't let it go. He took to the street, airing his lungs, challenging anybody who'd bother to look at him. I didn't know him then. I passed. The suffering edge on his voice made me shiver. I walked up to him. I put my hand on his arm, and led him away. I noticed, as he sat in my office, that he was in bad shape. The examination turned up the turning of his body toward premature old age and devastation. So I took him on. I was happy to do it. I started to repair his family—the diabetes, the hypertension, the benign prostatic hyperplasia, the cancers that turned up like relatives. I advised, I sent them on. I took the weight of their deaths. I'm a doctor. Do I have to say that? I have a responsibility. Frank Fawcett knows that. Here he is in the fucking mountains, turning up old bones he claims to recognize and rags he knows he's never worn. Subtle man, Frank Fawcett. Such a discriminating sensibility. He thinks he can bury my pride with his treasure chest. I'm not finished.

[*He takes up the shovel and leaves.* PETERS *has* FAWCETT'*s garment and box. He slowly examines them.*]

PETERS: Yes, that is a garment to cover or to adorn the body. Frankie. So many questions. Man or woman. I think the son-of-a-bitch doesn't know himself how this thing serves. Or perhaps he does. Maybe he knows that there is no one it can serve and no reason for the existence of this cloth. Think on it. We assume that someone has dressed, or draped a body with this cloth. So what have we done? We have conjured a body for this cloth, and a purpose for the cloth. So now we're in deep shit with the elements of design. It turns up, this cloth, in the hands of a man who counts his steps. And it takes its place in a shallow grave where it can be found, if one has an inclination, or an intuition. Or if one is threatened. There's the rub. We have to establish where the danger lies. Bob King looks at this, and sees a ghost shirt. He thinks of this burial as evidence of an aberrant cell, coursing the body. What do I think? Oh, well, I resent its spiritual indifference. But let us say that Frank Fawcett had a purpose that had to, has to, remain as obscure to him as it is to us. But let us say again that he was conferring dignity upon a life we ignore. I ask you, why compromise the mountain? And this funky box with its coins, its emblems, its inarticulate papers. Child's play. Why didn't he come to me with his ambition? All right. Here it is. Frankie's little secret. One that I now share. I don't think I'll return this box. I might burn this garment. Or I might simply bury them under Frankie's filthy feet, and see if he can sniff them out. One thing for sure, I'll make sure that Bob King keeps quiet about this. There's no reason to stir up a danger that won't even speak its name.

[*He leaves.* SAWYER *sits working on his computer.* KING *approaches.*]

KING: Don't you ever give that thing a rest?

SAWYER: This is my rest.

KING: Beautiful. Idle hands.

SAWYER: No. It's just that I let the world come to me, and the cosmos never sleeps, Doctor King.

KING: Thanks for the information, Sawyer. I see you were restless yourself early on. I heard you and Jeff traipsing off on one of Jeff's expeditions. He's never been able to explain to me why he has to compete with the owl for the night creatures. Did he show you anything, point out some feature of the landscape sunlight burns up?

SAWYER: I think he kept his secret places to himself.

KING: Good. I'd be jealous, if he had. I thought I heard you moving about again a little later.

SAWYER: I guess I'm a bit agitated by the silence. And I think I'm looking forward to the hunt.

KING: Not much hunting back east.

SAWYER: No, *sir*. I lost a lot of hours chasing the white tail in New Hampshire and Vermont.

KING: You've got family then.

SAWYER: Companions.

KING: Did you get very far on your own? I mean, when your agitation took you scouting the second time. It seemed you were gone for quite some time.

SAWYER: I took some time to meditate.

[PETERS *appears.*]

KING: Finished your prayers, Jeff?

PETERS: I can always tell when you're annoyed with me, Bob. Can't you see that, Sawyer? It takes a thorough annoyance for someone as pious as Bob to impugn my prayers. He knows that I will act efficiently. And discreetly. And, if it's prayer that I need, Bob King would never deny me.

KING: Damn, Sawyer, the man is about to preach.

PETERS: Not at all. I have laid aside the cloth, for the moment.

KING: Where's Frankie? We might as well get him up, and have an early breakfast. We're all cackling like roosters. What do you say, Sawyer?

SAWYER: Fine with me.

PETERS: Unfair to Frankie.

KING: Unfair to Frankie!? You're worried about Frankie? Frankie's ass, on this mountain, belongs to me.

PETERS: What a relief. I thought you were going to shut the mountain down.

SAWYER: Would it help…?

KING: It would help if you stayed out of this.

SAWYER: Sorry.

KING: Sorry's not a grandma. The best way to handle these things is not to go necking where you're not wanted.

SAWYER: I had no intention…

KING: Of what?

SAWYER: Of defending Frankie.

PETERS: Shame, Sawyer. A man of your liberal education who has no more sense of justice than that.

KING: The Scotus would be ashamed for you.

[SAWYER closes his computer.]

SAWYER: Maybe this was a mistake.

KING: What was a mistake?

SAWYER: This excursion.

KING: Excursion. He calls what we're doing here an excursion.

SAWYER: A face-licking time.

KING: Don't repeat my words to me.

SAWYER: There's something unspoken here.

[KING *makes for* SAWYER's *computer.*]

KING: Open up your computer. Maybe the cosmos has some idea about it.

SAWYER: What do you want to know, Doctor King? About me?

KING: About your purpose. Who are you, Sawyer?

SAWYER: I think I told you, I'm just someone who likes to tinker with old metal and numbers. Maybe that was in another life.

KING: You've never been here, Sawyer. Give me some passion.

PETERS: I think we could all do with some breakfast.

KING: What is this? Some kind of conspiracy? You all determined to hide things from me? Frankie!

PETERS: I'll get him.

KING: Frankie!

SAWYER: He was exhausted.

KING: Was? How do you know?

SAWYER: When I passed his tent on my way back.

KING: On your way back. From where? Which direction did you take? I hope your sense of direction is better than that when you're stalking. The deer, I mean, boy.

SAWYER: I knew what you meant.

KING: Jeff, you've got this boy disoriented with your talk. Hell, you're disoriented.

PETERS: Forgive me, Bob.

KING: Forgive you! What a hell of a thing to say. Well, no, I don't forgive you. I like to finish things. You get my meaning?

PETERS: Perfectly. I am, after all, like you. I like to see things come to a close. And I think we should apologize to Mr. Sawyer. We haven't given him a chance to see our better side.

[HOPE *enters above, out of their domain. He picks up one of the abandoned machines, and moves it off.*]

KING: What the hell is that?

SAWYER: Sounds like someone moving machinery.

KING: Ridiculous.

SAWYER: It could be functional.

PETERS: Len Hope salvages a lot of the abandoned equipment.

KING: You knew this?

PETERS: What's to know? It's a minor business.

KING: There you go, Sawyer. Old metal. You and your mines. You got to tell me about that sometime.

SAWYER: Oh, I'm sure, Doctor King, you know that to talk about old machines and old mines you need a certain leisure.

KING: Are you playing with me, boy?

SAWYER: I assure you, sir. I am as troubled by these deaths as you are. The landscape is a desert of skeletons. Uranium mines in the west. Coal mines in the north. Salt mines in the south. Water has abandoned us.

KING: Don't talk to me about that. I've got a belly full of Len Hope and his bullshit claims. Have you met Len Hope?

SAWYER: Briefly.

KING: I thought you had. Maybe he and Frankie will let you in on their mystical connection.

[FAWCETT *appears.*]

FAWCETT: What makes you think I have anything to do with Len Hope?

KING: Town records.

FAWCETT: I have nothing to record. Just my house. Which is under a heavy weight. But we can talk about that at some other time.

KING: Oh, my, such discretion. Observe, Sawyer, how he sidles up to the issue.

PETERS: This is scandalous, Bob.

KING: You're right. I'd prefer to bury it.

PETERS: We were in the way of eating breakfast. Weren't we? Frankie's here.

KING: Frankie is standing there. But he's not here. Right, Frankie? Your heart is somewhere else in the valley.

FAWCETT: Can't hide from you.

KING: Not at all. Here we are. Gathered. Dawn is breaking on the Watermelon. The season is upon us. There is something sacrificial about this moment. Don't you think? Shouldn't we have something ceremonial? What say, Jeff? Frankie?

PETERS: This is unworthy, Bob.

KING: Nonsense.

PETERS: I see, it's just fuck the old lodge brother.

FAWCETT: The house that was built has been destroyed.
Who does not see that it has been ruined?

KING: What the fuck are you talking about?

FAWCETT: I'm giving you what you want. Don't you recognize the words?

PETERS: What is this, Fawcett? Isn't it enough to bury your dirty laundry, and pollute the earth with your family garbage?

KING: I wouldn't go so far, Jeff.

PETERS: Cut the tolerant crap, King.

KING: Say, listen here…

PETERS: You had your ass up your nose about an hour ago. I expected you to look him up and pistol whip him.

SAWYER: *Do* you recognize the words? I'm interested in this ruined house. Where is it, Frankie?

PETERS: Maybe it's in the garment and box he buried out back.

FAWCETT: I better not find…

PETERS: You won't find…

KING: That's enough. I thought you had sense enough to let me handle it.

PETERS: With your ceremony.

KING: With my common sense.

[*The sound of a charging horse, coming closer.*]

What the hell is that?

SAWYER: It sounds like Len Hope.

PETERS: The idiot's riding toward the camp.

KING: Hope! Hope! The bastard is challenging me!

SAWYER: Call him off, Fawcett!

[*The horse goes by, fading in the distance.*]

KING: What did you say, Sawyer?

SAWYER: It was logical.

KING: Logical, you say. What makes it logical for a half-breed to challenge me? And why should you think it would take Frankie to stop him?

SAWYER: Frankie seems well-armed.

FAWCETT: I want my box. Give me my garment. I've lost patience with people who don't respect the dead.

KING: Well, now, who is it that died, Frankie? Nobody I know. And if that should happen, my pride would keep me from hiding it. If I hear right, there's a little matter of something that might have escaped the box. Do you have anything you want to tell me?

FAWCETT: Nothing escaped the box. I placed there a record of every pilgrim who ever entered your life.

KING: You others listen. I could have told you that Frank wanted to remove me from his life. I knew it on the day I went to his wedding. He said he'd been married before he came to Albuquerque, but for some reason he wanted to be married again here. I helped him with the wedding, certainly. I knew he wanted me to be there, too. Of course, the way we were, I would have thought I'd be more than just one of the guests. But he had this queer little cracker as best man, one Will Lewis, a poor soul I'd find it hard to vouch for in hell. Well, that was the way it was. People you never saw before or after, dancing, singing. Frank enticed us all to the tables. Ham so sweet there were honey bees around it. Ribs so boisterous they'd take your tongue out. Don't talk about the chittlings and the greens and the corn and the way he laid those potatoes in one saucy gravy. Pastry so light and fragrant the air around it was like spring. And this Will, who seemed to have some kind of genius with the still and homemade brews, kept a steady flow of barrels on the ground.

FAWCETT: You don't have to remind me of my kindness.

KING: Oh, but I must. Long about evening, when I figured it was time to walk politely away and let the party carry on, I went up to Frank and held out my hand, with a folded hundred dollar bill in it, just a little something more that my heart asked me to do for him. He pulled back from me, and looked at my hand as if I were holding a fiery branding iron, and started to bless me as everything but a Child of God. Fortunately, for him, nobody heard it. I put the money in my pocket, walked over to a gully he'd had dug to get rid of refuse, put my finger in my mouth and gagged up all that I had so happily put away throughout the day. I turned around and wiped my mouth. We looked each other in the eyes. He turned away. I stepped over the gully, and went on home. Next morning, I thought of it as just another nigger wedding. And Frank never brought his wife to call.

SAWYER: I don't understand. Why do you tolerate this man?

KING: Oh, don't you now, Sawyer?

PETERS: There's an interesting point here. Bob knew beforehand that Frankie would refuse him. But did he force Frankie into that refusal? And did Frankie know the moment when Bob would offer his kindness?

KING: You see what I'm up against, Sawyer? Your blindness. Jeff's frivolous fascination. And this nigger's belief that somewhere, at some time, God tied his miserable soul to mine. Goddamn it, I don't need to hunt anymore.

[*He makes to strike his tent.* PETERS *and* SAWYER *restrain him.*]

PETERS: Bob!

SAWYER: Leave it!

FAWCETT: He who has not killed
          is not fit to drink the beer
          brewed by a virgin.
          He who has not killed
          is forbidden to drink the beer
          brewed by a virgin.

    You wanted ceremony. Did it take you this long to realize that it takes purity to do this? Give me what belongs to me.

KING: Ho, Frankie. I thought we had business. Ten minutes of my time. An agreement. You turning away?

FAWCETT: Ask Sawyer.

KING: I meant to ask Sawyer.

SAWYER: Well, I'll be damned. I've heard of this. I can't believe it's happening to me.

PETERS: *What* is happening to you, Sawyer?

SAWYER: Why, the propositions of the book, Reverend Peters. [*He sits, pulls a small book from his jacket, opens it.*] I keep it with me at all times.

PETERS: Don't be offensive, Sawyer.

SAWYER: The light is bad here. But let me read you…

PETERS: Not here, Sawyer. Not now. Not before Frankie.

SAWYER: What book do you think I have here?

PETERS: It's obvious.

[SAWYER *begins to tear and to scatter pages from his book.*]

SAWYER: Why can I do this? Because this is not the book but an image of that book. You knew, of course, that I would damage my book. But you knew also that there was the possibility that I would not damage my book. So why am I doing this?

KING: Peters, you owe me for this.

[*The sound of the horse and buggy charging, coming closer.*]

SAWYER: [*To* KING.] I thought it was you.

KING: Is that Len Hope?

PETERS: What you see.

KING: I don't see anything.

PETERS: Perfect. [*To the others.*] Does anybody see anything? Good. Then we can go on.

FAWCETT: God's righteousness, I'll bury you before dawn. [*He walks away.*]

SAWYER: Hey!

KING: You surprised, Sawyer?

PETERS: Shall we take him through it once again?

KING: We owe it to him.

PETERS: Then we will. You see, Frank Fawcett, that is to say, our very own Frankie, has to hide. And we, that is, Robert MacIntyre King, or Bob King, and Jeffrey Peters, must discover him. And he must discover us discovering him. Oh, there's a contusion here. There's a certain latitude in transparency. Now, you ask am I, Jeff Peters, transparent, is Bob transparent, is Frankie transparent? Not cunningly so. Are we finally inscrutable? Not gracelessly so. So what is the point? The point lies aslant our own desires. We have, Mr. Sawyer, been pursuing a life that is as tellingly improbable as this mountain. That is our anguish, and that is our shame.

KING: I can't tell, Jeff, if that's danger I see in his eyes, or terror.

PETERS: I think it depends on the lessons he had in New England. Or what he heard when he passed through Chihuahua. Or what Frankie told him about *his* ancestors' ambitions.

KING: Is it too late to say, we shall see?

PETERS: It is never too late, but it may always be too early.

KING: Anyway, Sawyer, God's righteousness…

PETERS: If he cares.

KING: I love your categorical mistakes.

PETERS: Category, Bob.

KING: I'll take it up with the ritualist. And I will count upon Hope.

PETERS: Can we be of any help, Sawyer?

[SAWYER *moves quickly away.*]

KING: Who will take responsibility for us?

PETERS: I don' t know.

KING: Show me that garment again. I want to study it.

PETERS: This way.

[*They go.* HOPE *appears, polishing a miner's tool.*]

HOPE: Fucking Frankie, impugning my integrity, calling my purity into question. We'll have to see about that. When the time comes. I said that without thinking, that bit about time. Why should time come? Why should anyone be there to greet it? No one thought I could make sense of salvaging these old machines. You can see the astonishment when I begin to explain their structure and the way they work. They don't fool me. What really bothers the folk is that I seem to have a purpose for these machines, that I understand the life they serve. The bastards want to deny me that life. So, if they live the life, it's not my place, and, if they kill it, it's none of my business. I ought to let them know that I'm a connoisseur of graves.

[*He goes.* FAWCETT *shovels at the spot* KING *and* PETERS *uncovered.* SAWYER *appears.*]

FAWCETT: What do you want? They send you to check on me?

SAWYER: You ought to know by now no one can send me for anything.

FAWCETT: By now? I hardly know you.

SAWYER: Frankie, this is not you. You don't need a lifetime to make judgments. Intuition. Depth. Isn't that what we were talking about before?

FAWCETT: We?

SAWYER: Don't play me, brother. Don't try to make me into something you can toss in the gully. Listen, I apologize for what I had to do. You can understand the pressures I was under.

FAWCETT: You see what they've done here?

SAWYER: Who?

FAWCETT: King. Peters. They took away this space. Don't tell me you didn't know. And don't tell me you don't approve.

SAWYER: I'm sorry. I can't put this together.

FAWCETT: Look at this repository. They spied on me. They have things that are sacred to me.

SAWYER: I heard you say...

FAWCETT: You heard me say. You don't know what you heard. King was speaking in another voice. I don't know why. Peters I can understand. He had no reason to come into this valley.

SAWYER: That makes no sense.

FAWCETT: He had a greater imagination. That makes me wonder about you. Why has your imagination failed you, and brought you here where all you see are dead things? Why are you so friendly with people who want to rob you of what little spirit you have? You see what they're capable of.

SAWYER: King and Peters.

FAWCETT: Yes.

SAWYER: You drew a distinction.

FAWCETT: What difference does it make?

SAWYER: Every. How am I to take your warning? How am I to follow the course of this water without a map?

FAWCETT: Don't you play me. Look at this. Look at this. What did you do to stop it?

SAWYER: What did *you* do to stop it?

FAWCETT: Get out of my face. I don't recognize you.

SAWYER: Funny, you should put things in that way. Because, according to you, I should be perfectly familiar.

FAWCETT: Not anymore.

[SAWYER *takes the shovel, pushes* FAWCETT *aside.*]

SAWYER: What do I have to do? Look. Here. Maybe they missed what they were looking for. Maybe you buried things deeper than you thought. Maybe, Frank Fawcett, there was a fucking mistake. Maybe you missed a pilgrim.

FAWCETT: Impressive. Passion. You keep your ears open. Why did you betray me?

SAWYER: I could betray you now with the idea that I betrayed myself.

FAWCETT: But you won't.

SAWYER: No. We start fresh.

FAWCETT: What did you find?

SAWYER: Nothing. Like you.

FAWCETT: You knew that.

SAWYER: No, Frankie. You knew it. I had to discover it.

FAWCETT: How can I help you, Mr. Sawyer?

[SAWYER *stares.* HOPE *appears above, an image in his own domain.*]

HOPE: The man is a connoisseur of graves.

SAWYER: Tell me again. What is Len Hope to you?

FAWCETT: Nothing.

SAWYER: This is the truth?

FAWCETT: Why should I lie?

SAWYER: You called him your brother.

FAWCETT: Jeffrey Peters is his brother.

SAWYER: You're lying. That can't be.

FAWCETT: Why are you so upset?

SAWYER: So there is really no way to remedy things, is there? What if I buried you in this shallow grave, what good would it do me?

HOPE: Be careful. Only the impure have to beg.

FAWCETT: No good. You wouldn't have prepared.

SAWYER: Prepare me.

FAWCETT: Say, now, I'm like Jeff Peters. There's no need to insult me.

SAWYER: That's the easy way out.

FAWCETT: I don't have time…

SAWYER: Time? There's no one here. Oh, that's out of line. Certainly, you and I are here. I listen. I know that, because of you, we are not alone.

FAWCETT: I'll do for King. He put you up to this.

SAWYER: Never. He doesn't know I'm here. Let's go back. You were quarreling with time. It seemed an impediment to the act we, you and I, could accomplish. Accomplish. Finish, yes.

FAWCETT: Ho, now. You want me to prepare you to kill me.

SAWYER: Kill? Did I say kill? No, I said nothing about kill. I talked only of burying you. What I really want to say is I talked only of finding a remedy. A remedy for this confusion caused by a misconception of time. Your little box. Did it include the mathematics of family, Frankie?

HOPE: Hit him. He's dangerous.

FAWCETT: What do you mean?

SAWYER: I was simply calculating the possibility that somehow you and I are related.

FAWCETT: Could be.

SAWYER: Then you don't deny it?

FAWCETT: Leave me alone. Goddamn, haven't they done enough to me?

SAWYER: Oh, no, Frankie. This suffering is timeless. If I had my machine here, I could model it for you. I know you, Frankie. You're an unfaithful reader. You only want to justify your own vision of the world. Take me in, Frankie. Take me in.

[FAWCETT *wrestles the shovel from* SAWYER, *tumbles him.*]

FAWCETT: Get up, and get away from me.

SAWYER: Ah, Frankie, don't you get it? This is not fair. I am your only
hope, to help you accomplish what you said you would do before dawn.

FAWCETT: Why would you help me?

SAWYER: It was written.

FAWCETT: What?

SAWYER: I could say, in the great text. And that would be false. I could say,
in all those texts that inform us as we are. And that would be presump-
tuous. I could give no reason. And that would be insulting. I could say I
do it out of love. You get the point. This is another moment in...another
instant...But there I go making mistakes. Where is Len Hope?

FAWCETT: Where we left him, I suppose.

SAWYER: It doesn't matter.

HOPE: We'll see about that. [*He leaves.*]

SAWYER: What do you want to do?

FAWCETT: I don't trust you.

SAWYER: You trust King. Peters.

FAWCETT: You don't understand.

SAWYER: You need them.

FAWCETT: I do not.

SAWYER: You need me.

FAWCETT: I do not.

SAWYER: My point exactly. Can I get out of this grave?

FAWCETT: No chains on your ass.

SAWYER: We ought to be able to come to some agreement.

[*They go. The two figures reappear. They run the area, playing with the lines, the
lights, the machinery.*]

ONE: It's not going to happen.

TWO: What's not going to happen?

ONE: *Lo que tu me dijiste.*

TWO: *¡Cómo!*

ONE: I'll bet you would like to know what was in that pouch.

TWO: You heard the man. Tokens. Dead things.

ONE: La la la. You're envious. No such thing. Aluminum, iron, nickel, manganese, cobalt, tin, copper, lead, zinc, silver, gold, platinum. And ash. An eye into eternity.

TWO: That's what I don't like about you. You take anything to reason beyond your means. And ash? What about the ash? Are you going to tell me that the pouch was a coffin? I meant to tell you, get rid of this idea of eternity. It doesn't become you.

ONE: Ah, becoming. That is the point.

TWO: The point is you have lost your gift.

ONE: Oh, you innocent. I'm just coming into my gift. I am prepared to give us names.

TWO: You mean you mean to change our names.

ONE: Exactly. I've done it for all these others.

TWO: A little goddess.

ONE: Not at all. I've just been attentive. Aren't you curious about this Miguel Valdivielso? Who might be Len Hope, and might have migrated here as Clinton Napoleon.

TWO: Ridiculous.

ONE: Well, then, wouldn't you like even a peek into that box? Baptismal things. A death certificate, perhaps. Perhaps a deed in the name of Miguel Valdivielso.

TWO: You saw these things?

ONE: I saw what they saw.

TWO: Who?

ONE: The ones who prepared the box.

TWO: Frank Fawcett prepared the box.

ONE: Frank Fawcett had possession of the box. And the garment.

TWO: He said they were sacred.

ONE: He spoke of a sacred place.

TWO: That's what I said.

ONE: You've been around these folk too long. You think that what you say is what you say, and the truth is obvious.

TWO: [Sings.] I feel a song coming on. What folk do you mean?

ONE: The ones who abandoned Vernon Sawyer.

TWO: God, if I listen to you, it was Sawyer put the garment in the grave.

ONE: He did.

TWO: Jesus.

ONE: Belongs to Bob King.

TWO: Jeffrey Peters.

ONE: No, Jeffrey Peters belongs to an ancient tradition of measuring silence. Bob King will put his finger on the flesh. Why are you looking at me that way?

TWO: I just remembered. You were after chasing a flood.

ONE: So?

TWO: What did you find?

ONE: You were with me. It was the beginning of our imagination.

TWO: A natural failing.

ONE: Precisely.

TWO: I need a death to make sense of all this.

ONE: My dear, I will give you several.

TWO: So let's catch up with them.

[ONE *begins the series of balletic poses.*]

ONE: Look at this. You are an excellent teacher.

TWO: Only if you fall over yourself.

ONE: Like them.

TWO: Yes, like them.

[*They run the area again.*]

ONE: Prepare the ground.

[*They go.* KING *and* PETERS *sit, cleaning their guns and casually drinking.*]

KING: Jeff, do I seem quick to judge?

PETERS: It's not one of the seven sins.

KING: Give me an audience, Jeff. How long have we been out here this trip? Ten hours? Maybe. But I swear there's something disturbing about that boy, Sawyer. He refuses to learn.

PETERS: Can I believe my ears?

KING: Who is this son-of-a-bitch? Where's he from? Arizona? God, you need a map just to understand him. He's been out there among his Indians and wetbacks, and he thinks he has the world by the tail. I despise his corrupted innocence, his way of pretending that failure costs nothing.

PETERS: Are you asking me for a report?

KING: I am asking you to tell me I've failed. "Study me, then, you who would lovers be…"

PETERS: You're confusing your passions.

KING: Tell me about passion.

PETERS: Maybe we are wrong. Maybe Sawyer has already tied his desires to ours, and it's his serenity that speaks most loudly.

KING: That dogie has no right to his serenity.

PETERS: Bob, this is my hunting trip. I don't want to start the morning with an argument.

KING: Everybody on this mountain has a bug up his ass. What does Frankie want from me? Why didn't you just give him his stuff?

PETERS: I had to examine it.

KING: For what? You can't read that scribbling.

PETERS: Not at first. No. It requires a little patience to realize how elegantly Frank Fawcett has arranged his little world. I was taken with the way he understands that there's a certain necessary respite here, a time to think about the movement taking place.

KING: Tell me again, Jeff. What was in that box?

PETERS: Names you should recognize.

KING: Was Robert MacIntyre King one of them?

PETERS: My god, I think you're afraid.

KING: Of what?

PETERS: Frank saw you coming. You thought you were the perfect stranger. He knew you were mistaken.

KING: Is that what the Scotus says?

PETERS: As a matter of fact, yes. He does. Frankie will free you from doubt and deception, show you that you *are* Robert MacIntyre King who stepped on sacred ground.

KING: What sacred ground? Come to your senses, Jeff. You act like you're hunting for water. If Frankie can get you to believe in this shit...

PETERS: Believe. What can I tell you, Bob? Frankie believes in order.

KING: I do believe I have crossed over. My god, I'm about to testify. Jesus, if I could get Frankie here with his raggedy cassock, I'd have a right reverend congregation. A church full of fools who don't see that digging around in the scrub on the Watermelon is an insult to reason.

PETERS: You want me to return the box? Bury it? Burn it up? What is your pleasure?

KING: I want you to stop thinking about it. Wrap it up in that filthy cloth, and shove it up Sawyer's ass.

PETERS: Now, that is the most interesting proposition you've come up with. Yes, certainly. Why didn't I think of it? I thought *you* had missed it. You barely glanced at the papers, but you saw the logic of it.

KING: What the hell are you talking about?

PETERS: The way you have defined yourself as the perfect stranger to Fawcett *and* Sawyer. And before that, to Len Hope. You knew that they would understand the logic of your virtue. Whatever it is. You would have had to travel a long distance to see that, Bob. And you have always been here. Or have you?

KING: Don't insult me.

PETERS: How can I? I'm only half-way there myself.

KING: Something told me to keep an eye on you.

PETERS: No. No, don't say that. That is not the Bob King I know.

KING: You don't know Bob King.

PETERS: I agree.

KING: What do you want from me, Peters?

PETERS: I want your approval and help with some land I have my eye on. The Napoleon land, down by the river.

KING: What? Who's asking me?

PETERS: Frank Fawcett.

KING: They work on you, don't they? It's slow. But little by little, they tell their stories, or their lies. And they read themselves into existence, and read the death of certain forms into being. Then they say, look what we have, a new life. Don't think the place of your birth will be there when you return. Don't think you can recognize any star, any constellation. You'll have to swallow your pride when you realize that you can't even spell your proper name. So you are Frank Fawcett. Or Jeffrey Peters. Did you finish your examination?

PETERS: Of course not. There are names I didn't recognize.

KING: I thought so. Will Frankie enlighten us?

PETERS: Frankie believes that they are our names.

KING: Then we're saved, Jeff. The death certificate has already been written.

[*The sound of a movement off.*]

Sawyer?

[*Two shots.* KING *and* PETERS *fall.* FAWCETT *appears, holding one of Sawyer's rifles.*]

FAWCETT: Seven pounds. Three and a half feet of power. The stock is geared to the body. Jeweled. The sight is a gold bead. A work of art. Take this cartridge. A hundred fifty grains in a soft point. The rifle has speed. It's sure. It speaks softly in only one language. May God look upon your gifts, and forgive your transgressions.

[*Len* HOPE *suddenly appears, out of* FAWCETT*'s sight. He raises his rifle to fire.* SAWYER *appears.* FAWCETT *turns to aim at* SAWYER, *and sees that* SAWYER *has him in his sights.* FAWCETT *drops.* HOPE *makes a sudden movement, and* SAWYER *fires quickly toward* HOPE. HOPE *runs away.* FAWCETT, *quickly grabbing a small pack from which the cane and a wooden bowl jut, escapes.* SAWYER *comes forward, checks the bodies, gathers his small pack, and runs toward the vehicles. The sound of the jeep being started and going. The sound of the false starts of the truck. Silence.* FAWCETT *reappears. He sits, with the rifle cradled on his thighs, over the bodies. He speaks as though he were reciting. While he speaks,* SAWYER *appears, carrying a pole like a yoke on his back, and careens silently and at first slowly from side to side.*]

FAWCETT: Tears run.
           The hoe is broken.
           The hoe is broken.
           The axe is broken.
           He has taken the goatskin.

[*He claps his hands.* SAWYER *moves faster, with more frenzy.* FAWCETT *claps his hands.* SAWYER *subsides, moves with more grace, dances very slowly.*]

           Night has come.
           All men have their eyes on you.
           The women have run into their houses.

You must set out,
You must return to your canyon of stone.
Night has come.

[HOPE *appears.*]

HOPE: Stop it. They don't deserve this. This is the wrong place. Who are you, anyway, to think you can carry them across?

FAWCETT: Help me to strike the tent.

HOPE: I will not.

SAWYER: I'll help you.

HOPE: Guilty. You'd do anything.

FAWCETT: Stop thinking about yourself, Len Hope. I need you now.

[*The three lift* KING *and* PETERS, *one by one, and move them upstage. The large tent is struck and folded, so that* KING *and* PETERS *can be placed on it and covered by white sheets. Their bowls and spoons are set around them. A box containing some of their goods—whiskey, shirts, maps, old boots, books, paper, pens, ammunition and knives—is set above them.*]

SAWYER: I have to admit that I'm as afraid of those two as I am of you two. Who knows what they intend to do? Don't get me wrong. I'm uneasy, but I'm not ashamed. I'm not asking for their forgiveness. I just want them to lie still, now.

HOPE: I want nothing to do with this.

FAWCETT: You see why I had to kill them. Frank Fawcett shot these two murderers. I'm not ashamed. I hide because I know you'd lie. What is it with you, Hope? Do you want to give back the power I've put in your hands? Look at them. They are dead.

[*A grinding, clanking sound of old machinery begins in the distance.*]

Oh, I see. You don't need me.

SAWYER: Stop talking about lies and hiding out. Hope understands what needed to be done. Why, he would have killed you, Frankie. Great god, in his enthusiasm, I think he would have done you away. But there is something I heard that disturbs me, Frankie. Nobody killed King and Peters for me. I killed them. I made the decision. I planned it. I pulled the trigger.

HOPE: Then you're the nigger. Because it was a nigger standing in the smoke, a nigger I had in my sights and a nigger I would have killed, if you hadn't turned on me.

SAWYER: Get it in your head. There was no one there but me.

HOPE: I saw…

SAWYER: You saw me. You've got me depending on him. Am I to let you walk around with these ridiculous ideas, threatening my life? Frank Fawcett will die for it. But I killed them.

FAWCETT: I never knew how devious you could be, Vernon Sawyer. Vernon Sawyer. I don't even know if that's your name. You say you've come up from Sonora.

SAWYER: That's what it is about you. You get things turned around.

HOPE: I know this man, now. I met him on the road. He come talking to me about doing things decently and in order.

SAWYER: A lesson you obviously haven't learned.

HOPE: He insulted me, and the people with me. We were sheltering people who had just come over the border. We had finally got them to speak of unspeakable things.

SAWYER: Samaritans.

HOPE: You starting again?

FAWCETT: You never told me about this.

HOPE: You never asked. [*To* SAWYER.] You were lucky. I kept my people from paying you out.

SAWYER: Do I have to listen to this while we're trying to do something decent for these two?

HOPE: You turn your back on me now, and you're a dead man.

SAWYER: Frankie, what's happening in your house?

FAWCETT: Compassion is my power. This cradle in which these bodies lie gave me my power.

HOPE: I'm going to see that you both hang.

SAWYER: Well, now, that's up to you.

[*The sound of tapping on wood, like that of a woodpecker.*]

FAWCETT: That is the soul squeezing out of its cave.

HOPE: I told you to stop it. Those words belong to me.

FAWCETT: These dead belong to me.

[*The two figures appear downstage and opposite the others.*]

TWO: Release them.

ONE: And if I did?

TWO: It doesn't matter.

ONE: You're too squeamish. But, if I must.

[*They begin to run the space. Repeating parts of previous speeches, they sound like birds singing in counterpoint.*]

ONE: Frankie, what's happening in your house?

TWO: Compassion is my power.

ONE: Compassion is my power.

TWO: Frankie, what's happening in your house?

ONE: Those words belong to me.

TWO: Those words belong to me.

[*They weave these into an intensity.*]

FAWCETT: I thought, goddamn, you would understand why death called me to its service.

[FAWCETT, SAWYER *and* HOPE *gather the pole and other equipment, and run off under the figures' assault.* KING *begins to stir, slowly incorporating himself through the movement known as The Cat. When he is finally on his feet, he comes downstage, facing the audience, and speaks reflectively and intimately. While he speaks,* PETERS *incorporates himself.*]

KING: Well, now, get to that. Death called him into its service. Sawyer wants the franchise, or let's say he wants the profit. What would it profit him to gain the whole world and…you fill in the blanks. Sawyer, anyhow, would remain unprepared. And Hope? His position in this harmony is accidental. No, I would have left this circumstance to Frank Fawcett. I like the idea of taking the earth into account when you least suspect that it has any gift remaining. I will never forget that for my daughter's thirteenth birthday, Fawcett made it a celebration of the land. Venison and bear meat, buffalo—oh, yes—and wild turkey, trout and bass, corn and collards, beans of all descriptions, wild rice and berries and melons, a regular rainbow of God's gifts. He tamed them, civilized them and brought them to the table.

[PETERS *has now come down opposite* KING.]

PETERS: That lone bird singing in the wood made me think kindly once again of Frank Fawcett. I have been closer to his spirit than Bob, let Bob protest. Yes, I would have left this event to Fawcett. The depth and weight of it. He says from home. I say, yes, from home. Did I hear him say, let the dead lie still for a moment, let the water run smooth and the storms cease? I know he would have the fruit bird with the bright body call us, and we would hear. We would hear the shaking of a sacred bell upon a grave. Our bodies would be covered with white clay, and we would dance. Those others robbed us of a celebration that not even faith could touch.

KING: Forget about faith.

PETERS: You will have noticed that *I* didn't beg, or whimper, when I heard the movement. Oh, no, no, no, I wasn't resigned to my fate, and I wasn't looking for a miracle. Just at that moment, I saw that we had come to a logical conclusion, and I am a most logical man. So I come out of it, looking innocent and untouched by all that rage, a man of faith, who wouldn't compromise with such faithlessness. It attacks you and attacks you from every side, this faithlessness, the way another human being will reach out for you, and then withdraw his hand. I had to honor the same passion that Frank Fawcett revealed over the sight of his rifle. Let them bury me at their peril.

[PETERS *and* KING *turn, and walk determinedly back to their places, slowly re-*

suming them. The lights dim just enough to make it possible for one of the others to return, entering from a direction from which he did not leave, to kneel where he seems to be preparing something. Each actor should have borrowed some piece of clothing from one of the others, to make it difficult, at first, to distinguish one from the others. The sound of a spoon in a wooden bowl. The man eats frantically, anxiously. The lights gradually come up to reveal Len HOPE. FAWCETT *sneaks up on him, aims the rifle at him.*]

FAWCETT: Always catch you feeding your face.

[*Hope makes a move toward his rifle. Fawcett releases the safety.*]

You know I'd send you to hell.

[FAWCETT *circles* HOPE.]

Keep your eyes off me. [*He takes* HOPE*'s rifle.*] You got a knife, or anything else, you better drop it, now.

[HOPE *takes his knife and tosses it forward.*]

That's okay now. Tell me, Len Hope, why are you still traipsing around these mountains?

HOPE: I'm not in a position to appreciate your humor, Frankie. Why haven't you lit out?

FAWCETT: You. And Sawyer. How could I avoid you? How could I get around, or through, you?

HOPE: You're a dead man. There's no escape.

FAWCETT: You say.

[SAWYER *appears above and opposite to them. He seems to be following a trail, moving slowly, step by step, closer to them.*]

HOPE: I know I was a burden to you, Frankie. Old blood. Family business you didn't understand with the land and the water. [*He holds up his bowl to* FAWCETT.] Can I offer you some supper? Just a poor stew. But it's all I got. Unless you don't want to touch things touched by human hands.

[FAWCETT *slaps the bowl from* HOPE*'s hands.*]

I hope you make it.

FAWCETT: I'll tell you what got me about you. You treated my suffering as an impurity, and my liberation as a compromise only you could make. Somewhere along the line, you lost sight of me. It was easy for you to lie, to yourself, and to them.

HOPE: The good lord seems to have arranged our last supper together. Do what you have to do.

[FAWCETT *raises his rifle, aims, lowers it.* SAWYER *swiftly enters, thrusts his rifle in* FAWCETT's *face.*]

SAWYER: You should have. Put it down.

[FAWCETT *carefully lays down his rifle.*]

Hope, you may as well come over here. Family. You know.

[HOPE *suddenly ducks, retrieves the knife and lunges at* SAWYER. FAWCETT *strikes* SAWYER *with a rifle butt.* SAWYER *falls.* HOPE *slashes at* SAWYER's *falling figure, misses, then turns to stab* FAWCETT *in the right shoulder.* SAWYER, *recovered, shoots* FAWCETT *and* HOPE. KING *and* PETERS *set up a fierce moan, which continues and gradually rises.*]

God's righteousness, I said I would bury you before dawn.

[KING *and* PETERS *arise, and come forward to view the bodies.*]

KING: You did a good job, son.

SAWYER: I didn't ask for your approval.

KING: I didn't give it.

PETERS: Tell me, Sawyer, to whom did you make that promise?

SAWYER: You see. There's the evidence.

PETERS: I see two dead souls. But evidence is another proposition.

KING: Yes, you say you finished things up. But how do we know your intentions?

PETERS: Yes, this deed lacks a certain purity.

KING: Do we have to start again?

PETERS: No, we'll do what we always do, make do.

KING: No. This time, Jeffrey Peters, I'm holding out. There was no clarity here. The boy didn't come close to capturing my reasons.

PETERS: Stop it. We left that talk in the grave. This fetid self-expression. This strutting in individual desires.

KING: Are you accusing me...?

PETERS: Yes.

KING: I appeal to you, Sawyer.

SAWYER: Oh, no. What we need is a little logic. These are my dead. You don't offer them much hope. You fail to give them the one thing they ask for and the one thing you pretend to give them, to be saved. Can they be saved being here with us? Is that even the question? I don't think it is. The question is, what does it mean to be saved? And, if that's the question, why did we have to do what we did?

PETERS: Marvelous, the way you moved to implicate us.

KING: God, what arrogance.

SAWYER: Yours.

KING: I leave him to you, Jeff.

SAWYER: [*To* PETERS.] I'll trade you these dead.

PETERS: My god, he's asking me to stand surety for myself. And what about you, Mr. Sawyer?

SAWYER: I am a witness.

PETERS: Clever.

SAWYER: Help me to move them to a safe place.

PETERS: I hear Frank's voice.

SAWYER: The deal is between me and you. You know what we're trading. I give you a new name, and you give me power over the grave. That's it, isn't it? You remind me of the way down. You teach me to face the dark with the right kind of fear.

KING: This is outrageous.

PETERS: We ought to consider it.

KING: What? Where would we bury them? Here? I've had this ground set apart since before I was born. You see my possessions right there by the grave. And look around you. You see the way I've cut a life into the mountains. All that work, all that power only half-remembered in those bodies you find so fascinating, Sawyer. These are not common matters, gentlemen.

PETERS: We ought at least to discuss it.

KING: Let's just step off down there, where it's comfortable, and one doesn't have to suffer this thirst.

[*They go.* FAWCETT *arises.*]

FAWCETT: Get up, Len Hope. There isn't much time. You see what they're doing. This is the house. I draw a circle about this house. I bring the child to it. I take the child in my arms, into the shade of the house. We have come, on our serpent-canoe, past palm, cane and cactus, the high cloud of Bogotá, beach of Bahia, forest of Uxmal, Asante cocoa grove, dry plain of the Ogol, the high whiteness of the Mediterranean coast, the caverns of the south, the blue star and sheep grange of the north, to here. Child, you are the spirit of a *doñu*, the fox and toucan, prophet and minister of the rain forest, hammer of the midnight sun, blue bead and human bone of Ifẹ. I call you the golden oriole for the beauty of your plumage. Your life will be a reflection of light; your deeds will be good. You will live in peace with other souls. I place you forever under the sun's creative presence.

HOPE: That's all very good, Frank Fawcett. What about me?

FAWCETT: What about you? Didn't you enter with me? You heard the man. We're beans and cornbread. Corned beef and cabbage.

HOPE: Just when I think you're serious, you disappoint me. Wake up, man. This will be our last abode upon this earth.

FAWCETT: Misprision.

HOPE: Damn it, Fawcett, we're gone. This is our last chance for respect.

FAWCETT: Oh, forgive me, Hope. I had no idea you could be so grave about the grave they're digging for you. Consider my invocation nothing more than a momentary lapse in my courtesy. If you would rather be on your way to some other domain, don't let me keep you.

HOPE: Didn't you hear what he said? He wanted to trade our names for his power.

FAWCETT: I told you compassion is my power.

HOPE: Sawyer will have it.

FAWCETT: My compassion? Good.

HOPE: He's beginning to talk like you.

FAWCETT: Our lives are running water, brother. We can never, even among the dead, rest.

HOPE: I think I do want to try those graves we prepared. [HOPE *goes to them.*]

FAWCETT: You're angry with me.

HOPE: Why should I be?

FAWCETT: Look at me. Where'd I get this? [*He takes off the piece of borrowed clothing.*] It's yours?

HOPE: I've never seen it.

FAWCETT: I notice that you're a little raggedy, Hope, for one who is so concerned about his grave image.

HOPE: You're talking.

FAWCETT: I had a sacred garment. Silence. He can't handle it. [FAWCETT *lies on the tent/grave.*] All right. I'll try it on for size. Let me lie down here, and astonish them when they return.

HOPE: Frank Fawcett, save me.

FAWCETT: What did you say?

HOPE: Save me.

FAWCETT: Why? I mean how? This thing that has occurred doesn't speak in that language.

HOPE: I knew it. You're a fraud.

FAWCETT: Hope. Hope. Listen to me. I know the limits of my domain. Did I ever say I could save you? If I did, I'm sorry. God help me, I thought I had learned to live with my contradictions. Len Hope, forgive me for stirring the wrong passion in you.

HOPE: What passion did you mean to stir, brother?

FAWCETT: It has no name.

HOPE: Good. I see. Here we are. They've abandoned us, haven't they?

FAWCETT: It doesn't matter. Look. [FAWCETT *lifts the maps, books and paper in the box.*] They couldn't take it away.

[HOPE *scatters the material on the ground. Fawcett tries to protect it.*]

I'll kill you.

HOPE: Frank, we *are* dead.

FAWCETT: Yes. We have to consider that. What it means to be dead. Come here, brother. I need to embrace you.

HOPE: I don't want your touch anymore. Get out of my face. I'm fucked. I might as well crawl into that grave. I want to crawl into that grave. And the only soul who can cover my body and see my spirit away is you.

FAWCETT: Well, what would you think if we tried preparing ourselves, and pulling these covers over our own bodies with our own hands. That would work, wouldn't it? Why should we be forced into accepting these last ministrations from people we despise, or who despise us?

HOPE: You acknowledge that there was a missed connection, then?

FAWCETT: I acknowledge nothing.

HOPE: Yes, that makes sense. Keep the darkness in it.

FAWCETT: Perfect.

HOPE: There's something I don't understand.

FAWCETT: Speak. I wouldn't see you leave unfulfilled.

HOPE: I knew I could count upon your grace. Forget that I called you to account for your failings. Being here reminds me of the imperfections that kept us so close. You know, Frankie, I think of you as a gift. I think of this moment as a reward.

FAWCETT: You are too kind. But what was your question?

HOPE: No, I've changed my mind. It would be unfair to you. It was something you couldn't formulate, and, by that measure, something you couldn't answer. I beg your forgiveness.

FAWCETT: Damn it, you can't beg my forgiveness. I don't forgive you. Didn't I wake you? Get you up before the bastards came back with their improper attitudes? There was an exactitude in Sawyer's stupidity. He gave me a companion into bliss. We, goddammit, Hope, we're here.

HOPE: Oh, listen to him. He's discovered a passion. Shall I reward myself? At least let me credit myself for the disturbance that brought you to your senses. You love me again. Right, Frank Fawcett?

FAWCETT: Always.

HOPE: Then let me burn these books, these papers, these maps, this evidence that others have trafficked in our lives.

FAWCETT: Don't talk nonsense. Look around you. As you can see, it takes a long time for death to take hold.

HOPE: That's something Sawyer would say.

FAWCETT: Don't insult me.

[*The sound of the horse and buggy.*]

Listen. I think they're on their way. Trust them to choose a decadent manner of return. We're resolved, then?

HOPE: Irrevocably.

FAWCETT: Good. Let them bury us at their peril.

[*They lie on the tent/grave. The sound of the horse and buggy fades in the distance. A new sound, that of a mining car, takes over.* SAWYER *appears, driving the car. He stops, dismounts, walks around.*]

SAWYER: You do not, you cannot, negotiate with the dead. They have everything to lose, and they give up nothing. Well, I invested their grief down the road. I made them comfortable. Made them promises I may keep. Vernon Sawyer, *el peregrino*. I'll clean this field. I won't exactly start over, but I won't make their mistakes. Strange, I thought I'd left Fawcett and Hope near where we'd marked the graves. Family. Presences. People who won't leave well enough alone. I suppose now I'm alone, and these others have to suffer being carried by me. Those two, King and Peters, kept opening their book of accounts. I didn't pay much attention at first to where we were. We had reached the water, the three of us, who are five, but who may be four, or one. The light showed the banks thick with mud, the thick spirit flesh of the gods. They wanted to strip me, massage my flesh with the mud and the water. Was I with them at the water, or here where the grave seems to have been attended by someone who wasn't here before? I am not going to concern myself with this light. They got lost in it.

[*The two figures appear.*]

ONE: Oh. Pardon. We didn't know there was anyone here.

SAWYER: You can see I am. You're not the ones who prepared...?

TWO: Oh, no. We never interfere.

SAWYER: Strange, I think I recognize you.

TWO: Well, we have worked this domain for...years.

SAWYER: Then you're responsible...

ONE: We have no responsibilities here, other than keeping good order.

SAWYER: Which means?

TWO: To see that things are done decently and in order.

ONE: And that no one cheats by making claims.

SAWYER: Like what?

ONE: Like the one you have just made.

SAWYER: Which one?

TWO: You know.

ONE: We give everyone a chance at perfection.

TWO: The natural light that seems necessary.

SAWYER: These others spoke of you.

ONE: They know us.

SAWYER: Yes, I do.

TWO: Oh, look at the mess. We should get to work.

SAWYER: I'll help.

ONE: Of course.

[*As they work,* KING *and* PETERS *arise, sitting erect in the mining car.* FAWCETT *and* HOPE *sit erect in their tent/grave. They begin a deep, resonant moaning, which grows louder and more intense.*]

SAWYER: You know my name. I ought to tell you that I have a feeling for buried things.

[*The figures smile. The four dead stand, moaning at a peak of intensity.*]

THE PLAYING SPACE

[*The lights rise upon a round playing space, with two altar-like structures at the center. Four variously appointed and vigorous figures have arranged themselves so that each appears to be a "cardinal" point within this circle. Each figure seems at once aware of and negligent of the other figures. We sense a moment of rest, of quiet, balance, and a momentary composure that seems gradually to fade. The figures begin to rustle, all playing around an irritated fastidiousness, all beginning to display an impatience that each would prefer to disguise. The silence becomes a presence. The figures turn, facing away from the center. They suddenly, without any signal or any direction, begin to sing a wordless song, with an organization and harmonies that each appears intuitively to understand. The song continues as each figure interrupts its coursing with an improvisatory, intelligible statement. As suddenly as it began, the song stops.*]*

BRANDO: Gaudentius, look at me, brother.

[*No response.*]

You see how *I* am working hard at reconciliation. Can I do any more?

[*The others show a slight annoyance.*]

Well, that's an answer the evangelist didn't get from the river.

KALA: Perhaps if you were less satisfied with your efforts, you'd be more effective. That is to say, maybe reconciliation would take its natural place beside us.

BRANDO: Trust you, Kala, to remind us of nature.

KALA: And trust you, Brando, for putting us in the way of having to test it at every turn.

GRUS: Speaking of turn, have we forgotten our purpose?

GAUDENTIUS: There's no purpose in music.

GRUS: My god, how can you say that?

GAUDENTIUS: Because there is a god.

GRUS: Someone save me from this heretical kitharist.

BRANDO: I will beat the time.

GAUDENTIUS: Keep to your own office.

BRANDO: What is my office, Gaudentius?

GAUDENTIUS: Reconciliation, he says.

KALA: [*Looking around.*] There's something precise about this arrangement. Don't you think?

GRUS: I do hope so. I'd hate to be out here with no ritual to sustain me.

GAUDENTIUS: Here he goes begging again.

KALA: There's something to be said for supplication.

GAUDENTIUS: Impossible. There's no metric for it.

[*The others howl.*]

BRANDO: Cambridge, right?

GAUDENTIUS: Princeton. How could you not see that?

KALA: *Excusez-moi, j'ai déjà entendu ça.*

GAUDENTIUS: I sing for the intelligent.

KALA: I've heard *that* before.

BRANDO: Why, Kala is accusing Gaudentius of plagiarism. I might have to stop my ears to avoid the scandal of it.

GRUS: A very interesting proposition. Here we have our Gaudentius trying to establish a correct view...

BRANDO: That is not a proposition.

GRUS: A position, then.

BRANDO: Yes? Go on.

GRUS: What are we to think about Kala and his supplication?

KALA: Forgive me, Grus. I made a mistake. I thought I saw you trying on some old clothes. Oh, god, you've got me confused, can't make sense of wearing and hearing.

BRANDO: Swearing and shearing! Delicious!

GAUDENTIUS: Brando. An artisan of modulation.

BRANDO: The term does not exist.

GRUS: But it can be found.

BRANDO: Why should we bother?

GRUS: Because there is an order in things.

BRANDO: We have to be careful of our words, Grus. We are not just talking about beating air. Is it "in" or "of"? There's a fundamental judgment there.

GAUDENTIUS: Brando, the dancing master. Is this the man we followed out here?

KALA: I came on my own.

GAUDENTIUS: Listen to him. On his own. How can we speak of being on our own?

BRANDO: Don't go any further, Gaudentius. You can see the delicate balance we have to negotiate. So. Turn around. Face the center.

[They do.]

KALA: And the music?

BRANDO: It will come.

GAUDENTIUS: Nay, sir, it has already embraced us.

GRUS: Let's not take anything for granted.

GAUDENTIUS: I simply call attention to the tone of this occasion.

GRUS: Certo.

GAUDENTIUS: You see that now?

GRUS: No, I don't.

KALA: God, Grus, you do or you don't. There's nothing hard about this scale.

GRUS: The scale, no. But what about the intervals?

BRANDO: The relationships.

GRUS: Exactly.

BRANDO: The dance.

KALA: Which seems to have escaped our grasp.

BRANDO: The body is our guide.

GAUDENTIUS: That does it. He just casts aside all music. How are we to appear without the harmonies?

BRANDO: Harmonies do not matter.

[GAUDENTIUS *adjusts his clothes, prepares to withdraw.*]

Before you abandon us, Gaudentius, give us a demonstration of harmony.

GAUDENTIUS: I cannot believe the inelegant, indecorous, cacological, Doric nature of such an assertion.

BRANDO: I asserted nothing.

GAUDENTIUS: You've spent too much time at Cambridge.

BRANDO: St. Andrews. How could you not see that?

GAUDENTIUS: *Basta.* I came on the proposal of a performance, an emptying of the heart's miseries. But, no, that doesn't appeal to you; you need to prosecute some hidden recollection, and subject the rest of us to your disorderly behavior.

KALA: Stop it. Pay attention to succession, Gaudentius.

GRUS: To the numbers.

BRANDO: I told you, Gaudentius, I have prepared our reconciliation. [*Pause.*] You don't believe me. What can I do to convince you that I suffer, too? Look at me, Brando the dancing master, out of phase with himself. Oh, don't deny that you see me bereft of my skills, sitting at the apex of ground that has no recognizable shape.

KALA: Stop it. Sequence, Brando.

GRUS: He preens himself on his ecstatic resignation. We don't need it.

KALA: Not at all, unless we provide a space for a decent confessional.

BRANDO: I thought that...

GRUS: You could have thought nothing.

BRANDO: I am always conscious of my responsibilities.

KALA: That's the kind of talent coming up on the continent, people who think they have solved every mystery.

BRANDO: That sounds like nothing other than jealousy. And it will fester...

GRUS: Fester! Lovely word. You sense the royalty in it, don't you?

BRANDO: ...fester...

GRUS: That takes talent, Gaudentius. Think about the improvisational fortitude it took just to pluck that word from the surrounding air, and to use it with such deliberation. Admirable, admirable. Go on, Brando.

BRANDO: This jealousy...

GRUS: Of course, of course.

GAUDENTIUS: Stop it, Grus.

BRANDO: I get it now, Kala. You simply want to delay our dance. Or should that be, betray our dance? Don't deny it. I remember the last time we met in this position, and you came forth, in the midst of our ceremonies, with your meat-stealing dance.

GAUDENTIUS: He's caught you, Kala. What a picture, vulgar on the face of it.

KALA: Who accuses me...?

BRANDO: No one accuses you, Kala. Think on the propriety of our innocence. Precision, Kala. Will you step up, sir? I'm talking about that rhythm that was here a moment ago.

GAUDENTIUS: Thank god, some of us can't be deceived.

KALA: What does that mean?

GAUDENTIUS: Show us the rhythm you prepared, Kala.

KALA: I refuse to be examined in this way.

BRANDO: Places!

[*They resume their original positions.*]

That's better. Now, shall we go on? Or shall we admit that our spiritual deficiencies have just done away with us?

[*The others protest.*]

Then, I will beat the time.

KALA: Who appointed you?

BRANDO: Appointed me? Why don't you ask about that ordered pair? [*He points at the altar-like structures.*]

GRUS: Why don't you ask about the color of my robe?

GAUDENTIUS: Or the mathematical inclination of my feet as I stand here.

KALA: We did begin on a good note, wouldn't you say? The song. The improvisatory majesty we drew from the air. Why did we stop? Why didn't we just fall into our figures, and provoke the benevolent intercession of this space?

BRANDO: We all sensed the shadow. It came before we were properly prepared.

KALA: And we had no way of going back.

GRUS: Suddenly, we didn't know left from right.

GAUDENTIUS: In that instant, the measure seemed empty.

BRANDO: So. Have we lost our courage?

GRUS: Not at all.

[*He gestures; the others dance, following individual figures. They repeat their opening improvisational song.* BRANDO *moves toward the center, raises his voice above the singing.*]

BRANDO: "The celestial vault was filled with rejoicing, cloudless, radiant; in the lull of the air the winds stopped their impetuous flight; Nereus appeased the fury of his roaring floods; so did the great ocean who... [*He hesitates.*] Gaudentius, give me the measure.

GAUDENTIUS: I told you to leave the words to the choir. Now, look at you, suffering from a loss of memory.

GRUS: That doesn't make sense. You can't lose memory. I appeal to the others. You don't lose memory—*sono le cose stesse.*

KALA: Impossible. Things can only die with you. You see that, don't you?

GAUDENTIUS: So Brando is dead. Pity.

BRANDO: Why, these pilgrims want to bury me.

GRUS: Nay, sir, only your fanciful story.

KALA: I propose an illustration.

BRANDO: Of my song?

KALA: Pay attention. I meant to expose the deviousness, the malignancy of our sainted mother, memory.

GRUS: And how will you do that?

KALA: I will have to tell you my dream.

[*The others howl.*]

I can wait. And you, Brando, should welcome the solace.

BRANDO: How can I find solace in a composition that seems to have gone astray?

KALA: I knew it. You all want to bandage your eyes, stand around this circle, pretending you have nothing to do with grace.

[GAUDENTIUS *abruptly drops on his bottom.*]

GAUDENTIUS: Could we have the beginning of that hymn again, Kala?

KALA: Pay attention. I give you a veiled figure, as she sits in a throne-like chair, her whole aspect covered with a shapeless garment that is ruddy with her own blood. Her uncovered face glows with the grime of sweat, tears, traces of blood. Her bared arms seem sliced into ribbons. The body appears to dance from exhaustion and an unspeakable trauma. She does not speak.

GRUS: You call this a dream?

KALA: Call it a divestiture.

GRUS: As always, he plays us.

GAUDENTIUS: So, tell us, Kala, which grace do we have?

GRUS: There you go. He can't even tell a good story. He gets bogged down in pictures. Then he leads us up some back road with a metaphysical assumption he thinks will appeal to those whose ears have gone dead. *Badare*, Kala. Let Brando dig his own grave.

KALA: Most enlightening that you should refer to the grave, Grus. These others will think us in collusion, at odds with the mother whose bitch of a daughter shows every sign of an appetite for ethical error.

BRANDO: *Párate*, Kala!

KALA: And I will. I won't go on to tell you what the mother said.

BRANDO: Good.

GAUDENTIUS: No. This has gone too far. Let's hear the rest of it. *À toi*, Kala.

KALA: It doesn't matter.

GAUDENTIUS: Then, by god, why did you bring it up, this flagellant fable?

KALA: Call it exorcism.

[GAUDENTIUS *turns away.*]

Even a flagellant fable can serve. Look at him dance. But I do note an ethical failure in attendance, even here, now. And I refuse responsibility for your souls.

[GAUDENTIUS *attacks* KALA.]

BRANDO: Gaudentius!

GRUS: Come now, Kala, shall we have the third crowing of the cock? Twice you've sounded that dactyllic assault upon our spirits—ethical. So you can't back out now. Continue your fable, master Kala. Show us your theological skills.

BRANDO: He had finished the story. The woman would not speak.

KALA: The daughter would not speak.

GRUS: But the mother would. And said...?

KALA: No. The moment has gone by.

GAUDENTIUS: I thought so. A fraud.

KALA: She looked me in the eye. She turned to clear her daughter's face, and, looking deeply into the daughter's eyes, she said, my daughter has won both her matches. I knew then where we stood at that moment. The mother wanted the daughter's failure, wanted me to acquiesce in the devastation I had before me. You ask why I didn't examine the situation, why I didn't ask for evidence of an abandoned battle, a skirmish where some overpowering love had set its course. [*He turns away.*] Brothers, I ask your forgiveness. I entered that desert, and brought nothing back.

GRUS: Well, we seem to have settled that.

GAUDENTIUS: Settled what?

GRUS: A Ptolemaic point, my man, that any moving body occupies any one geometrical point only for an instant, that is, as the master would have it, for no time at all.

BRANDO: I say that Kala lost his nerve. He began to think about his purity, or about the space that would make him pure. The daughter's devastation was a dignity he couldn't approach. Right, Kala?

KALA: If you say so, *maestro.*

GAUDENTIUS: He has no right to say so.

GRUS: Give us the measure, Brando.

[*They move about their circle, each improvising upon rhythms to which the others cannot, and will not, respond. They fall into a decorous dance, approaching the altar-like structures.*]

BRANDO: This reminds me; there is a flaw here.

GAUDENTIUS: Nonsense, we've just come.

GRUS: You say. But suppose part of us had been here before.

BRANDO: Grus, those buried here would consider that indelicate.

GRUS: They are not bound by delicacy, Brando.

BRANDO: Did you approve of my song?

GRUS: I assume you mean to go on with it.

BRANDO: As soon as Gaudentius gives me the measure.

GAUDENTIUS: *Miren, caballeros,* how he solicits my weakness, or scouts, perhaps, a failing in me. Where did we stop? Can we go back to that point? Don't tell me no one remembers it. That's why we have measure, to tune the mind. *Aspetta*, Brando, I don't accuse *you* of any weakness. I simply call attention to the fact that the great ocean seems to have abandoned you.

KALA: "As rivers flow onwards towards the sea, they experience a considerable diminution in their fall, and a progressive increase…"

GAUDENTIUS: "…in the basin which they drain, owing to the successive influx of their various tributaries…"

BRANDO: Whose story is this?

GRUS: Why, theirs, Brando, the indelicate ones.

BRANDO: I refuse this carnival of misconceptions.

KALA: [*Mockingly.*] *Carnaval! Carnaval!* How do you spell that, Brando?

BRANDO: I'll spell it on your ass in a minute.

KALA: Well, now, a palpable invitation to the field.

GAUDENTIUS: I hate these distractions. Where did we stop? "…gradually their current becomes more gentle and their discharge larger in volume and less subject to abrupt variations…"

KALA: "and consequently…more suitable for navigation…"

GAUDENTIUS: There you have it, Brando. Your measure.

BRANDO: So, you'll play me. And you, Grus, what do you have to say about these magical rivers?

GRUS: Who speaks of magic with regard to these rivers? I think Gaudentius meant to assure us of the natural inclination of our desires. With respect to rivers, that is, having nothing to do with your great ocean, which seems to have escaped our regard.

BRANDO: Nonsense. You can feel the flow of it, even here, just resting upon your fissiparous bottom.

KALA: Does anyone else hear that noise?

GRUS: Noise?

KALA: Sorry. I thought I heard a bell, and some flapping of garments in the wind.

BRANDO: You won't give up, will you? Listen, we won't get very far along our road if you persist in washing your fantasies here in the open.

KALA: Twice, now.

GAUDENTIUS: No disrespect, Kala. You have to realize how fragile we all are, having come this far without our emblems.

GRUS: Why, this gets more ridiculous by the hour.

KALA: I simply want to call our attention—again, mind you—to the space we seem to have inherited.

BRANDO: Thank you for embracing me, Kala.

KALA: Can no one hear that bell?

GRUS: What bell?

KALA: Let's finish our business. Suppose someone comes, and sees us all, standing around, compromising the space. Could we justify our presence here?

GAUDENTIUS: Brando has it right. You have lost your nerve. Let me finish. Why didn't you ask, could we justify not being present here?

BRANDO: Ah, Gaudentius, why implicate me in setting out on a journey I can only refuse? I did not accuse Kala of disappearing. I only wanted to point out the contradiction of his inheritance, which seems to frighten him into calling for a retreat.

GRUS: Contradiction.

BRANDO: Decidedly.

GAUDENTIUS: That reminds me of the happenstance in Veracruz. We suffered a tropical storm that had no right to call. You will never understand the *Veracruzano*, unless you bunk in one of those shacks on the beach and submit your person to a weather that has no credentials. Can I tell you what had me in that place, at that time? You will suspect a woman. Right? What if I proposed the danger of storms, or a plaza filled with inexhaustible dancers?

BRANDO: You would be well on your way to enchanting us.

GAUDENTIUS: The perfect point.

KALA: Why is he telling this story?

GAUDENTIUS: Why not?

GRUS: I do hear that bell.

KALA: No need to mock me.

BRANDO: Ah, the light's fading. Does anyone have a light for the altars?

GRUS: You called them altars.

BRANDO: Do you approve?

GRUS: Why wouldn't I approve?

BRANDO: Well, when we came on this scene, you refused to dance.

GRUS: Who made that a requirement?

BRANDO: You can't hide, Grus. You understood our agreement.

GRUS: Nonsense. Ask the others about our agreement.

GAUDENTIUS: Own up to it, Grus. What other speech did we have at that time? Don't pretend you thought we could get by with just the enchantment of song, without touching upon that deep rhythm buried in our bodies?

GRUS: Contradiction.

GAUDENTIUS: I see. Grus wants his release, a *désinvolture*.

GRUS: My learned Gaudentius. Trying to do away with me.

KALA: I have an ending for your story, Gaudentius.

GAUDENTIUS: Forget you.

KALA: Point of order. The master of measure can't see the difference between one rhythm and another.

GAUDENTIUS: Spell that for me, Kala.

KALA: Your story has no beginning, no cadence. How could you expect us to follow you?

BRANDO: Give him a break, Kala. Gaudentius learned his narrative skills among warrior-hunters who have every tale at their fingertips.

KALA: I refuse. I will not forgive him for taking us for granted.

GAUDENTIUS: I won't forgive Brando for shoving me into his anthropological box.

GRUS: I see. Gaudentius wants his release.

GAUDENTIUS: Forget you.

BRANDO: I suggest...

[*They stop.*]

I suggest that we light the altars, and see if we can recover any warmth there.

GRUS: In the light?

BRANDO: In our presence here. What do you say to that?

[*The others grumble.*]

KALA: I'd welcome a body on the other side of that bell. We seem to have tattled our way into an immobility. Did I say that? Yes. Suddenly, our bodies are mute, our tongues are stillborn. We shouldn't delude ourselves that we have been liberated. We have just reached the point where our stories cannot account for us. And we have fetched up here, as one.

GAUDENTIUS: You chocolate eating grave digger, you would come up with something like that. [*To* BRANDO.] You put him up to it. [*To* KALA.] Can't you even get the coordinates right? Nothing you've said belongs in that space.

KALA: Well, where should I stand?

GAUDENTIUS: Not there. At least not where you seem to have moved. I had you placed south-southwest, but here you seem to have turned up hovering east-northeast, or somewhere about there.

BRANDO: I admire your geometry, Gaudentius. If we leave it to you, you will find some algebraic dimension to the soul. You have us all fascinated, with your circular ingenuity. So why don't you "place" Kala? Again.

And the rest of us will shuffle around until we come up with the right proportion.

KALA: What about my space!?

GRUS: Good god, you don't buy this business, do you?

KALA: He has a point.

GRUS: Who has a point?

KALA: Gaudentius. Brando. The two of them together.

GRUS: That does it. I could expect some sanity, a little commonsense exploratory temper. One can see that we are an unusual gang of tuppers. Hey, let me tell you, I've seen the envy in those others' eyes, even before we set out for here. But do we have to fall over a cliff, chasing every Pythagorean rainbow?

KALA: Brando, you speak to him.

BRANDO: What do I tell him?

KALA: A story, if nothing else.

GRUS: Contradiction.

[GAUDENTIUS *paces evenly toward the structures in the center.*]

What the fuck are you doing?

GAUDENTIUS: Sounding the board. Obviously.

GRUS: A little kitharist who thinks he can compose.

GAUDENTIUS: Come on, Grus. Give your syrinx a ride on imagination.

KALA: Aren't we getting a little too fancy for the circumstances? Think of where you are.

BRANDO: Exactly. I don't want to hurt anyone's feelings. But this playfulness puts a damper on our purity...

GRUS: Say wha'!?

BRANDO: ...on the order of our disorder, makes it easy to make mistakes about the rules—the relationships, you understand; so what do you get? A bunch of lies that any fishwife could tell.

GAUDENTIUS: Listen to him! Insulting the mothers! [*Singing.*] "Have you no conscience...?"

GRUS: Precisely. And we can't let him get away with it, insulting the mothers. You have got to keep in mind that we have all come from somewhere. So, I apologize, Gaudentius, if I misconstrued your relationship with your mother, the truest of true composers.

GAUDENTIUS: Well. Oh, yes, well I must say that I hadn't noticed. But there you have me. I never lose sight of the real narrative, so these interruptions and carpings never disturb me. Maybe we should let Brando get on with his proposal.

BRANDO: Thank you. I didn't suspect such graciousness in you, Gaudentius.

KALA: I sense an accusation.

BRANDO: Save me.

KALA: No. You forget our symposium in Albuquerque where you accused us all of being blind to some primordial flaw that only you could see.

BRANDO: Well, you had failed; we all had failed. You dredge up these places—Albuquerque, Cambridge, the Okefenokee, Tlaquepaque, some flowering desert or other graced by the presence of scholars—and pretend that you have everything in hand.

GRUS: I haven't stepped over that puddle of fishwives with their lies and intimidated purity. Can we go back to that?

KALA: I think we need a contradance.

BRANDO: Don't mock me.

KALA: I believe in you, Brando, in your ability to invent a primordial flame and barbecue it for us. *Caballeros*, this is a celebration. Am I right or wrong?

GAUDENTIUS: Rhythm, rhythm, it gets you into difficulties. So the master of measure, being in this instance, *su jodido servidor*, would like to warn you against taking everything too playfully, or too solemnly.

KALA: But the fucking primordial flaw. Let this *piccolo uomo* tell us what it is.

[*They come to mocking attention.*]

BRANDO: You thought I wouldn't. You thought I didn't know. You thought we couldn't find one. Or that it would stay hidden or inaccessible. You could live with that disappointment, couldn't you?

[*The others show impatience.*]

Aspetta. It speaks. I must name the primordial flaw—existence.

GRUS: I knew we couldn't trust him.

GAUDENTIUS: Rhythm, rhythm. What did I tell you? Come on, Grus, listen to the music.

KALA: [*Melodramatically.*] If music be the food…Speaking of which, this idiot seems to have forgotten that we haven't eaten, that we haven't even come close to finishing our duties here.

GAUDENTIUS: Duties!? Where did you come up with that?

KALA: I found it in the choir of that primordial flaw. Of course, Brando offers this trisyllabic beginning to an all-encompassing cursus. And he has you, Gaudentius, to pretend that this rhythm has a natural fall. You might even say that it has us by the balls. Albuquerque, he cries. Oh, yes, he insists we left something—shall we say—plausible in Albuquerque that miraculously our brave and good Brando discovers right here in the absolute light of these altars, before our very eyes.

GAUDENTIUS: You would have done better if you had left off the tag.

KALA: Well, forgive me.

GAUDENTIUS: No, I will not forgive you. You want to talk duty? What about your duty to speak precisely of what disturbs Brando?

KALA: What disturbs Brando?

GAUDENTIUS: He's told you.

GRUS: Sense, expense, tense, dense, rinse, quince, immense.

GAUDENTIUS: What the fuck are you doing?

GRUS: Testing the rhyme for the primordial flaw.

GAUDENTIUS: None of those words rhymes with existence.

GRUS: I refer you to Emily Dickinson, my man. Oh, sorry. I didn't mean to expose your literacy.

GAUDENTIUS: I see. I've landed among a band of cutpurses, slyboots and pimps, who had me persuaded we had set out on the same pilgrimage. Thank you, thank you. Perhaps I should just toddle off into that twilight you refuse to acknowledge.

KALA: We all know you'd make a narrative career out of being abandoned.

GRUS: Brando. My apologies, man. We interrupted just when you were about to dress this primordial flaw for the tale. I mean you were in the way of proposing figure and ground for this *ens* you call existence.

KALA: But this time we want real toads in the imaginary garden.

GRUS: You have it all wrong. This time we want to see real blood on the parchment.

BRANDO: So. I am being inquired.

GAUDENTIUS: You are being questioned, Brando.

BRANDO: I had it right!

GAUDENTIUS: No. Listen, we all make mistakes. Cor-rig-i-ble. Lovely word. How could we get along without it? Even the primordial flaw must submit to correction.

BRANDO: You percolating spider, you have nothing to say about the quality of those stones there. Run from it, Gaudentius, run from it, this great loveliness. *Orgullo, dicen.* Not at all. I have gone beyond that, and beyond every touch of humility. [*Surveying the others.*] Do you dispute me? Or can I count upon your blindness? Well. Speak up. Give me at least a dignified rag to wear.

GAUDENTIUS: That is up to you, Brando.

BRANDO: You want no part of it.

GAUDENTIUS: Say that Grus's rhymes have captured me, that I now understand their necessity.

BRANDO: Nonsense. They have nothing to do with our text.

GAUDENTIUS: Text. Our text.

BRANDO: With that space I thought you had so aptly defined. You did correct Kala.

GAUDENTIUS: Kala has no feel for syntax.

KALA: I beg your sheep-shearing pardon. I didn't have us prancing around a plaza filled with "inexhaustible dancers."

GAUDENTIUS: You remember that, do you? There you go, Brando. You see how paying attention to details keeps you from confusing your clock. I salute you, Kala, for reminding the assembled that every occasion has a shape.

GRUS: Even in a Veracruz that no longer exists.

GAUDENTIUS: Forget you.

GRUS: No, Gaudentius. We have come to the point where you might, and perhaps should, forget yourself.

GAUDENTIUS: I can't stand it! I refuse. You bloody hacks won't make me lose the shape of this instant.

GRUS: The imperial flaw.

BRANDO: My god, I've done better than I thought I could. I've invented you, all of you. Stand in homage, brothers. You won't find any improvisatory lassitude in Master Brando. *¿Verdad?* No one answers.

GRUS: Shall we go back to the ocean?

BRANDO: If it pleases you.

GRUS: I just wanted to point out the unpredictability of our circumstances here.

KALA: I protest this usurpation.

GAUDENTIUS: Listen to the robber baron. He shows up here, all innocence and ambition, and stakes a claim, some place to park his rootless behind so he can savor grace. He keeps his ears open for some phrase he can use to convince us that he belongs, that he has always belonged, to that grace he doesn't understand. He mumbles his fable, and hopes that it will serve to establish him. And then he takes advantage of the first misapprehension—I mean that primordial flaw—to cry injury, and ask for our solace. But, god help me, I protest this fabling conspiracy. Do you understand me, Brando?

BRANDO: Observe, brothers, my skill at blinding.

GRUS: Oh, don't preen yourself. Why the fuck do we need eyes to see what our bodies already tell us? Why don't you flog us, Brando, beat this understanding out of us? You and your goddamned light that you intend to take away when it pleases you.

BRANDO: That sounds like a chariot speech.

GRUS: Well, I thought you needed an escape.

BRANDO: Well, yes. I guess that will have to do for now. Places!

KALA: Has anyone noticed? The altars, as you can see, have disappeared.

GAUDENTIUS: Impossible.

KALA: Why wouldn't they? Would you want to hang around folk who pay no attention?

GAUDENTIUS: Do we have to put up with this idiot's frivolity?

BRANDO: I hate to point this out to you, Gaudentius. But what was there seems not to be there.

GAUDENTIUS: Have we all gone out of our minds? Grus. Speak up.

GRUS: I notice you haven't looked at the altars. Or should I say, looked for the altars. Because they have, by demons or design, unmistakably abandoned us.

[They all urge GAUDENTIUS to look toward the center.]

All right, Gaudentius, tell us. Is that space more spatial than it was a moment ago?

GAUDENTIUS: Ah, no. You won't catch me in that. Wake up. Somewhere along the line, engaged in our joyous and enlightening narratives, we moved, that is to say, with respect to each other—that is, with respect to the altars' relationship with each other—we reorganized, reordered, however you want to put it, our spatial configuration by which we had oriented ourselves before, that is, before this new relationship became operative.

BRANDO: Then it's no more than a question of perspective.

GAUDENTIUS: Exactly.

KALA: Then we can retrieve the situation by going back to the status quo ante?

GAUDENTIUS: Exactly.

GRUS: Now where would that be, Gaudentius? Here? Or there?

KALA: Damn you, Gaudentius, you've emptied me of my sense of east-northeast.

BRANDO: Don't blame Gaudentius. We are all at fault. Shall we wait here until things return to normal? Or should we risk an exploration to facilitate our return?

GRUS: Strike that. I don't want to return to the situation we had.

BRANDO: Why not?

GRUS: Think about it. What would we have to do to assure ourselves that we had come back to our place, reconfigured the proper relationships, if you will? We'd have to go over the same ground, tell the same stories, get into the same quarrels, talk about the same proposals, visions, dreams. And consider this, brothers, we'd have no idea of what had transpired in the altars.

GAUDENTIUS: Nonsense.

BRANDO: What do you propose?

GRUS: That we wait right here.

BRANDO: Upon our bodies.

GRUS: I didn't say that.

GAUDENTIUS: What did you say?

KALA: Grus needs another language, one that isn't circumscribed by bones or blood.

BRANDO: What shall we do while we wait, Grus?

GRUS: I haven't constructed any altars, Brando.

GAUDENTIUS: What a charming way of calling attention to your innocence. I suggest that we subject this Pythagorean to an examination. He can't tell me he didn't see this coming. Talk about conspiracy. Just recall, brothers, what Master Grus said during our celebrations. How could you not have seen that smug reticence on his face?

GRUS: Say wha'...!

GAUDENTIUS: Don't deny it. That look of will he or will he...

GRUS: Hold your Hebrides tongue!

GAUDENTIUS: I will not. No. I will not. You couldn't have been more transparent, practically preaching from some private prayer book.

GRUS: The one you gave me.

GAUDENTIUS: Ho! Now he wants to turn state's witness, and turn you all against me.

BRANDO: *Cálmate*, Gaudentius.

KALA: Yes, your instrument seems out of tune.

GAUDENTIUS: Let me see if I have this right. Who has put us in this trick?

BRANDO: Your point? I see no trick.

GAUDENTIUS: Well, get to that. The man who blinds finds himself blinded.

BRANDO: You make too much of an accidental occurrence. Wouldn't you say? Just particles scurrying through an underground chamber, looking for a home. Don't you see it that way, Gaudentius?

GAUDENTIUS: I really don't like the way you use your baton, Brando. You've got this orchestra confused.

KALA: There! Doesn't anybody else hear those bells?

GAUDENTIUS: Oh, let's have done with your fucking bells, Kala.

KALA: *Maravilla*. Copulative bells. I admire your denotational ingenuity, Gaudentius. But nothing will make the bells go away, unless they don't exist, or unless they arrive. Brothers, I submit that our metric *maestro* has lost his bearings, or his hearing. Oh, god, Brando's misguided baton must have disoriented me. My rhymes can't seem to marry, to copulate. Gaudentius, you owe me some space— south-southwest, east-northeast, whatever you choose. Do you hear me?

GAUDENTIUS: Rhythm, rhythm.

GRUS: καὶ δὶς γὰρ, ὃ δεῖ, καλόν ἐστιν ἐνισπεῖν.

GAUDENTIUS: What does that mean?

GRUS: It means your Pythagorean remains unhappy with the way the altars walked away.

BRANDO: They did not walk away. You said so yourself.

KALA: Yes, Grus. You had me convinced that the fault was not in our stars.

GAUDENTIUS: *I* made that specification.

GRUS: No. You blamed our unrooted desire to be on the move.

GAUDENTIUS: Don't try to slip out of this.

BRANDO: An unfortunate choice of verse.

GAUDENTIUS: We all agree the altars did not slip away.

KALA: *Certo.* They deliberately shucked us off.

GAUDENTIUS: They did not. We—the altars and *nosotros mexicanos*— made a reciprocal arrangement.

GRUS: Impossible. We were in no position to do that.

GAUDENTIUS: We were there.

KALA: Where?

GRUS: "For one after another all the limbs of the god were shaken."

BRANDO: Remove that figure. It will bring no solution.

GRUS: As you wish. Why don't we take up our narrative where we left it?

KALA: I don't have the heart for it.

BRANDO: Besides, which narrative would serve us best?

GAUDENTIUS: I sense a sly movement toward separation.

GRUS: Really.

BRANDO: Yes, Grus. Realism.

GRUS: So we can't start over?

GAUDENTIUS: My question exactly.

KALA: Brando puts too much faith in his "accidental occurrence."

BRANDO: Don't provoke me, Kala.

KALA: My god, no, Brando. Think of this as a challenge, an attempt—I mean your attempt, *por supuesto*—at an *explication de texte*.

BRANDO: I think you're all barking at a knot. But go on, Kala, instruct me.

KALA: I will. You thought you had bought your place by being anonymous. We all must have thought that, standing in the little circle that draws us toward those two stars in the middle—such a saintliness of voices and good intentions. But now we have this accidental occurrence, and where before we could live on the unbroken thread of our exhilaration, now we have to live on the silence of our stories. And we don't know how to recover that silence.

GAUDENTIUS: [*Mockingly.*] Bravo. Oh, well done. [*To the others.*] Wouldn't you say? [*To* KALA.] But, of course, that story you started had nothing to do with you.

GRUS: I thought he had offered it in defense of our sainted mother, memory.

KALA: Haven't you been listening?

GRUS: I have, for the return of those two stars.

BRANDO: Ah, Kala, have we gone back to Albuquerque, just picking up where we had left off?

GRUS: "But I shall return again to the passage of songs..."

BRANDO: Leave it to you to talk about something we never had in hand.

GRUS: Of course, we had it in hand. Do you think I've been sitting here in this passage forgetful of my own fucking name, careless of my own imagination? No, sir, the crows haven't eaten my soul.

GAUDENTIUS: Good for you, Grus.

BRANDO: Oh, don't encourage him in his ludic behavior.

GAUDENTIUS: That came close.to being a prayer, Brando.

[KALA *begins to search himself for something.*]

What's the problem, Kala?

KALA: I had something I wanted to read to you. Something quite appropriate to the occasion, something you'd appreciate.

GRUS: Thank god, you've lost it. Haven't we had enough of this "reading for the occasion"?

KALA: Not yet. [*He finds a paper which he unfolds.*] There. Hold still. I'll have it in a minute. [*The paper unfolds and unfolds.* KALA *becomes more and more disheartened.*] My apologies. This seems to be no more than the sketch for a sacred dance. One, as you might guess, I thought would serve us here.

GAUDENTIUS: So you were prepared?

KALA: Prepared! Prepared! What does it mean? I came hoping I might be of service. Isn't that why you came, Gaudentius? Isn't that why you accepted an anonymous invitation to come into a silence you hadn't yourself prepared, or even conceived? So let me stand here with my miserable choreography of gods, goddesses and saints, and weep because I haven't discovered the steps.

BRANDO: Don't just stand there, Gaudentius. You can see that Kala wants to see your invitation.

KALA: *Bárbaro!*

BRANDO: No, no. He has every right to know why we have to accept your presence here.

GAUDENTIUS: How in the hell did you come up with that?

BRANDO: I didn't. The altars did. They chose a most opportune moment to veil themselves.

[GAUDENTIUS *walks to the center, spreads his arms, whirls.*]

GAUDENTIUS: Observe, *caballeros*, this atmosphere of absence, this clamor of silence. Should good Gaudentius take credit for this? This? Nay, I should watch my language—these events. I ask you to consider that nothing took place here. Nothing started here. So, can we have a finish, a new beginning and a solution to that Brandissimo problem, the primordial flaw? So, what invitation does kind Kala have in mind?

GRUS: Delicious.

BRANDO: Pull yourself together, Grus. This southern Jersey cleverness simply avoids the question.

GAUDENTIUS: What says kind Kala? No bells?

[KALA *prepares to leave.*]

Wait a minute, Kala. What about that symmetry that caught your eye?

GRUS: Yes, show a little courage. Things don't just fall into place. Tell him, Brando. Strike that.

BRANDO: You've made your point, Gaudentius. Those material objects— oh, let's just call them altars—did not walk away; they simply removed themselves. But, of course, we couldn't know that because we could not have been here.

GAUDENTIUS: He wants out.

GRUS: *Certo.*

KALA: Well, if no one minds. [*He walks away.*]

GAUDENTIUS: Where do you think he'll go?

GRUS: It doesn't matter.

BRANDO: I think it was all prearranged. Didn't you notice that he went in the same direction as the...?

GRUS: Yes? Go on. Tell us what you know about the direction.

GAUDENTIUS: *Tais-toi*, Grus. He can't know anything about that.

GRUS: Well, whether he did, or didn't, he seemed perfectly willing to specify a direction.

GAUDENTIUS: As any mathematician should. Right, Brando?

BRANDO: You say so.

GAUDENTIUS: No, the altars say so.

[KALA *returns.*]

KALA: I couldn't do it

GRUS: Do what?

KALA: Bury myself.

GRUS: It must be that twilight, Brando. Say, I declare myself about to boil over. Maybe you can tell me what makes this innocent take his ass into the dark, and then come back talking this graveyard shit. Don't smile, Gaudentius. I don't have a whole lot of use for your "atmosphere of absence."

GAUDENTIUS: Hey, why don't you listen to the man? Speak, Kala.

KALA: I will, Gaudentius, in spite of your discourtesy.

GRUS: Delicious. *Vale*, the resurrected Kala.

KALA: Misprision. I began to die when I came back to this.

BRANDO: This?

KALA: This little configuration of souls that pretends to sustain us. We have to pretend that death alone will open the space we thought we had established. Master of the dance. Master of metric, And what is Grus? My friend, or my ancestor? Or the gravitational possibility that ties me to this place? Does anyone hear that bell now?

BRANDO: Playful. But you have to know, Kala, that, while you went on your walkabout, everything here changed. Take Grus, for example. You know what he did? He came up to me with a petition to be your father.

GRUS: Nonsense.

BRANDO: Sorry. Uncle, was it?

GRUS: Stop it.

BRANDO: Don't deny that you had designs on Kala's place in our circle.

KALA: Did he now!?

GRUS: Oh, come on, Kala, use your head. We couldn't even talk about a circle without your point.

KALA: My point exactly.

BRANDO: No, not your point. And not exactly.

KALA: So I had become essential.

GRUS: You were dead. You said so.

KALA: I did not. Listen, we no longer had a circle. I mean those material objects, that metal, that granite, that sand, that blood, call it whatever you want, but that double-headed eccentricity that stood there had disappeared. I kept stepping, stepping away, and then I realized that I could never find it, them, out there. All of a sudden, I felt the altars' indifference. So I started back. I really didn't care if I found you here.

GAUDENTIUS: Bury myself, he says. What does that mean? You get buried, if we bury you. Don't think you can slough us off.

BRANDO: Yes, Kala. That's a skill you cannot have mastered. You see that, don't you? [*Pause.*] I say. I've neglected you all. So let's do what no proper dramaturg would have us do, and pause for a festive meal, *una borrachera,* singing and prevarication, *una vez, une fois de plus, ancora una volta* and once again.

[*A chorus—a split band, wearing dark robes, carrying various instruments and bags—flows from doors on the left and right into the space.*]

CHORUS ONE: What have we here?

CHORUS TWO: A mess from the look of it.

CHORUS THREE: Pitiful. But look at it from their point of view.

CHORUS FOUR: Please.

CHORUS THREE: No. Hear me out. Look at us. We didn't even get the entrance right. [*He turns on the others.*] We seem almost as confused as they are. I told Archie...

CHORUS ONE: Don't call me Archie.

CHORUS THREE: What should I call you?

CHORUS ONE: Not Archie.

CHORUS THREE: I refer to the office.

CHORUS TWO: Your point.

CHORUS THREE: The approach is all.

CHORUS FOUR: Oh, my god, another of his slogans.

CHORUS THREE: I don't know where you got your training.

CHORUS FOUR: The same place you got yours.

CHORUS THREE: Then why did you stumble out of the wrong door? And where did you get that robe? Archie, I hold you responsible for this mess.

CHORUS ONE: Which mess? Ours, or theirs?

CHORUS THREE: Oh, you want to play, do you? You know what I mean. I remind you of propriety. I remind you of our sacred purpose.

CHORUS FOUR: Please.

[CHORUS ONE *turns to the first group.*]

CHORUS ONE: You can see how it goes. Did you even think about these things when you showed up here? Listen, I don't apologize for my colleague. He has a point. You can't just turn a cathedral into a brothel.

CHORUS TWO: No need to go that far, brother.

CHORUS ONE: You want control of this episode, brother?

CHORUS THREE: Don't forget the symmetry, Archie.

CHORUS ONE: Stop it with this Archie!

BRANDO: Who are you?

CHORUS ONE: Oh. Let me introduce my fellow pilgrims, my *mathematikoi*, though I think that at least one of them thinks of himself as *Akousmata*. But these distinctions shouldn't disturb you. Anyway. [*He points to each in turn.*] Two. Three. Four. One. The names don't matter, that is to say, not the familiar names. You see us reduced in strength. That, again, should not bother you. As my fellow pilgrim has said, I refer to the office.

CHORUS TWO: [*To* BRANDO.] What did you do with the altars?

CHORUS THREE: What could he do with the altars? He had to suffer.

CHORUS FOUR: *Stai zitto*, Flavio.

GRUS: I thought you had no names.

CHORUS FOUR: That one will do for now. If the situation changes, he'll get another. Besides, we have to address more important matters. You can't account for the altars, can you? Never mind. They haven't disappeared. Perhaps your usurpation provoked them into this strategic retreat.

GRUS: What do you mean, usurpation?

CHORUS FOUR: The fact that you are here, and insisting upon your rights to some emotional, intellectual, social behavior, some theological dogma you can't even specify. [*In a preaching tone.*] Am I right or wrong?

[*The other chorus members grunt their assent.*]

GAUDENTIUS: Stop it right there. I've seen this game. I remember...

CHORUS FOUR: [*Mockingly.*] He remembers. Yes? Go on. What do you remember? Say, you haven't heard such singing.

GAUDENTIUS: Oh, my, we have sheepherders dealing in dithyrambic delights.

CHORUS TWO: Notice his accent. He can't even do the word.

GAUDENTIUS: But I can do you.

CHORUS TWO: Oh, a proposition.

CHORUS ONE: *Tais-toi*, Pierre.

BRANDO: Obviously, we got started on the wrong foot. You acknowledge that yourselves. That stellar absence has disoriented us.

CHORUS ONE: What do you propose?

BRANDO: That you go off, and enter again.

CHORUS ONE: Ah, he believes in the value of historical discontinuity.

CHORUS THREE: It makes sense.

CHORUS TWO: Leave it to you to confuse things. What do we do with these footprints? And what about that hymnal cacophony we heard on our way here? Songs, prayers, whatever they choose to call them. Pay attention, Willie. You can see they have filled up the space.

CHORUS FOUR: *Certo.* They lose the altars in this rubble, and then they pretend that they have been abandoned.

KALA: No one said...

BRANDO: *Tacete*, Kala. [*He approaches* CHORUS TWO.] You remind me of an old wrangler I met just two steps out of Socorro. He had plotted the whole state on the basis of the measurements he had made in his front yard. Don't laugh. Someone, who called himself a chancellor, had floated down from Santa Fe, with a retinue of saints twirling their instruments and dancing in the backyard, looking for a divided poplar that would mark the space for eternity. What did the old wrangler say? "You will come up empty." So tell me about these footprints, these songs, these prayers, whatever you choose to call them.

CHORUS TWO: I salute your diplomatic skills, my man. Notice, brothers, how he has veiled the appearance of those altars that you see right there. [*He indicates the altars that have suddenly returned to their places.*]

KALA: I did not come back for this.

GAUDENTIUS: No, of course not. You came back to be jacked around by these citizens.

CHORUS THREE: Let's get it straight right now. These citizens, as you call them, have a purpose.

GRUS: I don't doubt it, but I don't see how it should concern us.

CHORUS ONE: Ah, but there remains that Dionysian exactitude that would benefit us all. Why don't we come to some agreement about this configuration?

GAUDENTIUS: Don't fall for it!

CHORUS ONE: How innocent of you. Why should we deceive you? We now belong to this space, or haven't you noticed?

BRANDO: Correct me. But didn't you refuse a new beginning?

CHORUS ONE: We don't deal in such contradictory terms—new, beginning.

GRUS: [*Slapping his neck.*] Oh, forgive me. I felt that bug of propriety on my neck.

CHORUS ONE: Yes, I remember now. You couldn't decide between the "in" and "of" order of things.

GRUS: You cannot have heard that.

CHORUS ONE: Perhaps not. I find it hard to distinguish among your storytellers and your dancers. You all seem capable of surprising allegiances, even if you disappear and return.

KALA: I don't need your judgment.

CHORUS ONE: Sensitive. But, here, let us determine which direction says left and which says right.

BRANDO: If they exist.

CHORUS ONE: Well, then we will simply have to improvise upon these terms.

GAUDENTIUS: [*Pointing to the altars.*] And they?

CHORUS ONE: They will have to accommodate themselves to this harmonious order.

BRANDO: Let me count. [*He does, pointing at* KALA, GRUS *and* GAUDENTIUS.] Four, three, two. [*At himself.*] One.

CHORUS ONE: Do they agree?

BRANDO: There is no room for such improbability.

CHORUS TWO: I don't like this figure's fumbling with the cardinal points.

BRANDO: Or with the songs, prayers, whatever you choose to call them.

CHORUS THREE: Smart. A legacy of repetition.

BRANDO: Which we had before you came with these costumes and flamboyant signatures. Why should we believe in you?

CHORUS FOUR: Why indeed. Our lyrics speak only of sensation.

KALA: [*Pointing to the altars.*] When they walked away, sensation departed.

GAUDENTIUS: I refuse…!

CHORUS TWO: I refuse…!

GAUDENTIUS: After you.

CHORUS TWO: No, citizen, after you.

GAUDENTIUS: What refusal did you have in mind?

CHORUS TWO: No, sir, I defer to your good sense regarding this sensuous matter.

GAUDENTIUS: Ho! That confirms that you have lost your pussy-footing way. Who writes your lyrics?

CHORUS TWO: God, what a hypocrite. Let me see your ticket.

GAUDENTIUS: What do you mean?

CHORUS TWO: You and that one [*He points at* KALA.] seem out of place.

CHORUS FOUR: *Calma*, Pancho. We can't give them up just yet.

GRUS: I don't like the sound of that.

CHORUS FOUR: I refer to the mathematics of the situation, sir. The space lends itself to the perfect discontinuity.

BRANDO: That sensation arrived with you.

CHORUS ONE: Ah, back to sensation. We apologize for having come late. I almost said we apologize for having come at all. Did you need us? We can only imagine how cozy things had become. And then you had this fraudulent episode where the altars danced away, following some ancestral configuration that had you pissing in your pants. Don't deny that you looked forward to such a delicious emptiness. The stories would begin again. You could dress in new clothes every lie you had ever told, or you could think of them as new clothes.

BRANDO: Would you do me a favor? Stand over there next to Gaudentius. You recognize Gaudentius, don't you?

CHORUS ONE: I don't recognize a need for Gaudentius.

BRANDO: So much for your improvisation. I wonder anyhow about the mathematics of the situation. Help us out. Why don't we take a turn around the space?

CHORUS FOUR: I won't stand for this trivialization of my space.

GRUS: Your space!?

BRANDO: Down, Grus.

CHORUS FOUR: No, you idiots simply haven't prepared…

BRANDO: Yes?

CHORUS FOUR: Well, look at you. You don't even seem to recognize each other. I won't refer, sir, to the disastrous dance we saw in progress when we arrived.

CHORUS TWO: *Certo.* You should thank your stars that we came along to put you in your places.

CHORUS THREE: Exactly. So the altars would express the proper relations.

KALA: I think you go too far. You've given the altars eyes and ears.

CHORUS FOUR: Scandalous. This idiot can't see that the altars have no need of eyes and ears.

KALA: What then?

CHORUS FOUR: Judgment.

BRANDO: I recognize *you* now. Brothers. welcome the mighty Eshu-Elegba.

CHORUS FOUR: Say wha'…?

BRANDO: Calm down. I won't do away with your disguise.

GRUS: What about taking that turn around the space? Why don't we yoke the [*Indicating the chorus.*] reverend followers of a mass that never sounds and [*Indicating his four.*] pilgrims with stories that never change.

BRANDO: Thank you, Grus, for the compromise.

CHORUS ONE: I refuse such a compromise.

BRANDO: I hate to point out to you that your presence here has taken you beyond compromise.

CHORUS ONE: Yes. I sensed a didascalian error along the way. So we have become subject to your inventiveness, if not your sacrality.

BRANDO: *I* didn't come in the wrong door.

CHORUS ONE: I don't expect sympathy. But, given the way this problem has evolved, I would hope that you wouldn't mind hearing our story, part of that *nouvelle dualité.*

BRANDO: Should we listen?

CHORUS ONE: Suit yourself.

BRANDO: *Pace,* Archie.

CHORUS ONE: Don't call me Archie.

BRANDO: I refer to the office.

CHORUS ONE: Don't mock me. You can't understand the office.

GRUS: Right? Or left?

CHORUS TWO: [*To* CHORUS ONE.] You needn't bother, Jerome.

CHORUS ONE: The story needs no justification, brother. And I have it in hand.

[CHORUS TWO *starts to leave.*]

Wait.

[*He stops.*]

BRANDO: Say, this is an occasion. Let's make a home for this story. Here. Gather around. Organize yourselves.

[*He conducts them into a jumbled configuration, and coaxes them to sit.*]

There you go, a different syntax. [*To* CHORUS ONE.] *C'est à toi, mon frère.*

[CHORUS ONE *begins an elaborate preparation of his robes and voice. He signals to his chorus. They spark what seems a scriptural text that quickly, in the moment it appears, turns into a twelve-tone exercise that mimicks the four figures' first song. Isolated words get distributed among the voices. We hear, and lose, "deep," "dampen," "colloquy," "bed." The spark quickly fades; they grow silent.*]

CHORUS ONE: We all must have had the grace of dreams. Even here I can see the signs.

GRUS: Will you get on with it!

CHORUS ONE: I will. [*Narrative tone.*] Field: a set (of numbers or functions, for example) together with ways of adding and multiplying members of the set, that satisfy rules similar to the rules for the addition and multiplication of rational numbers.

GAUDENTIUS: Get this idiot out of my face.

CHORUS ONE: [*Continuing.*] Given any element in the set, we must be able to add any element to it, subtract any element from it, multiply it by any element, or divide it by any nonzero element, and in each case obtain a result in the same set of elements.

[*The other chorus members launch another brief twelve-tone scheme.* CHORUS ONE *speaks angrily.*]

Not yet.

KALA: Surely, you must have finished. This is your dream?

CHORUS ONE: Don't burden me with your misconceptions, Kala.

KALA: He remembers my name.

CHORUS ONE: Shall I go on?

BRANDO: You have nowhere to go.

CHORUS ONE: You say. Have you ever worshipped in the Santuario de Chimayó?

BRANDO: Don't give us your impossibilities.

CHORUS ONE: I'm simply trying to establish a symmetry here.

GRUS: In dreams? In worship? Or in the existence of this instant you have so carefully arranged?

CHORUS ONE: Why, Grus doesn't trust me. So I have entered twice on the wrong foot. [*He indicates the chorus.*] You hear them trilling the same anxiety you brought here. You see me slightly withered, my robes more than a little tattered. I do understand that you would like to keep your distance. I took you up an old trail where the wounded might find grace. Will you imprison me now in my own desires, or let me find comfort in the story of my numbers?

KALA: What about them? You stopped their singing.

CHORUS ONE: Oh, they'll let me go on. [*Resuming his narrative tone.*] Axiom: a statement used in the premises of arguments and assumed to be true without proof.

CHORUS TWO: *Basta!*

CHORUS ONE: We cannot abandon them.

CHORUS THREE: You say.

CHORUS FOUR: No sanctuary here.

CHORUS ONE: Speak to the space!

CHORUS TWO: We have done with it.

BRANDO: There's no reason to go any further.

CHORUS THREE: Stick to your office.

GAUDENTIUS: Has anyone noticed? The altars have exchanged positions.

CHORUS ONE: Well, then, we have come to the wrong place. [*He pulls himself together.*] Brothers. I ask your indulgence.

[*He and his chorus walk away, singing the twelve-tone antiphon they had begun.*]

BRANDO: Well, now what do we do?

GAUDENTIUS: We keep the fire.

BRANDO: Fire!? Do you see any fire there, Gaudentius?

GAUDENTIUS: Brando the pragmatist. But my rusticity tells me you have a problem, brother. You never see what you see. And fire here seems so out-of-keeping.

GRUS: Hold your Carolingian tongue, Gaudentius. You can see that we're in trouble.

KALA: Did anyone notice how the little ragged peasants picked our metaphysical pockets?

BRANDO: What nonsense!

KALA: I only refer to the office. You must admit we hadn't been well-defined before they came.

GRUS: He has a point. That didascalian rogue understood that something would always exclude him—them, if I might put it exactly—from the inevitable process we had going before they came. You said so yourself, Brando.

BRANDO: A manner of speaking.

GRUS: No, no, no, I won't accept such failure. You counted us. Four, three, two, one. I quarrel with your priority, of course.

BRANDO: Oh, you do!?

GRUS: Yes.

GAUDENTIUS: I didn't want to make too much of it. But the equation couldn't balance in the way you proposed it.

BRANDO: And now?

KALA: You can see it makes more sense. Listen, they did us a favor, getting us to take a close look at our alignment.

GAUDENTIUS: Yes, how could we move on, if we continued to occupy ourselves with these idiosyncrasies?

BRANDO: I refuse to be the butt of this joke.

GRUS: Don't take it that way. For example, take this business with the primordial flaw. Who would propose it? Who could propose it? Why, all of us have contributed to that passion.

BRANDO: "As rivers flow onwards towards the sea, they experience a considerable diminution in their fall, and a progressive increase…"

GAUDENTIUS: Exactly.

KALA: Rhythm, rhythm. "For one after another all the limbs of the god were shaken."

GRUS: Who is the metric *maestro*?

BRANDO: Yes, yes, how clever we have become. Do we need that intrusive chorus of peasants, with their archaic instruments? Why, we could make out of driftwood and rusting tin better instruments than they displayed.

GAUDENTIUS: And certainly, they do not have our ingenuity.

GRUS: *Certo.*

BRANDO: But suppose we rearrange events, the space; reorder the intervention of the instruments, the singing. We wouldn't feel any loss, would we?

GAUDENTIUS: Nothing has disappeared; nothing can disappear.

[KALA *indicates the altars.*]

KALA: Let's not get carried away. Let us approach and see how they take this situation.

BRANDO: Thank you, Kala, for your modest suggestion. We should go down there. I don't much like the way they have remained silent through all of this.

GAUDENTIUS: That should tell us something. We can't just pop down there, and have them receive us with open arms, as though nothing has happened. I mean, think of the offense of it.

BRANDO: Offense!? Of what? To whom?

KALA: I must say that I had that in mind. Look at us. Do we consider ourselves properly dressed? I say nothing about our attitude, and the way we scuttled our companions and made it impossible for them to support us.

GRUS: They don't understand support.

KALA: I don't believe you, Grus. Do you deny that they had a function?

GRUS: Oh, my, the mathematical Kala. What do you propose?

GAUDENTIUS: We do appear a little threadbare. And I, for one, feel a little exposed in my awkwardness. Oh, don't frown, Brando. Even you have to agree that we would have a more presentable case if there were more harmony in our bearing.

GRUS: Well, how should we approach these mute intensities?

KALA: Hold it right there. I suggest we go no further.

BRANDO: Kala and Gaudentius think I will stop now that I have these mute intensities at hand. I'll sort it out. They'll recognize me. I'll know them.

KALA: What about us?

BRANDO: You'll have to determine whether your decorum means more to you than your inquiry.

GAUDENTIUS: Clever, Brando. You've configured a new domain.

BRANDO: No, their silence did that.

GRUS: God, I wish we had the other pilgrims. We wouldn't have this argument over whether we waltz or two-step. Such majesty.

KALA: Strike that.

GAUDENTIUS: Don't abandon me, Kala.

BRANDO: Do we go on? I mean, enter that space and take our chances?

KALA
GAUDENTIUS } Only if we prepare.
GRUS

BRANDO: We prepared when we broke all our connections. Certainly, you see the continuity in that.

KALA: What do they say?

BRANDO: Strange. But I see they have turned their faces from us.

GAUDENTIUS: Oh, great Brando, *mathematikós* who has intelligence of faces. I'll go with you, and I will dance.

KALA: So will I.

GRUS: Damn me, I have to live with my errors. Who will sound the first note?

BRANDO: Rearrange your garments.

[*They do. They straighten. The old chorus is suddenly beside them.*]

CHORUS ONE: No, we offered you a statistical possibility. And we see you haven't got very far. Oy! *Mathematikoi.* You would have done better if you had simply sat with your illiterate spirituality. But go on. You won't find what you proposed.

BRANDO: What happened to your instruments?

CHORUS ONE: You noticed.

[*He gestures to* CHORUS TWO, *who sounds a weak bell.*]

Satisfied? We call it reconciliation. My colleague, the third among us, convinced me that words such as that should come only after great suffering. Have you suffered? No, I can see the ecstasy in your faces. Ecstasy, out of oneself. [*He gestures toward the altars.*] They understand. You don't understand. You can't just boogie down to the space without some preparation. Call it protocol; call it reconciliation. Look here, let's send the third among us to open the way.

GAUDENTIUS: *Sono io!*

CHORUS ONE: There you go. [*He indicates* CHORUS THREE.] He'll go with you.

BRANDO: What a preening bastard!

CHORUS ONE: Watch your mouth. There are ladies among us. Oh. Sorry. Didn't mean to call attention to your failings. But they should go, shouldn't they?

BRANDO: Well, you've stacked the deck.

CHORUS ONE: *Atani*, Brando. *Giocare.*

BRANDO: [*To* CHORUS THREE *and* GAUDENTIUS.] Go on, then.

[*Flowing, they go.*]

Ah, the rhythm of it. You really don't need any special light, do you?

CHORUS FOUR: [*Producing a flame.*] No. But we have this.

GRUS: What do you intend to do with that flame?

CHORUS FOUR: I hope to illuminate the orbit of their pilgrimage, and to clear the space for our further concern.

KALA: [*Producing a small axe.*] I had hoped I would not have to use this.

CHORUS ONE: So. Shall we sacrifice the two who trusted us?

BRANDO: So. It has come to that, has it?

CHORUS ONE: Oh, don't be absurd. You knew you could never measure what you see there. And they had already taken your measure. I'll never forgive you and your associates, Brando, for your ecstatic resignation, for parading your dignity, for dying well, even if you had to corrupt those who had made no claims.

BRANDO: We have a problem.

CHORUS ONE: Not your primordial flaw, I hope.

BRANDO: No. We need a new definition of syntax. No one can write anything here anymore. You've made sure of that with your evasions, your contradictions, your change of clothes; why, you've even changed your smell. You did well to bring a flame. We should burn everything to the ground.

CHORUS ONE: [*To the other chorus.*] Berkeley. They teach them how to audition. But perhaps not to listen.

BRANDO: You accuse me, sir, of being tone deaf.

CHORUS ONE: That. And for having no eyes for the balance of things.

GRUS: [*Pointing to the four figures below.*] They seem to have forgotten us.

BRANDO: Impossible. They know why we sent them.

CHORUS FOUR: A felicitous agreement. We should celebrate how quickly they've accomplished our intent.

KALA: Yes. I did hear it, when you came knocking at the wrong door back then.

CHORUS TWO: Listen to him. We found you standing on your own arc, counting up your injuries, and hoping someone would come along to rescue you.

CHORUS ONE: *Calma*, Benjamin. That ceremony he now sees simply unnerves him. And the others can't get over the astonishing pleasure of their fear.

BRANDO: What about you?

CHORUS ONE: What about me?

BRANDO: Why did you rehearse our steps? What made you so sure of the emptiness you would find?

CHORUS ONE: I think we should move on. Look at them down there. Dressed, embellished, flamboyant, exhilarated by indiscernible ambition. They don't need us.

BRANDO: No. I suppose they don't.

CHORUS ONE: Well, we're off.

[*They gather, loosely group, and start to walk away.*]

Perk up, pilgrims. There is a multitude of these harmonies.

[*A violent light and overpowering wind sound arise to fill the space. A sudden red darkness.*]

LEMMA

[*Lights come up on a sextet of actors, each one carrying a particular property that each will use as a subtle shift in movement in the action that involves that actor—call it a change in direction and a new placement of relationships. The actors move at first in a single line, then begin and carry out a series of differing positions with respect to each other, as though they were looking for the proper and perfect configuration of their group. They choose, and come to a first rest. Each one now sings an individual prologue.*]

VOICE A: Death steps on the garden egg, and the garden egg drops suddenly.

VOICE B: The geometer draws no conclusion from the existence of the particular line of which he speaks, but from what his diagrams represent. Furthermore, all hypotheses and postulates are either universal or particular, but a definition is neither.

VOICE C: Why, after all, should the earth fall? If the universe is symmetrical, there is no more reason for the earth to move down than up.

VOICE D: Night Mare, "Her nests, when one comes across them in dreams, lodged in rock-clefts, or the branches of enormous hollow yews, are built of carefully chosen twigs, lined with white horse-hair and the plumage of prophetic birds and littered with the jawbones and entrails of poets."

VOICE E: It happened just about the time I thought I had a solution to the problem of identity. The identity of indiscernibles. Well, this doesn't concern you.

VOICE F: Every day begins with a silence that has earned its keep. This morning requires a translation.

[*A sudden darkness. We hear what seems a fluttering of cloth or of birds' wings. The six figures have disappeared. Through the silence, a distant* agógó *sounds, gradually growing louder as it approaches, seemingly with* FUADACH's *entrance, now lit by an exceedingly white light.*]

FUADACH: You think you know me because you hear my bell. You have captured the red tail feather of a parrot, so you think you see me. Such blindness. Don't make me embarrass you. All this business about an egg, birds who don't bathe but wrap themselves in oil. Did you like the way I sang? I sing under another name, Tibio, a shadow of what you see before you.

[BRICCO *enters, carrying a long pole and a white cloth.*]

BRICCO: Still lying, I see. Whatever happened to the woman who had your cock in a sling?

FUADACH: Bricco, I don't play.

BRICCO: Fuadach, neither do I. I just want you to remember the text we want to establish here. The room where we find Kafka washing the wine stains from a white shirt.

FUADACH: Trivial matter, my man. These people don't care about that. I resent your getting in the way of my story.

BRICCO: Put your mask on.

[FUADACH *does.*]

Now, go on with your story.

FUADACH: Nothing begins that easily. Do you hear me? Nothing.

[BRICCO *indicates the pole and the cloth.*]

BRICCO: Shall I put these near the shed?

FUADACH: Give them to me. I know how to place them.

BRICCO: And I don't? Well, will you go on? I want to know what happened in that third hour.

FUADACH: You confuse things. The woman had nothing to do with that.

BRICCO: But I saw you in the café near the baroque church, waiting for someone. Stuffing your face with refritos and sour tortillas.

FUADACH: Bricco, you don't understand. Nothing keeps its place in prayer. I said no prayers upon my departure, though I had been concerned all night with a fraudulent physician whose words astounded me in their innocence—"to give light to those who sit in darkness and the shadow of death, to guide our way into the way of peace." To give light, light to me. I remember they cut into my body. A reconfiguration of entrails. An opening for the scar, unrecognizable and durable, that designs my days. Nothing remains that easy.

[*The light fades from* FUADACH. *He disappears.* BRICCO *puts on his mask, stands to one side, as though disguised.* SPALLA, *rustically adorned, flows into view. She stands some distance from* BRICCO, *pins him down with her eyes.*]

SPALLA: What did you have in mind, Bricco?

[BRICCO *remains silent, looks away from* SPALLA.]

You have my permission to speak.

BRICCO: You have no right to ask.

SPALLA: In this environment, who has rights?

BRICCO: That attitude got you into some trouble before, didn't it? Of course, if you don't recognize the claims of this environment, as you call it, you would hardly see the things that must remain unspoken.

SPALLA: Oh, well spoken, Bricco. But didn't you just try to divest Fuadach of his office?

BRICCO: You did not see that.

SPALLA: I felt it.

BRICCO: Spalla, leave me alone. I have to stand here until I figure out how to save Fuadach.

[SPALLA *laughs.*]

SPALLA: But, Bricco, who will save you?

[*She flows away.* BRICCO *kneels, and begins clawing at the ground.*]

BRICCO: I will put it here. I did not want the pole at that shed. Why should we hesitate where some creative deception gives us an opportunity? Evening. A cabin. So many unanswered questions attend this amber light. Kafka's hands in water, a sacrificial stain on the white shroud of a shirt. Oh, god, we will have a great feast. Perhaps not the marriage that Spalla wants. But we shall see.

[*He rises and walks away.* LORG, *loaded with utensils and provisions for a meal, comes out of the darkness, circles a spot, settles, prepares for a meal.*]

LORG: *Ese pájaro que canta arriba.* Ah, singing, singing. I will get that Bricco off his ass. What melodies does he know that I haven't taught him? Does he ever say that? Forget it. [*He begins to savor his meal.*] That taste reminds me of Colima, an ugly little place with master chefs. I think it improper to sit with my mind carried away by my loneliness. After midnight, hours lose their definition. I'll just sit here a while.

[*He nods.* BRICCO *appears.*]

BRICCO: We meet again, Lorg.

LORG: By chance, of course.

BRICCO: Does it disturb you, my man, that I always know how to find you?

LORG: Well, I don't hide from you, Bricco. [LORG *gestures to his meal.*] Such as.

[BRICCO *refuses the offer, pulls a brown bag from his pocket.*]

BRICCO: People don't drink coffee at this hour, my man.

LORG: You trying to corrupt me, brother?

BRICCO: I know better than that. [*He sits, takes a drink from his brown bag.*] You know, too many fools down in the village fail to make a fundamental distinction between you and me. They mistake your delicacy for a deep energy, and have no idea that whatever energy you have you get from me. They won't admit it, but these town folk approve of your detachment. Your tales, your lies about where you come from.

LORG: Do you see me that way?

BRICCO: Which way, Lorg? Which of the you shall I use to translate you? To here. To this moment. Speak up, Lorg.

LORG: I don't have time for this, Bricco.

BRICCO: Oh, he talks to me about time. You do remember the obsidian knife we bargained for?

LORG: When?

BRICCO: [*Heating.*] When, when. So we've lost it, the connection? I tell you that knife served as the ritual motive of knowledge. Through it, I knew you, and you knew me.

LORG: As you say, we must have lost it.

[BRICCO *is suddenly upon him.*]

BRICCO: You arrogant, sniveling little concoction. Do you think I'll release you? Think again.

LORG: Thank you for reminding me of the solar prominences.

[BRICCO *shakes, dismissing and releasing him.*]

Such blindness. Don't make me embarrass you. I thought of you. An hour ago.

BRICCO: [*Inattentively.*] An hour.

LORG: But I know that you have no ear for music, and, therefore, no sense of the time you parade so assiduously. [*He ignores* BRICCO's *impatient gesture.*] But you must hear the music. Don't you see that I have adopted you, Bricco?

BRICCO: Get out of my face.

LORG: Listen. [*He sings.*] Ese pájaro que canta arriba...

BRICCO: Stop it.

LORG: [*Persistently.*]...que el corazón me lastima...

BRICCO: Stop it.

LORG: And *you* have designs on Spalla.

BRICCO: Shut your mouth.

LORG: You have a place for the altar, a place for the shed. A theological architect, if you please.

BRICCO: You cannot know that. How do you know that?

LORG: Know what, Bricco?

BRICCO: What gives you the right...? Don't you know that this place has become a haunted cemetery?

LORG: Make up your mind, Bricco. You searched *me*, instead of searching yourself.

BRICCO: My, my. Lorg. Lorg, a vicar of injury. Quick eyes. You sit here on your night watch. Clever, how you managed to find your way here.

LORG: So you did place me.

BRICCO: As far as I know, I can read your road's pathologies.

LORG: Then you know that I have transformed every landscape I have traveled.

[BRICCO *searchingly approaches Lorg.*]

BRICCO: I want to touch you.

LORG: Do. Perhaps you will feel in the bone that I have no reason to lament the patchy juniper, the balding Ponderosa pine, the desiccation of trees and shrubs that supposedly thrive here. I might have become a prospector of stream beds, a connoisseur of caves and natural faults; someone who can appreciate the disastrous configuration of adobe and glass, of aluminum and steel, a world piled high with activity that fractures the very things it builds. I sit reading hours, the narrative of authoritative absence. There you have it. We must impose our perfect ordinariness upon the flagellant day. With no apologies.

BRICCO: What about the knife? Have you forgotten that?

LORG: I thought that you had.

BRICCO: Not at all. I meant to use it to repair us.

LORG: And Fuadach?

BRICCO: Don't concern yourself with Fuadach. I don't need your help. Or Spalla's.

LORG: So you've set the boundaries, have you? You always surprise me, Bricco. You take your instruments to measure something that only you can see. You turn up these little ethical dilemmas to show us how we stand with respect to your measure.

BRICCO: Lorg, I've got to go.

LORG: Sit down, Bricco. Let me show you a new measure. Patience.

[BRICCO *starts to walk away.*]

Fuadach will never tell you what happened in that third hour.

BRICCO: What did you say?

LORG: I said divination doesn't suit you. I said your impatience doesn't fit the knife you say I stole from you. Look at this. [*He produces a small plate, and slowly fills it with cowrie shells.*] I assume you can still count.

BRICCO: Don't.

LORG: Pay attention.

BRICCO: To what?

LORG: To the configuration you seem so anxious to avoid.

BRICCO: Can you play that for me?

LORG: [*Sings.*] *Ese pájaro que canta arriba…*

BRICCO: I'll bury you all.

LORG: Bricco, put on your mask. There you'll see yourself spinning in the same dance.

[BRICCO *forces his brown bag into* LORG's *hands.*]

BRICCO: Here. You need this more than I do. Say hello to midnight for me.

[*He goes, limping away.*]

LORG: What does he understand about my music? A melody makes no sense unless we remember each step in its progression, and, once established, we can reconstruct it from the smallest successive units. Just as here. Will we grow into these reconfigured and inescapable instants? Will Ginocchio sing for Bricco?

[*He slowly subsides into stillness; the light leaves him.* BRICCO *returns, now masked. He speaks to the audience.*]

BRICCO: Did you notice the trick I played on him? That business with the bottle? Should have been a bottle of gin. But that would have taken us somewhere we might not have wanted to go, at that moment. I won't get you involved in all that. Wait a minute. You do recognize me, don't you? We've met, you know. Righteous. Say, let me tell you, Fuadach will play. Take for an instance how he throws out all those names for the sun: *kílí blé*, a red egg, the *kílí bá*, a mother egg, the *fá bá*, the great egg. You think Lorg understands that? Does his music encompass these hidden harmonies? No, sir, that would diminish me. Clever Lorg, with his *pájara pinta*, his *guirigay lírico*. I heard him talking about a molecule in a stationary state. Leave that. I want to tell you something that happened to me, something I had done before I understood it. Picture this. We have this naked woman, her eyes covered by a big straw hat, sprawled in an *equipal*. Another woman, in a white choir robe, attends to the hair of a shabby little man, who leans against the woman's belly. The room smells of unfulfilled desires. Strike that. ¿Speculation, *verdad*? Anyway, there we stand, all of us, waiting for something we might call service. The woman in the chair mumbles an almost inaudible and unintelligible phrase, ending "there," the only clearly enunciated word. The other woman says, "What?" The man says "What?" twice rather aggressively, holding his ear under the woman's hat. The woman seems distraught, diffident. She repeats the phrase. The others turn away. The naked woman turns to me, and says, "He has no pockets in his hair, nothing to hold the messages." The woman in the robe says, "Pay no attention to the money; the currency has no face." The little man bows his head and says, "*Benedicto benedicatur.*" At that moment, I conceived a great feast. [*Aggressively.*] Tell me what I must do.

[LORG *seems to have awakened.*]

LORG: *Pájara pinta, guirigay,* indeed, Can't you at least give me credit for unstated action?

BRICCO: I leave it to you, Lorg. This wandering.

LORG: So you know I set out for Damascus without knowing why. Bully for you.

BRICCO: When you wake up, you'll sing it for me.

[*He goes.* LORG *falls into his darkness.* POLSO *appears, stepping lightly, ringing an* agógó *in a syncopated rhythm. He moves in a series of circles over a small area. Lorg tentatively approaches him. Polso stops.*]

POLSO: You have to rehearse.

LORG: Rehearse what?

POLSO: Sorry. I can't tell you that.

LORG: I know you, don't I?

POLSO: You do seem familiar.

LORG: Remind me. Where did we meet?

POLSO: I don't know. Where have you gone?

LORG: Wrong question. Where did you come from?

POLSO: In a minute, I think you'll ask me for my green card.

LORG: Ah, yes. Now I see. Or let me put it this way, now I've heard something that I've heard before, a little tremor of *orgullo*. Wouldn't you say so, Giuig?

POLSO: Nobody calls me that. Not now.

LORG: Why not? Hey, don't try to hide on me, Giuig. This business with your audition. You haven't changed.

POLSO: Neither have you.

LORG: Spoken like the spiritually impaired son-of-a-bitch who got lost in Davenport, Iowa.

POLSO: What do you know about that?

LORG: Everyone knew the story, man. You and Donald Byrd, on your way to Montana for some joke of a gig. You would have done better if you had tried to sing in the Mormon choir.

POLSO: You can't measure me, can you?

LORG: I see a small spirit, trying to elevate his confusion into a mathematical divinity.

POLSO: Yes, but when the light comes I know how it got there, and why. Can you say as much, Ginocchio?

LORG: You called me Ginocchio.

POLSO: You called me Giuig. Let's start again. We can forget that sacrificial knife. We can dress Rufino Durán with Kafka's white shirt. You don't have to walk all the way to Damascus by yourself.

LORG: What did you say?

POLSO: I said call me Polso. The names mean nothing. Listen, you remember Soslayita Perea, the taste of her biscuits. Sure, you do. Why not? She had the trick of the flour, or in the lard, or in the water. Don't get tied up with Bricco and this Kafka.

LORG: You ask me for blindness.

POLSO: I ask for imperfection. Enough of this destruction. Come here. [*He pulls Lorg toward the spot where he seemed to be constructing his designs.*] You see that now, my geometry, that little imperfection no speech can repair.

LORG: You go too far. Think of the music that fits it.

POLSO: Then dance, Lorg. I give you license.

[LORG *stops, his mind drifting.*]

LORG: She...said something similar to him.

POLSO: Stop it. Don't let these voices embarrass you.

LORG: Polso, I can't think of imperfection. I can't think of these little figures you've made without my music.

POLSO: Then give it up, Lorg. Get off my ground

LORG: *Your* ground?

POLSO: Yes, mine. Look around you. Everything. Even the patchy juniper, the balding Ponderosa pine, the stream beds, the caves. I did not have to invent them.

LORG: [*Deliberately.*] Oh, I see. A little counterpoint. A sorting out. A small but self-fulfilling rhythmic pattern. In other words, I have to kick your ass.

[POLSO *straightens.*]

POLSO: At your service. Put on your mask.

[*They put on masks.*]

LORG: I must have told you about Abelardo Sánchez, my *socio* from Guatemala. You must know those *cuentos* of brother birds, whose emerald green always set Abelardo to dreaming. He used to sit with us near the Rio Grande, and touch his sober toe to a distant stream. Think carefully before you disdain such an embrace.

POLSO: So you want to preen yourself at my expense? My scholar, who has given us these deficient tales, reminds us that Seferis finds a weight upon Cavafy's hand, the "material that has grown old in monasteries and libraries."

LORG: I don't read in that dictionary.

POLSO: Sound your "a."

LORG: What will that do?

POLSO: Bring us some distance toward unveiling what Bricco has observed.

[LORG claws at his own mask.]

LORG: Unmask, unmask.

POLSO: What did you expect? You chose the wrong part of the year to open this ceremony.

LORG: Strange that you should speak of ceremonies.

POLSO: Well, there for your *pájara pinta.*

LORG: Careful. We'll end with a burial under your design.

POLSO: Stop it with your number crunching melodies, these harmonies that don't go anywhere.

LORG: I insist that you dance on your own ground.

POLSO: Oh ho, now he wants to abandon me. But how does it go?

> The moon's my constant mistress
> and the lonely owl my marrow,
> The flaming drake
> and the night-crow make
> the music to my sorrow.

LORG: Nay, sir, you have mistaken all my Pythagorean blessings.

POLSO: Ah, blessing.

LORG: I accepted your invitation. And now you want a different form of enchantment. You will never recognize yourself. So don't come to me with your silly account of Bricco's failings.

POLSO: Bricco loves me. I love Bricco.

LORG: You forget. *I* brought the white cloth home.

POLSO: Did your Fuadach even notice?

LORG: He has the cloth.

POLSO: No, Ginocchio, the altar has the cloth. But you have your mask. Will it satisfy you?

LORG: Why shouldn't it?

POLSO: Reasons, reasons. When he doesn't understand, he falls back on his reason, though his reason does nothing for his understanding, or his understanding does nothing for his reason. Listen. [*Taking a large red scarf from his pocket.*] I've brought this to adorn your stiff neck. I'll let you have it, if you'll let me have that cross you have buried under your shirt.

LORG: I'd rather go blind.

POLSO: Lorg, you will go blind. The text requires it. [*He shakes the scarf before* LORG*'s face.*] Take it.

[LORG *rips the scarf from* POLSO*'s hand, throws it on the ground.*]

LORG: There. Did you see something that makes you angry, Polso? Something that you can't just let pass?

POLSO: I know you will pick that up, fold it carefully, and hand it back to me.

LORG: To do that, I'd have to bend over, perhaps go down on my knees, make a fuss over something that doesn't mean anything to me.

POLSO: I see. Well, that scarf, my man, has sacramental duties, which mean something to me. Someone so conversant with the cloth should understand that.

LORG: My, what a gift for confusion.

[POLSO *produces a knife, holds it at* LORG*'s throat.*]

POLSO: Indeed.

LORG: Ah, you do the pawnshops, do you?

POLSO: Take another look, Lorg. This has uncommon qualities.

LORG: So why would it involve itself with such common blood?

POLSO: There you go. You see how modest it makes me feel.

[SPALLA *appears, walks forward without noticing the knife.*]

SPALLA: Lorg, I think Bricco has found the…

[LORG *escapes* POLSO'*s touch, runs away.*]

What does this…?

[POLSO *gets tangled with her, while trying to push her aside.*]

POLSO: Can't you get out of the way? Look what you've done. [*He stops, notices her eyes, flashes the knife.*] This? You did not see it. [*He goes up to her.*] I'll put it to you. This doesn't exist. [*Pocketing the scarf and knife, he walks around* SPALLA.] We understand each other, don't we? [*He points at his designs on the ground.*] Don't step here. If you want to bathe, take your little bird body where the women know the feel of the oil that suits you.

[SPALLA *rushes away.* POLSO *is alone for a moment.*]

Every day begins with this silence. They all make the same mistake. They take me for my own motive. They don't understand, I have no motive. I once got turned around inside that argument for a language I could propose as my own. That moment passed, as you might have thought. I didn't need such uncertainties; I needed my stories. Consider this, a dream. The harpy has my right ankle clamped in the vise of her left hand. Her right hand flits like a bird toward the seeds of my trouser buttons. I find myself aroused, a new sensation, since I myself have set the boundary I dare not, for the love of myself, transgress. The harpy cackles and smacks at me; her exhilaration flames my anger. I want to let her go. I turn my body to light. I shimmer in an attempt to fly from her. The more I struggle, the easier it seems for her to restrain me. She lays a body as light as summer air over my trembling bones, and breathes the orange marmalade of her breath into my left ear. I would cry, but I know that would not appeal to this angel. I have heard the word for what I should do to her, but I cannot effect the necessary reversal. Helpless, I lie still, submitting to a force that seems now to want nothing from me. I have stepped over the threshold of surrender.

[*The sound of several* agógó, *a seeming choir that brings* POLSO *out of his stillness. He appeals to no one in particular.*]

You left me the space. Now get out of it.

[BACÁN *appears.*]

BACÁN: What a disingenuous greeting. Have you no sense of *Xenia*? Do I have the honor of encountering the infamous and abstemious Polso?

[POLSO *stares.*]

No answer. Then I shall assume that they misinformed me down below. Of course, the temper of their talk told me I had probably made a primary mistake.

POLSO: Do you always talk this way?

BACÁN: Don't let it disturb you, Polso.

POLSO: You have some nerve. You do some chancy due diligence. You scout me out, and then you turn up, with this intimidating shine on your sleeve, trying to pretend that we have something to do with each other.

BACÁN: I didn't come on hope. I came with absolute assurance that you would embrace me and take me in. But I told you that, didn't I?

POLSO: Give me a chance to wake up here.

BACÁN: Every day begins with this silence.

POLSO: Carry on with this mockery, you won't see too many more days beginning.

BACÁN: I get it now. I caught you dreaming of unruly women, and you wake up, and what do you see? Another one, who has already marked you with a prepositional arrogance. Or should I say, a propositional arrogance, culling a mystery of masteries, with a hidden mistress marking malicious and malleable assumptions. Why, Polso, should I believe in you, or attend to anything you say? [*She begins a false exit.*] Well? Nothing? No pleading? No serious disturbance, no fetal flow…oh, forgive me, I didn't mean to get that close to the proposition, fatal. Given that you have no assurance that you have ever come forth, and flowered. Polso. Let us come to a compositional rest. Put on your mask.

POLSO: You made this up with Spalla, didn't you? Quick as that. You wanted to pay me back for the knife. Right?

BACÁN: Who or what answers to this Spalla?

POLSO: Clever, clever. Throw in a little fragility. Read the text again. Exhaust every permutation of perplexities, Oh, ho ho, you have me, and you have this instant to hold me to account for the divinity in me.

BACÁN: Lord...

POLSO: Stop it.

BACÁN: I can't believe you said that.

POLSO: You want to touch me?

BACÁN: Where have I heard that before?

[GINOCCHIO *comes crashing into their conference; lurching, he threatens to step on* POLSO's *designs.* POLSO's *eyes straighten him.*]

POLSO: Recovered your courage, Lorg?

LORG/GINOCCHIO: Who said I lost it?

POLSO: You left town in a hurry.

LORG: [*Appealing to* BACÁN.] Do you concur in that, my lady?

BACÁN: Don't call me your lady.

LORG: A form of courtesy.

BACÁN: I see we will never agree upon courtesy.

LORG: [*Appealing to* POLSO.] Ah, don't worry, Polso. I see the family resemblance. I would not insult your presence, my man.

POLSO: You riddling chicken scratcher, this woman has nothing to do with me.

LORG: Of course. But consider this, these instances never happen on their own.

POLSO: Meaning?

LORG: These suddenly disappearing women who have no function. You haven't asked me why I came back. Don't you want to hear what I discovered?

POLSO: About what?

LORG: I can keep it to myself, just overlook what you've hidden in your designs. She knows enough to let sleeping...

POLSO: Stop it.

BACÁN: *Anima*, Polso. As one of those variables without a function, I always look for a purpose. Maybe this chicken scratcher has a pertinent idea.

POLSO: Wake up. He has nothing to tell us.

LORG: He'll wiggle his way out of facing a memory he knows we share. Not that easy escape he gave himself, the ritual trembling, the surrender.

BACÁN: *Anima*, Polso. I want to hear about this surrender.

LORG: No. We start at another place. You see I passed that oak orchard at the far end of the park.

POLSO: Nonsense. What park? Not here.

LORG: Polso, you've seen the stripling malls tighten their grip around the shaded *veredas* strung through the park. We know the place where families could picnic under a sliver of moon, the place where truckers and other innocents could find rest, settle their urges. Even you, Polso, cut off from any commerce with the waters. Transcendental purposes always beggar definition. Right, Polso? You have to remember the light in that very park when we decided, you and I, to sacrifice the union official who had refused us entry into a warehouseman's union. The fringes of desire we wanted to loosen because someone had refused to acknowledge our names. You remember the gun, the figured moment of a moon in conjunction with a shaded path in a garden, on an evening that spoke prematurely of fall. I could speak of this event as memory, and place us next to a scandal. Take these elements—the gun, moon, shaded path, advancing fall—as a mirror of a broken continuity. Yet there remains something familiar about the closing of another season, something that calls a certain fervor of discontent out of that familiarity. Picture this, the two of us waiting for a union official who has promised to come only upon the promise of silence. You must remember now our discontinuous discontent, our isolation, how we had almost given up our names.

BACÁN: Who tells a story like that?

POLSO: Believe him at your peril. He does this.

LORG: Don't do this, Polso. Don't you see that this soul here understands you?

POLSO: Which soul, Lorg? Yours? Or hers?

BACÁN: Do I have a say in this?

POLSO: No. You do not. I can see that you've let this hazardous conception of a musician…

LORG: Ah, he's given me my union card.

POLSO: …this hazardous conception of a musician tune your ears to harmonies that don't exist. He wants to leap from square to square until we find ourselves placed where we have never belonged.

BACÁN: Here?

POLSO: No. In the third hour.

BACÁN: Don't play with me, Polso.

POLSO: Get out of my face.

BACÁN: No. I will put on my mask. [*She does. Speaks to* POLSO.] Can you put away that knife?

POLSO: If you'll get rid of that gem in your pocket.

BACÁN: You have made a serious mistake.

POLSO: [*Holding up the gem.*] Nimble fingers.

BACÁN: Don't brag.

POLSO: I mean you. I caught your electronic gambit in transition. The attentive eye knows when to intervene.

BACÁN: What will you do when Lorg joins our dance?

POLSO: Oh, I have Lorg's measure. I refer you to that oak orchard and that silly translation of moon.

BACÁN: Defend your eyes, Ginocchio.

LORG: I refer to the absurdity of this instant.

BACÁN: My, a veritable suicide. Well, I will walk among these lines.

POLSO: I don't advise that.

BACÁN: Nervous, Polso? Don't you trust your calculations?

POLSO: I don't advise that.

[BACÁN *takes two steps toward the lines. Sudden darkness. The light returns to* BACÁN, *alone, sitting on a small three-legged stool.*]

BACÁN: Why should you pay attention to the story of a veritable suicide? He missed his chance, there at the shed. Say that, moving to that place, he passed granite, and refused to measure it. Say that he found some comfort in scruffy spruce, white pine, alders, and a rambunctious crew of lightning-scorched maples. He might have turned hemlock, blue spruce, paper birch into a living sheath around a divided heart, a layer of growing and dividing cells. You must understand that a force has carefully installed the heart, to function until the elastic flare of artery grows small with age and stress. I would tell you my mother's story, written in sugar leaves, soil minerals and water, an intricate chemistry that endangers my spirit. My mother died. I live like a rat, nibbling at grain, excessively in motion. An old, defrocked professor gave me the word for my peripatetic intensity, called me a *flâneuse*. A *flâneuse*, I return to that body constructed from the means at its disposal, that unpredictable complexity of activated depth. I mark that first event on this landscape, and feel it changing shape long before I rip it from its nest. Why do I solicit a systematic assault on my spirit, and rely upon a collateral vessel structured by simple desire?

[*She stops, listening. She fusses with her appearance, satisfies herself, resumes her stance.*]

Oh, you lie, everyone, and insist upon your ability to sense the flow of loss and acquisition. No, I will not allow you to speak this way, foisting the flimsiest valences and interpretations upon an arbitrary event, my mother's death. Does Ginocchio think that the third hour will simply subside?

[SPALLA *is suddenly there.*]

SPALLA: What do you think? I remind you that you have scattered us, your associates, just because you can't make up your mind.

BACÁN: What tells you that?

SPALLA: Look at you. Sitting there in contemplation. *Anima*, Bacán. How far do you think you will get, just sitting there? I recall you to that activated depth.

BACÁN: I resent your judgment.

SPALLA: Judgment, she calls it. I have no interest in judging you, Bacán. The text doesn't call for it.

BACÁN: What does the text require, my lady?

SPALLA: Don't call me my lady. I haven't forgiven you. You will recall that you pretended not to know me.

BACÁN: A tactical procedure.

SPALLA: An ambiguity.

BACÁN: Well, no.

SPALLA: An ambivalence.

BACÁN: I wouldn't say.

SPALLA: A subversion.

BACÁN: Close to that, yes.

SPALLA: Agh. I give you up. Why did I even bother to come back to this darkness? You can't even recount the epiphany of your mother's death.

BACÁN: Watch your mouth.

SPALLA: Why didn't you warn me to watch my heart?

BACÁN: Watch your heart! Show me how to do that.

SPALLA: Get your ass off that stool.

BACÁN: A test, a palpable test.

[SPALLA *looks at the ground.*]

SPALLA: You can still see the lines.

BACÁN: I don't see anything.

[SPALLA *is suddenly upon* BACÁN, *forcing her head down.*]

SPALLA: See anything now? Or do you choose blindness?

BACÁN: Let go.

[SPALLA *applies more pressure, forcing Bacán to her knees and to a writhing figure on the ground before releasing her with a gesture of disgust.*]

SPALLA: So, we spin around each other, not even noticing the path. We sound a slight note, without regard to an advancing melody or a constraining harmony. Where did this begin, Bacán? In a square, near a church, in Guanajuato? Or in a white room in a cheap hotel in a coastal city? Or did I come to have you justify a movement that has never begun? Tell me, Bacán, as one who knows our higher quantum state.

BACÁN: What do you want from me? I can't account for a radiant movement that still escapes me.

SPALLA: You'll abandon me, then?

BACÁN: Abandon, abandon. I wasted much time as a thief engaged in a pretence of service. You must have taken me at my word, whenever we met.

SPALLA: [*Looking away from* BACÁN.] I interrupted you. Do you want to go on…with your story?

BACÁN: Oh, she wants to appear a complement to my story.

SPALLA: What nonsense.

BACÁN: No, no. I sense it. You want me to redraw those lines. [*She points at them.*] I have to tell you that my mother never learned to dance, with me, or with the swirling universe.

SPALLA: Stop it. This forgetfulness. This uneasiness with the complement that brought you here, to this space.

BACÁN: Ah, you see that now.

SPALLA: In spite of your evasiveness, I do. I know you, of course, by the quality of your evasions.

BACÁN: Oh, I wouldn't brag of such virtuosity.

SPALLA: There, you see what I mean? You like to draw your strings rather tight to play sharper than the music requires.

BACÁN: So delicately stated, Spalla. You show such skill in this conjuration of a text that remains obscure to those who *do* play.

SPALLA: Strange. I thought you knew our text.

BACÁN: If I could, surely I would, tether myself to the music that modulates into our situation, as we stand. One day, I will have to astonish you again with that crystal winter morning.

SPALLA: Don't.

BACÁN: An impossibility?

SPALLA: Perhaps.

BACÁN: Better to have no voice.

SPALLA: Did you learn that from Ginocchio?

BACÁN: Please. Don't make me embarrass you.

[SPALLA STOPS, *listens.*]

SPALLA: Don't move, Bacán. Stay right there.

[*She runs off.* BACÁN *takes the opportunity to rearrange herself. Satisfied, she sits again on the stool. We hear the sound of heavy equipment, tools, or instruments, being moved. Silence, then the movement, accompanied by sounds of effort, resumes.* SPALLA *appears, supporting* FUADACH, *who seems spent, disturbed and thoroughly angry.*]

SPALLA: [*Pointing at* BACÁN.] There. [*To* FUADACH.] I apologize for such an abrupt introduction. But, of course, we didn't expect you.

FUADACH: I didn't expect you. I didn't expect to make that turn, and end up on this side of the ledger. [*He goes up to* BACÁN.] What do we have here? Don't get me started. I can tell you've let that little circuit rider get to you. You know who I mean. That Polso.

BACÁN: I don't know any Polso.

FUADACH: You deny it?

BACÁN: Deny what?

FUADACH: [*Appealing to* SPALLA.] You think she's bought his story? The garden, the egg, all that business that makes me sick when I think of it.

SPALLA: Come to yourself, Fuadach. I didn't bring you here for this.

FUADACH: Whoa. Haven't we got things turned around? Hey, I understand. That circuit rider got here speaking in tongues, and you believed him.

SPALLA: Stop it. Pay attention to what you see.

FUADACH: Ah, my lovely, we don't always hear what we see. All right. I admit it. I came too late to save you.

[SPALLA *pulls at* BACÁN.]

SPALLA: Let's go. I have to get you out of here.

BACÁN: I can take care of myself.

SPALLA: Really!? Well, you could have fooled me.

FUADACH: You see. The little angel has more sense than you think. She doesn't want to leave here. Leave me, you see. She will wait for the third hour.

SPALLA: Stop it.

FUADACH: [*Continuing.*] I said, wait for the third hour. I had no reason to credit this little sister with such an understanding. No, Spalla, you did me a favor. Look at her. I had to recover myself. Everything falls into place. Those Parthians, Medes, Elamites, those residents of Mesopotamia, Judea, Cappadocia, Pontus, Asia, Phrygia, Pamphylia, Egypt, parts of Libya belonging to Cyrene, all, mind you, all speak in tongues. I recognize a touch of genius in this lady we have before us. She wouldn't let Polso escape. [*He confronts* BACÁN.] Well? Did he tell his story? Tell us what he said. Or didn't you give him time?

BACÁN: You assume that Polso inhabited the mask I met.

FUADACH: Delicious. [*To* SPALLA.] I warned you of her delicacy.

BACÁN: Thank you.

FUADACH: Thank yourself. But I haven't forgiven you. I need that circuit rider's story.

[POLSO *is suddenly there, masked and significantly changed.*]

POLSO: And you will have it.

FUADACH: Look at you. No more cringing. Right, Polso?

POLSO: Every day begins with a silence.

FUADACH: Don't strut, joker. It doesn't suit you. You know what she wants from you. Strike that. What we want from you.

POLSO: Yes. Fifteen measures to provision sight. Such sightful confusion. Everything comes borrowed. But I have my measure and an accounting of its place within this world. Fifteen of them, if I move the body backward in time. Oh, the labyrinth, the density of walking through space. Someone wakes us to the distance that will fit; someone invokes the name for distance. There you have it, an accounting of measure, or place. Why should measure so concern the body, so ensnare the mind? I speak now, accounting for distance, or movement, the borrowed words no one saw fit to teach me. We cannot get out of this labyrinth.

SPALLA: Conspiracy! [*To* FUADACH.] I owe you a hiding. You don't have to tell me why you've let this disaster burden us with his fantasies. [*She starts to walk away.*] I have work to do, thank you.

BACÁN: So have we all, Spalla. Don't preen yourself. And don't pretend you've seen a light that missed our circle here.

POLSO: Please. I haven't mentioned the light, or called my inner for that fable of discovery. You see me awkward about light. I cannot begin again before measure, the movement. Now I would say Sun, Sunday, Moon, Monday, nowhere apparent in spring or summer. How can I persuade myself that I have arrived?

BACÁN: You don't have to apologize to these two.

SPALLA: Well! I like this new configuration. Let's all mask up.

POLSO: Say, I've had a fine time entertaining you. I see you noticed the change in my tone.

FUADACH: Spalla can go along with you, if she wants, but I despise your disguise. [*To* SPALLA.] You fooled me, talking compassion. You put me here. Do you understand? You put me here.

SPALLA: Where? I don't understand your anger.

FUADACH: Do I have to have a reason for my anger? I do not like this astronomical joke this idiot performs. [*He goes up to* POLSO.] Why can't you tell the simple story of your miserable existence?

POLSO: You say. I look for that crystal light in the analysis of such small events. Does that disturb you?

BACÁN: I suppose we'll have to wait for Fuadach to create his own motive for leaving that third hour without a resolution.

FUADACH: What do you know about it?

BACÁN: Yes? About what?

FUADACH: The fog in London.

BACÁN: I thought so. Citizens, I want to undress this gentleman.

FUADACH: Take your hands off me.

BACÁN: *Calma*, Tibio, we don't intend family matters. The necessary report occurs in the text. And here you stand like an ass between two texts, one of which seems to blind you, my man. [*To the others.*] Can I get a witness?

[SPALLA *and* POLSO *grunt in assent.* BACÁN *spins* FUADACH *away from* POLSO.]

Look me in the eye, buster. Wouldn't you say you have a lot to answer for? You've forgotten Kafka and the wine stain, the orchard, the midnight assignation, the small events. They do disturb you, don't they? So put up or put down your intimidation. You will not scare me into silence.

FUADACH: How did I get into this? Can't you just leave me alone? Look, I have a shed. I have things under my care. I don't need this.

SPALLA: *Pobrecito.*

BACÁN: You didn't bargain for this, did you, Spalla? Now, look what you've got. An angry man, turning his anger into a lament and doesn't even know the difference.

POLSO: *Basta.* Give the man a break.

BACÁN: Where the fuck did that come from, Polso?

SPALLA: Yes, Polso. When did this evangelical Polso arrive? Can you say?

POLSO: I just don't want this small event to escape.

BACÁN: Escape, escape. *C'est à toi*, Polso.

POLSO: No. I leave it to Fuadach to reveal what lies in his heart, if not anger.

SPALLA: Ah, I thought you meant to assess his motive.

BACÁN: The coursing of an atom of distrust through disregard.

SPALLA: The momentary surfacing of a notion Fuadach has never experienced.

[POLSO *tries to draw* FUADACH *into a brotherly embrace.*]

POLSO: Come along, Fuadach. They will never understand us.

[FUADACH *pushes* POLSO *away.*]

FUADACH: Don't confuse me with your borrowing, your measure.

POLSO: What did you want? I sang what I knew.

FUADACH: When? Now? Or then?

POLSO: At the third hour, my man.

[FUADACH *attacks, and wrestles* POLSO *to the ground.*]

BACÁN: Let him up, Tibio. I want to finish my story. He rang a bell with his fog in London. I recall you to the dissonance in which we started this composition…

SPALLA: Don't go on. We don't need such an improvisation.

FUADACH: Redemption! Let her continue.

BACÁN: Tibio sees that evening.

FUADACH: I remember a card game.

BACÁN: Exactly. The motive, if you will, for all of our forgetfulness.

SPALLA: Ginocchio!

POLSO: Leave him out of this.

BACÁN: I continue. Elzbieta Polkinghorne steps off that trolley that runs from Los Angeles, through Compton, and ends up on Sixth and Main in San Pedro by the Sea. Spalla, don't deny the beauty in that fog. But you could never accept Elzbieta, could you? You preferred Carmen with her roseate hair, an improvisor of the first water. Leave that aside.

FUADACH: Nay, nay. I won't let you forget that the two of them had a pact with poets.

BACÁN: But only to bury them, wind them in their own entrails.

SPALLA: So you approve?

BACÁN: I sing what I know.

POLSO: Exactly.

FUADACH: Elzbieta Polkinghorne. Talk about music. What a night. Not half the scandal in a scribbler's winey peccadillos, or that ugly sensation that invaded us when we had to endure going to the theatre to suffer for Arthur Adamov's rehearsal of Wright's adaptation of Beckett's Trinity thesis. No, no, no, no, save me from that. Continue, little angel.

SPALLA: She will, unfortunately.

FUADACH: Why don't you go and retrieve this Ginocchio person.

SPALLA: I see. Selective memory. The beginning and existence of that garden egg.

FUADACH: You cannot embarrass me.

SPALLA: I wouldn't try. How do we stand now, in this ecstasy of home-coming, though no one here belongs to the place?

POLSO: Envy. *You* see that no marriage will occur.

FUADACH: Stand out of the way, Polso. This little genius has found my motive, or the thing that speaks to me.

POLSO: What answers to this category, "the thing"?

[FUADACH *tries to draw* POLSO *into a brotherly embrace.*]

FUADACH: Forgive me, Polso. I know the music often commands a trun-cated harmony, and demands more than we might want to give. Think of it. How absences sustain us. Strange minors surface and die. Let's let our little genius return us to that evening.

POLSO: So you already know the story.

FUADACH: Did I say that?

POLSO: Your body did.

FUADACH: [*Turning to the women.*] Get to that. Giuig has a hidden talent.

POLSO: Get to that. He wants to diminish me by decomposing my name.

FUADACH: Spalla, see what you've done. I don't know this man.

SPALLA: What makes you think I do?

FUADACH: Ah, so the numbers don't add. I told you before that I don't like this idiot's astronomical jokes.

SPALLA: You've said.

FUADACH: Don't contradict me.

SPALLA: Tibio, I know better than that. Besides, you know our composition thrives on counterpoint.

FUADACH: Well, now. I don't think you discovered me by chance. I'd forgotten the delicacy of your ears. Here, here. Let me reconstruct the music of that evening. You must remember, surely, that first phrase of the String Quartet in G minor, just as Elzbieta stepped down from the trolley. Continue, my angel. Set the table.

BACÁN: Carmen had set the table, prepared to deal the cards. Oh, I almost forgot about that Norwegian speaker of the house who sat to my right.

FUADACH: You never mentioned him before. And you said nothing at all about your presence.

POLSO: Tibio, maybe you don't know the story.

FUADACH: I know the story.

BACÁN: Then I have no reason to continue.

FUADACH: Reason continues. Don't you understand?

BACÁN: Don't contradict me.

[FUADACH *starts to hobble away.*]

Wait. You got me started on this.

FUADACH: Not this. Not this joke of a Dog Star chasing doves across an empty sky.

POLSO: Bricco!

FUADACH: You remember Bricco, do you?

POLSO: I do. I would call him now to get us back on track. I deplore these deviations. The woman pushed me aside with these simplicities because she knows they appeal to you.

FUADACH: The man flows from absurdity to absurdity. Don't interrupt.

POLSO: I just want to call the choir to order. This text Bacán wants to sing makes no sense.

BACÁN: Tibio, shall I go on?

SPALLA: My, my, such cantankerous harmony. Do you have an answer to this, Bacán?

[FUADACH *waves his arms before* BACÁN *as though he would conduct her narrative. He begins to sing.*]

FUADACH: You innocents ought to understand that a melody makes no sense unless we remember each step in its progression, and, once established, it can be reconstructed from such small events of which Polso seems so fond. Can I get you all to consider that erotic page that began on that night?

SPALLA: That erotic page cannot travel on its own recognizance.

BACÁN: Elzbieta told me...

SPALLA: Elzbieta?

BACÁN: Yes. Elzbieta.

SPALLA: Not...Carmen?

BACÁN: Carmen had no standing at the table. She had given it up with some companionable afternoon with Kafka in that seedy hotel by the docks.

SPALLA: Oh ho, Tibio, I see your intention. We caught you nibbling at another text. Now you have this little catholic to help you to overlook your failure. Please, Bacán, you have us fascinated.

BACÁN: I have a page of an old text I have endeavored to memorize, but, even failing so, it haunts me.

SPALLA: I don't recognize that voice.

BACÁN: *Tant pis.*

SPALLA: Tibio, call her to attention.

FUADACH: Spalla feels frightened by an attendant spirit. *Coraggio*, Spalla.

POLSO: Let her continue, Spalla.

[SPALLA *slowly folds her arms, spits on the ground.* BACÁN *slowly laughs.*]

BACÁN: Let me tell you about St. Peter and his calculation. Peter heard the prophet say that he, Peter, would betray his master, and so, our scholar says, he did his moral sums. He knew the truth of the prophecy, and determined not to do it. Perhaps we have nothing to do with Peter's language, a report, after all, he never made. But the thought could occur to one attuned to the idea of intention, and the possibility involved in staying true to intent. The subtlety of the occasion astonished. Peter questioned the fulfillment of the prophecy. Our scholar tells us, "thus St. Peter could do what he intended not to do, without changing his mind, and yet do it intentionally." Now you see what Elzbieta might have seen in Carmen, standing with Kafka at a yellowing basin in a cheap hotel, rinsing the wine stain from a white shirt.

POLSO: You learned this from Elzbieta?

SPALLA: Polso!

BACÁN: I did.

SPALLA: Your point.

BACÁN: I hold this page in reserve against any narrative fiddling of those other voices; Cino, Guido, you can forget the name.

SPALLA: You haven't finished with that night, or with us. Tibio has no reason to celebrate the small event embodied in this melody.

BACÁN: So perhaps we've arrived at an indefensible notion. The story might set us a challenge that modulates through a dissonant discourse upon propositions, or to speak more clearly, upon the impossibility of propositions.

SPALLA: Clever little catholic. And you, Fuadach, how clever of you to arrange to sit us in a measure that only you can feel. I do protest most willingly.

FUADACH: Oh, stand still for a moment. You said yourself that we hadn't finished. [*He gives* BACÁN *a downbeat.*]

BACÁN: You could, I suppose, accuse me of a transcendental realism, a form, as my text would tell me, of illusion.

SPALLA: Elzbieta.

BACÁN: No. Elzbieta anchored the night. Don't try to take that away from her, away from me.

POLSO: I see it now. I see it.

SPALLA: God in heaven. Talk about an Oxonian fog. What do you see, Polso? Do you see any sense in the report of a card game that never took place?

POLSO: Well, if you have no memory of it, it never took place.

BACÁN: Nobody gets off that easily. What does Spalla want, a photograph of the table, the cards all laid out, the drinks sparkling, the food? She ought to remember the Norwegian speaker of the house. He made a play for her after all. Or didn't he? Does she want to deny it?

SPALLA: I don't like the way this has turned to make me the one who brought the house down.

[BACÁN *goes up to* SPALLA, *attempts an intimacy.*]

BACÁN: I won't tell. [*She pulls away.*] I continue. We had all those fishing boats tied to the dock near where we sat. Tibio fell off one, came up to us, and dropped a small bag of gold dust in the center of the table.

SPALLA: [*Attacking* BACÁN.] I won't take any more of this abuse.

[FUADACH *claps his hands.*]

FUADACH: What do you find so offensive about this ethereal vision?

SPALLA: Nothing happened.

FUADACH: You say. Ask the others. We have to defend ourselves against your petty fear of compromising yourself. You don't dream.

[*Pause.*]

SPALLA: It happened just about the time I thought I had a solution to the problem of identity. The identity of indiscernibles. Well, this doesn't concern you.

FUADACH: Get this woman out of my face. I followed her here, with an understanding. [*To* SPALLA.] Do you deny that we had an understanding? Surely, that probing in indiscernibles, as you now claim, gave you a little bit of courage to speak to me. And then I find you, as I could believe, as I did believe, married to this story you now want not to believe.

SPALLA: Tibio, I've already released Bacán.

FUADACH: No, you haven't. Bacán lodges in rock-clefts, in the branches of hollow yews. You must think very carefully of the devastation of dreams.

SPALLA: I did not...

[FUADACH *stops her.*]

FUADACH: Don't make it worse. I don't like the way you've accused me of a certain discontinuity that displaces these pilgrims who breathe with us here. [*He once again starts to stumble away.*] I should have kept going. I should have resisted that flame I saw in you. I should have resisted the desire to construct my shed on such sand. [*He looks around at the others.*] Will you forgive me? I won't bother you any further.

[GINOCCHIO *is suddenly there.*]

GINOCCHIO: Fuadach, you don't need forgiveness. You need to have your ass kicked. You have something you want to say to me? [GINOCCHIO *corrects* FUADACH*'s posture, straightens and brushes his clothes.*] There. [*He notices the stillness of the others.*] I see I got back just in time. Now, about this story our little singer seems to have in hand. No, no, no. Put on your masks, and give me time. I have the substance of that evening. Bacán dresses Elzbieta near the water in San Pedro by the Sea. A category mistake. We had arrived in Mexicali, a confusion on the border. Carmen stood there with her emptiness. She felt the imposition of Elzbieta, the danger of Fuadach under his other hat.

[POLSO *and* SPALLA *now become a chorus of two members. They begin the passage from left to right, from right to left, around* GINOCCHIO. GINOCCHIO *turns to address his narrative toward the audience.*]

You saw me enter from the right door. Didn't you? And you saw these [*Pointing at the dual chorus.*] eyes, eyes you trusted enter with me.

SPALLA
POLSO } No one can forget.

GINOCCHIO: Of course not. We had come up from Cananea, or down from Tucson. Someone had engaged us to deal with his brother-in-law. Oh ho, the blood stirs at the mention of brothers, or even at the mention of sisters, say. Carmen. Elzbieta. *Peregrinas.*

SPALLA } He thinks he can stick us with a pilgrimage we don't understand,
POLSO } or with a death we cannot justify.

GINOCCHIO: [*As though shouting down the chorus.*] I haven't given you license to contest the impulse of my story.

SPALLA } Where does the impulse lie? Where does the lie build its own
POLSO } garden with festering roses?

GINOCCHIO: Pull yourself together. Roses do not fester. Don't interrupt. What did Fuadach want, other than his own journey?

SPALLA
POLSO } You play with us. What bound us to the place?

GINOCCHIO: Your patience.

SPALLA
POLSO } We thought so. You had lost the measure of the composition.

GINOCCHIO: And you have surrendered your eyes to light that never appears.

SPALLA
POLSO } It appears in song.

GINOCCHIO: Nonsense.

SPALLA
POLSO
} We have given you enough time. Did the sisters survive?

GINOCCHIO: No. One night we discovered a mother who came to claim Elzbieta. Well, of course, Tibio, who now knew himself as Tibio, stood astonished by Carmen's deception.

SPALLA
POLSO
} What did Carmen have to do with it?

GINOCCHIO: Please. You cannot stop the world from spinning.

SPALLA
POLSO
} You abandoned her.

GINOCCHIO: I gave her a new face in Elzbieta.

SPALLA
POLSO
} Who spoke to the mother?

GINOCCHIO: Carmen had gone. I had no part in that geometry.

[FUADACH *howls frighteningly and beyond measure. The others come to themselves, as though they had just awakened from a nightmare.*]

Fuadach, don't despair. I've brought you something for our island.

[BRICCO *now appears, walking majestically. He has a small clock and a miniscule metronome strung from his neck and lying on his breast. He holds a large white cloth, as an offering.*]

BRICCO: Fuadach, so have I. [*He tries to settle the cloth upon* FUADACH.] You certainly shouldn't forget this.

FUADACH: What do you have there?

BRICCO: Something that Ginocchio thinks you might need, and that he probably thinks has walked away. But you and I know better. Don't we, Fuadach? What, have I interrupted some narrative?

SPALLA: I leave it to Tibio to tell you about Mexicali.

POLSO: We had just about come to some conclusion there.

BRICCO: Conclusion? Where? Tibio, what have you got these people believing?

BACÁN: I'd say the history of a love.

FUADACH: Don't play with me.

BRICCO: Fuadach, let them play. Let your disciples instruct me again in your good graces. Well? Who wants to go on? I see. Ah, the history of a love. You and I share a discretion. I'd never betray you.

SPALLA: Oh? That smells itself of a betrayal. You know nothing, Bricco, about Mexicali or of docking boats, or of a man lurching from moment to moment searching for an hour he thought he had left behind.

FUADACH: Elzbieta!

BACÁN: They didn't let me finish...

SPALLA: With Carmen.

BRICCO: Fuadach, where have you led these people? I have to tell you, you have all gone out of your minds with this history of a love that does no service to my *compadre*. Right, Fuadach? Shall I tell the real story of our Fuadach?

FUADACH: Shut your mouth.

BRICCO: The heart speaks.

POLSO: You know what they say, Bricco. Things and these small events can withstand our gaze.

BRICCO: Don't make me embarrass you. Why, after all, should our earth fall?

BACÁN: You insist.

BRICCO: I do. On a rainy night in Buenos Aires, where the three of us gathered to pursue the ambience of the Café Tortoni. I remind you of Josefina, Fuadach. This Elzbieta, or this Carmen—save them—offer nothing to our symmetry. That evening requires a translation. Buenos Aires remains with us. Five floors up on a corner at Las Heras; a window above Charcas y Maipú; *un zaguán* in Calle Arcos; a garden in the Plaza Italia;

a Mali awakening structured at La Recoleta. What do you think about all that? Did we sit comfortably with our librarian, and wrestle with the presence of Josefina? Ah, perhaps I should say, while you, Fuadach, struggled with Josefina's presence, or absence, if you will. *Mneme*, lovely word. You others should not think of this as an exchange, Josefina *por* Elzbieta.

[*All except* FUADACH *begin to grumble and stir.*]

Wait a minute, while I put myself on this clock. [*He fiddles with his clock, which seems not to work. Flustered, he sits, angrily removes the devices. He places the metronome on the ground at his side, starts its movement, approves.*] There. We need some definition of this moment that threatens to get away from us. I haven't asked you for anything…yet. But I know you feel the dance beginning in your bodies. I ask you to consider that sweet new song that shook Fuadach. I felt myself *de trop*. What could I do but continue speaking about an unsatisfied desire that had traveled with us, and sat at our table gloriously bereft of its own beginnings.

FUADACH: Look at him, mesmerizing the lot of you with something that should only concern me. He conjures this Josefina.

BRICCO: Go on. I can wait. [*He continues his narrative.*] I tell you I felt scorched by words I didn't understand. Our librarian went on about land and family, the juice and jubilation of a city that surrounded us even then. Fuadach listened. Fuadach laughed at every turn of the librarian's history. Fuadach searched Josefina's eye for her approval of such an entrancing narrative. Fuadach searched Josefina's eye for something he thought it should show. She cunningly removed it, at that moment. Why, after all, should she give herself up to one who thought that it never rained in Buenos Aires? Why should she reveal herself to one who thought that love never appears in Virgil, as our librarian claimed?

POLSO: Your metronome seems to have stopped.

BRICCO: Keep out of this.

SPALLA: Fix the measure.

BRICCO: Fuadach, don't you have anything to say?

FUADACH: Does my silence disturb you, Bricco? And when did this librarian come on the scene, with his intimation of love's failings?

BRICCO: Nay, brother. You won't escape. He came to our table when Josefina knew she would need some sustenance, some defense, against your *epithymia*.

FUADACH: Oh, John, we don't have to go back that far.

BRICCO: I beg to differ. That distance embraces us even now. You can shield it, and call it a new measure. These others will staunch you in your evasion. I won't. You loved Josefina.

GINOCCHIO: Tibio, defend your loneliness.

[FUADACH *kicks at* BRICCO's *clock and metronome, trying to overturn them.*]

FUADACH: This astronaut with his clicking spiders that have nothing to do with what happens here. [*He kneels into* BRICCO's *face.*] ¿*Verdad*, Pancho?

BRICCO: Don't abuse your spirit, Fuadach.

FUADACH: Bet on it. I won't. [*He unwraps the white cloth from his arm, shakes it before* BRICCO.] What do we do with this?

BRICCO: You know why it has to appear where it does.

FUADACH: No. You tell me. Better still, why don't you show us how we ought to display this garment. Here. Take it, my counselor. Doesn't it belong to you?

POLSO: It belongs to everyone.

FUADACH: Really!? I think I need a witness. My god, why should I constrain myself? Look at all these witnesses I have here. We ought to have that celebration.

[*He dances with the garment, flings it in the faces of the others.*]

SPALLA: I won't stand for this.

FUADACH: What disturbs you, my lady?

SPALLA: Your naked ass. Now, get out of my way. [*She puts on her mask, and starts to leave the assembly.*].

FUADACH: I admire your courage. To step into that danger. Look at the others. You can see the fear knocking at their bones. They won't question this Bricco. They won't ask why this *gaucho* had to impose himself, to tantalize me, to propose my love for one Josefina who cannot witness that third hour.

BACÁN: Tibio, you must remember, love always has two faces.

GINOCCHIO: What does that mean?

BACÁN: Why do you pursue me, Lorg?

GINOCCHIO: I resent your circuitous route into Fuadach's disordered embrace.

SPALLA: Forgive him, Bacán. He has lost the sense of our composition. Lorg would like to forget this geographic displacement we seem to have discovered. My lord, not once, but twice. Oh, god, my numbers turn awry. Remind me. How often has this trickery happened, Tibio and his maidens, those who need such a mantle as he now pretends to display.

FUADACH: I don't pretend.

[BRICCO, *fiddling with his clock and metronome, tries to reset them.*]

Give it up, Bricco.

BRICCO: Everyone seems to have turned against me, as though what I have seen doesn't count. What did I do? I had nothing to do with a librarian talking shit about a dagger.

SPALLA: I don't know whether to charge you or Lorg. You, and your misguided metronomic measure. What did you intend to prove about those hours?

BRICCO: Oh ho, oh ho. She removes us from the most pertinent hour, and the danger that sits with Fuadach's various, if not to say variable, affections even now.

POLSO: Why don't we just go back to that moment at the church in Oaxaca?

FUADACH: Oaxaca!? You see what I have to fight, this thorough confusion. When, Polso, did you get to this baroque church in Oaxaca? *Platícame del agua.*

POLSO: When you started your fantastic story, Fuadach.

FUADACH: In the garden?

POLSO: No. You had already abandoned the garden.

FUADACH: Impossible. The story wouldn't make sense outside the garden. Fuadach wouldn't make sense outside the garden. And Polso wouldn't...

POLSO: You needn't go on.

FUADACH: Citizens, I give you your own kinetic Polso. He changes places with Bricco. He quarrels with the way I walk, with the way I tell my own story. Think about that. He thinks I don't have the strength to keep my place out here.

BACÁN: No one does. No one can call this home.

GINOCCHIO: Why in the world would I want to call this home?

BACÁN: Stop your posturing, Lorg.

BRICCO: Well, that surprises me. We caught you singing your mathematics, a new configuration you seemed so anxious to impose upon us.

GINOCCHIO: Tibio.

SPALLA: Why appeal to Tibio? He got lost from the start, and led us astray, each little mask going its own way. Where did he come from? Perhaps he hadn't removed himself from some place, but the place had removed itself from him.

FUADACH: Don't bother to argue with her, Ginocchio. She'll tie you up in these tidy fables.

SPALLA: At least I've come out of my tree.

FUADACH: Whoa. Where did that come from?

SPALLA: From the third hour.

FUADACH: You remember that, do you?

SPALLA: I remember the language. I remember my own desire. I thought I would meet someone on my way. I thought I could do away with that rainy night in Buenos Aires, and the dagger the librarian strung above our table.

[FUADACH *flouts the white cloth, and exaggerates his dance.*]

FUADACH: Oh, she'll take credit for the shape of anything, won't she? Polso,

I think you've taught her how to cover her refusals so that they seem adornments, embellishments that only she understands. [*To* SPALLA.] Go on with your accusations, your defense of individuals you yourself have abandoned. [*Calling.*] Elzbieta!

[SPALLA *remains impassive.*]

Carmen! Mexicali. San Pedro by the Sea. Have I forgotten anyone, any village that feels a need for a protector? Speak up. Or let's speak no more.

POLSO: I will. To give this situation some shape, some purpose, some efficient cause.

FUADACH: A smart individual, trying to withdraw from us. Shall we approve of that?

POLSO: Surely, I've heard that bell before. You use it to disguise your failures.

FUADACH: That does it.

[*He throws the white cloth to the ground. The others rush to pick it up.*]

Leave it. Listen, what do you want from me? I put up with your wandering, with your strutting blindness. Let somebody else lead this parade.

BRICCO: There you go. You did the same in Buenos Aires. Don't think we didn't notice. Don't make me embarrass you. I ask you to recall, Tibio, that you saw Josefina displaying her unfaithfulness, the way she fiddled with her jewels and solicited the *carabinieri* on the other side of the room.

SPALLA: Exactly.

POLSO: We could have predicted that.

GINOCCHIO: Give the man a chance. After all…

FUADACH: I don't need your help, Lorg.

[GINOCCHIO *nods, and withdraws.*]

BACÁN: Oh. I don't like the way the sunset has run from my story.

POLSO: We could have predicted that.

SPALLA: Will you stop it with your clocks and mirrors.

POLSO: What would you prefer, rock clefts and horse hair?

BACÁN: I could tell you about that.

GINOCCHIO: Oh, of course, she studies those *espejos rotos* through her Kantian veil.

SPALLA: Do we find that in Mexicali? What happened to the *carabinieri*?

BACÁN: They buckled up, and walked away.

POLSO: That involved the docks at San Pedro by the Sea.

FUADACH: Have you forgotten about me?

SPALLA: Why do you ask?

GINOCCHIO: We've gone along with you this far.

BACÁN: Oh, beneficent one, no one wants to abandon *you*.

POLSO: I didn't want to bring this up, but Tibio has no ear for music.

[*The others grumble.*]

    Ese pájaro que canta arriba...

GINOCCHIO: Why you thief, an unsophisticated choir master. I ask you ladies...

SPALLA: You can ask us nothing. The bird has married you to your nostalgia.

FUADACH: Exactly.

BACÁN: Quiet. I think Tibio wants to speak of his antiphonal design.

FUADACH: You think I've made a mistake.

SPALLA: What do we know about your mistakes, the shell of these harmonies you use to cover that third hour.

FUADACH: Get up!

[*They stand to attention.*]

    All right. You want my resignation? Who will you appoint as the curator of this love I've discovered?

BRICCO: Why, he takes credit for music he can't hear.

FUADACH: Clever little idiot, changing the *siri* from sight to sound. You think you can confuse me, lead me away from *memoria*'s scriptural colors. But I won't let go. Sure, you hurt me. I assume you mean to hurt me. This business belongs to midnight, the night watch. I think my difficulty began on that evening, in a moment where I stood like an ass between two texts, unable to imagine how I would speak or what to speak about.

BRICCO: You refer, of course, to Buenos Aires.

FUADACH: No. I refer to my friend Abelardo Sánchez of Guatemala, with his *cuentos* of brother birds whose emerald green always sets him to dreaming.

SPALLA: Stop it.

FUADACH: Abelardo likes to sit with us here at the water. He touches his sober toe to a silent stream.

SPALLA: *Basta.*

FUADACH: Oh, but we must think carefully before we disdain such an embrace. Forget about it now. We differ in our wounds. I spend too much time on the road, thoroughly adamant concerning the road's pathologies.

SPALLA: Will you continue with this charade?

FUADACH: Not until I tell you about the Pereas who pretend to descend from Córdoba along the Guadalquivir, though some folk whisper that the origins lie further north in thirsty villages near other borders.

POLSO: What do the Pereas have to do with us?

FUADACH: You must know that Emiliano's father had once hired a poet to compose a psalm the family could parade through every lenten festivity. That ought to appeal to you, Polso.

GINOCCHIO: *Tacete*, Tibio. I didn't realize…

FUADACH: Realize what?

SPALLA: I think Tibio wants to charge us with a failure he proposed to us much before.

BACÁN: Yes. We interrupted his singing.

SPALLA: His composition.

FUADACH: There you go. Now, you can see why we had to approach love as though we knew it.

[SPALLA *turns to* BACÁN.]

SPALLA: I name you Elzbieta.

BACÁN: [*To* SPALLA.] I name you Carmen.

[*They retrieve the white garment, dance around each other until they fall into each other's arms, melodiously laughing.* FUADACH *stands sternly until they subside.*]

FUADACH: Finished?

GINOCCHIO: Don't hold it against us, Tibio, this small misunderstanding of your character.

FUADACH: Misunderstanding he calls it. The seal of the universe, and he doesn't recognize its death. [*He points to* SPALLA *and* BACÁN.] You dress these maidens, if you want. They have nothing to do with the souls that accompany me, or with that botched composition of which you accuse me. Perhaps, I should follow my own desire, and disappear.

[POLSO, LORG *and* BACÁN *complain.*]

SPALLA: Let him go. He had nothing to tell us.

BRICCO: Had? Or has?

SPALLA: Save you, Bricco, the cleverness doesn't suit.

POLSO: He brought up that boy.

SPALLA: What boy?

POLSO: The one in Mexicali who drove the lady preacher around in a Lincoln Town Car. Surely, you remember him.

BACÁN: Surely, the memory of that air has turned you silly, Polso.

BRICCO: Have we forgotten why we followed this bookish apprentice, who needs the exemplification of a baroque church, out here to this emptiness?

FUADACH: There you go. You have no purpose. I don't need you. [*He starts again to limp away.*]

BACÁN: Wait a minute! [*She goes to* FUADACH, *stands him erect, searches him, relents.*] There, you can go now.

FUADACH: What did you expect to find, daughter?

BACÁN: Probably a knife. A stained white shirt. A term for nothingness.

FUADACH: Get to that. [*He brightens.*] Did you like the way I parceled out these little instances, variations on a theme, so to speak? Why, I gave you more substance than you would acquire if you all struggled on your own. Think about it.

SPALLA: You didn't fool me.

FUADACH: Oh?

SPALLA: No. Your narratives have no pace. They have no temper, no resonance.

BACÁN: You make sense only when we embellish your body.

POLSO: Yes. And you always seem too willing to run away from your own place in the story.

FUADACH: Hey, I've had enough of this confession. I gave you voices; you misused them.

POLSO: Misused, or refused them, Fuadach?

FUADACH: Choose your own disappointment, Polso.

GINOCCHIO: Have we forgotten that we agreed to sing only the thread of a lovely composition?

SPALLA: And how, Lorg, could we do that?

GINOCCHIO: By paying attention. [*The others laugh.*]

FUADACH: There, you see. Even Ginocchio has his own theory of failure.

BRICCO: We can't get around you, Tibio.

FUADACH: I thought you had disappeared,

BRICCO: No. I wait for that Virgil moment when you acknowledge that love has defeated you. Or when you admit that Elzbieta knew more than she ever told you.

FUADACH: You conjuror. You spy. You followed us to our secret place. Go on with your betrayal.

BRICCO: I have no voice in this. [*His voice takes on a coaxing quality.*] Elzbieta...

FUADACH: Yes. Not everything lay in that moment by the docks. A lantern of easiness, notwithstanding. Forget all jealousy. Forget that I disguised all prior assignations. Elzbieta had no family other than the one I gave her.

SPALLA: [*Harshly.*] You gave her.

FUADACH: Please. I gave her an inheritance. I gave her an office, something to do while she prepared us for death. Does that surprise you? Does that disturb you, Spalla? [*He points at* SPALLA.] She can't hide her discontent with what you can all see, that Elzbieta loved me.

POLSO: Do you intend to offer that as a sentence?

FUADACH: What do you mean?

POLSO: I mean, how do we examine this love?

FUADACH: Oh, I see what you want, Polso. A performance.

[POLSO *shows his annoyance.*]

Tell me what would make you happy, Polso. I can't give you any of those moments when Elzbieta lay with me in contemplation.

BACÁN: I don't think you should go any further.

FUADACH: No. I want you to understand what depth of feeling we never reached. Elzbieta and I. She told me she had changed her name. She told me she had come from a place where she had to deny her sister's presence, had to deny the spirit that surrounded her day by day.

BRICCO: Tell us about Elzbieta. This office that you supposedly gave her.

FUADACH: You don't believe me.

BRICCO: You haven't given us any reason to think that you understood the measure of her love.

SPALLA: Ah, Bricco, Tibio approaches love as though we had known it, or should have known it.

BACÁN: In all of this confession, Tibio, you've told us nothing. These burials you call up mean nothing.

FUADACH: Strange that you should speak of a grave. Elzbieta and I had taken a wrong turn while wandering. We had no map. We had no plans. We had made an orderly exit from a village we had only recently discovered. We walked along, singing a Lydian scale.

SPALLA: Impossible.

FUADACH: Fortunately, we never met anyone like you, Spalla, along our way.

SPALLA: You know me, Tibio, a woman of grand design.

FUADACH: Pity. You lost your chance to speak to Elzbieta.

SPALLA: The woman you loved.

FUADACH: Let me finish. You haven't asked me why we had abandoned the village for this crossroads.

POLSO: Tell us.

FUADACH: We had awakened to a magnificent morning, one that had embraced this marvelous discovery that we felt alive with each other. I tell you, we felt the orderly advance of eternity within us. We leapt out of bed. We said, let the day take its own design. An outrageous sun can do that to you; it can make you forget that you have debts to an unspoken moment, to an unacknowledged past. We had to forget all graves. We had to remember that the god has no home.

POLSO: Talk about betrayal.

FUADACH: Let me finish.

GINOCCHIO: Impossible.

FUADACH: *You*, Lorg, *you* deny me the complexity of that moment?

GINOCCHIO: I deny you a blindness that will make no sense here.

[FUADACH *looks around at them.*]

FUADACH: Why didn't you tell me that you saw through my mask?

SPALLA: We thought that Elzbieta would wake you up with the memory you proposed.

FUADACH: [*Loudly.*] San Pedro by the Sea.

GINOCCHIO: That disappeared into the water.

POLSO: You know that she cheated you. This Elzbieta. She had you convinced of love's eternity, and death no more than a passing fancy. You see that now?

FUADACH: Oh, my philosopher, Polso. Give me another phrase. Something that would appeal to your logical temper. Go on, master Polso. Something that would show me that you didn't die that evening when you saw her arrive and walk toward me.

POLSO: I appeal to those gathered here.

FUADACH: I refuse to accept your misunderstanding, Polso. The woman loved me. Death will have to bow before that.

BACÁN: Death never bows, Tibio.

FUADACH: Stand!

[The others shuffle. For a moment they seem confused.]

SPALLA: Don't let him get away with this barreling about among unopened pots.

BRICCO: "We have a winding sheete in our mothers wombe, which grows with us from our conception, and we come into the world, wound up in that *winding sheet*, for we come to *seeke a grave*."

SPALLA: You've corrupted this man, Tibio. He'd buy you a way out of that third hour, keep you cuddling the misapprehension of your women.

FUADACH: She reads me.

SPALLA: I read myself.

POLSO: I have a question for Spalla. [He hesitates.] Did you ever get around to disarming Carmen?

[SPALLA goes after POLSO who charmingly and provocatively backs away.]

I only ask. Whatever happened to the knife, or shall we call it a dagger?

BACÁN: Your point, Polso.

POLSO: Spalla likes to traffic in these pots. Do they contain anything?

FUADACH: Stand!

BRICCO: Oh, Tibio. We've done that. What did you think of my instrument? Didn't you find my dithyramb fascinating? I floated it once for Carmen. She came up with this intriguing name she wanted to attach to the sound of my *aulós*.

GINOCCHIO: I despise this asymmetry in you, Bricco.

BRICCO: What do you mean?

GINOCCHIO: We thought we had gone beyond the ingenious mathematics that would tie Tibio to feelings he had suppressed, or surpassed.

BRICCO: Why, of course, if you mean the mode of Mexicali. We, of course, would have to abandon Carmen.

FUADACH: [*Slowly.*] Wait a minute. I smell a dead bird. Face up to it, Bricco, my woman scared you to death.

BACÁN: Stop it right there. Your woman.

FUADACH: Don't tell me you didn't notice, Bacán?

[BACÁN *and* SPALLA *begin again the mockery of becoming Carmen and Elzbieta.* FUADACH *rips the white garment from them.*]

There. [*He looks around, finding nowhere to put the cloth.*]

BRICCO: I'll take it.

FUADACH: No, not you. You've taught me not to trust your eyes.

BRICCO: Well, then, trust my voice. [*He sings a Lydian scale.*]

FUADACH: Well, bravo for you.

[BRICCO *approaches* FUADACH, *asking for an intimacy.*]

BRICCO: Can any of these others do that?

POLSO: Stand out of the way, Bricco.

SPALLA: Yes. Tibio can conjure his own evasions.

[FUADACH *seems suddenly overcome with emotion, shaking with and silently suppressing tears.*]

FUADACH: Say, carry on. I'll help you to bury me.

BACÁN: Oh, then we don't need this business with Carmen?

FUADACH: Tame your tongue, you bitch.

BACÁN: I assume you mean Carmen, or that you speak for Carmen. *Platícanos del agua, maestro.*

GINOCCHIO: Gently, Bacán.

[FUADACH *begins a quiet story, one almost self-enclosed.*]

FUADACH: I told her no one would believe her fragility. She looked too competent in breaking mirrors, or taking a hammer to Mary's image in the garden. I had heard of her residence on the docks, her cinnamon hair spread out, making her seem like spun lightning when she moved. She made it clear that she didn't need me, or need my approval of the devastation she had left on the docks, or in a cheap hotel room, or on a train crossing an ambiguous border. She marked our time together almost as a slippery vindication for her own redemption.

BACÁN: Judgment.

[FUADACH *raises his hand to assist* BACÁN's *protest.*]

FUADACH: The water courses, Bacán.

SPALLA: Polso. Does your dithyramb account for all of this, or even for the woman herself?

POLSO: Don't mess with my music, Spalla.

SPALLA: Get to that. He teaches you to sing, and then runs away when you find your voice. Go on, Tibio. You have us involved in your redemption.

FUADACH: No, no, no, you have it all wrong.

BACÁN: My, what a conjuration. Salvation that finds a body, then abandons it.

FUADACH: She did not abandon me.

SPALLA: Do you still have the wine-stained white shirt, Tibio?

FUADACH: [*Wanting to continue his Carmen story.*] You see, she had no way of knowing that I had followed her. Or that I knew her intimately, knew the very things that would occasion the violent breaking of her spirit. The Norwegian card players meant nothing to her. She left that. She ran away from you. She bought passage on a second-class bus traveling through banana groves, unfamiliar territory.

BACÁN: I don't think you should go any further.

FUADACH: Why not, Bacán? Do you think I'll put some distance between you and Carmen?

BACÁN: I think you got lost.

FUADACH: *We* got lost, following an asymmetric pattern that promised us a real love.

BACÁN: *Orgullo.*

FUADACH: No. Call it courage. You know that Carmen always carried a knife, a dagger, if you want to call it that.

[SPALLA *begins a dance, snapping her fingers like castanets.*]

Nothing of that. But you must acknowledge the recurring possibility of the cutting.

BACÁN: What do you know of the cutting?

FUADACH: And what do you know of ecstasy? Or even how one chooses the moment of a particular cutting?

POLSO: Don't tell me you think you had achieved that moment with this woman.

SPALLA: In a minute, we'll hear about the old affliction.

FUADACH: She loved me, yes.

POLSO: Why, of course, a real asymmetry for which you had always prepared.

FUADACH: I stand convicted of consciousness, Polso.

POLSO: I thought you might find some help among the Parthians, Tibio.

FUADACH: Thank you, Polso. For reminding me that some of us do speak in tongues. Carmen for example...

BACÁN: Indecent.

[FUADACH *shakes the garment in* BACÁN'*s eyes.*]

FUADACH: Do you want this?

[*She remains silent and motionless.*]

Then let me finish. There we sat in the plaza, near the heedlessly baroque church. Carmen understood how I had hoped to avoid that third hour.

SPALLA: What a scandalously impoverished imagination. *Zut alors*, the man thinks we don't recognize his borrowing.

GINOCCHIO: What borrowing? Clearly, he wants to tell us about what happened.

SPALLA: Where?

GINOCCHIO: In him.

SPALLA: Tell us about that, Lorg. This festival of sensations that touch you, even now.

[LORG *slowly and mockingly observes* SPALLA.]

GINOCCHIO: Do we have to speak of those sensations with such disdain, Spalla?

FUADACH: Spalla wants her portion of what we had.

SPALLA: You and Elzbieta?

FUADACH: Of course.

[SPALLA *laughs shrilly, sharply.*]

BACÁN: You mean, of course, Carmen.

SPALLA: *Le dejo en tu cargo*, Bacán.

FUADACH: You won't distract me, Spalla. "I will attempt to lead you, by way of experiencing, through very simple and very common means, into a sacred darkness."

BRICCO: You've tried that before, but you got tied up in some silly argument about absolute rest.

FUADACH: You remember that, do you? Then you ought to get it right. I said nothing about absolute rest. [*Holding up his hand.*] Don't contradict me.

BRICCO: Go on, then, Tibio. You have us fascinated.

FUADACH: I discovered that when we met there in the plaza we had crossed *un zaguán*. Ah, you see me there, don't you? The *zahareño*, masquerading as *un garrido*. Count upon it, Carmen would beat that out of my body. All that vanity of refusing to live, all that uncertainty in death.

POLSO: Did you ever touch her?

FUADACH: Did I ever touch her, he asks me. Of course, I did.

POLSO: At the third hour.

FUADACH: Don't rush me, Polso. Imagine a village as simple as a ceremony that only she could understand. She takes my hand. We get up; we walk away. Where could we go to pretend that the church had removed itself? She asked me to imagine, without saying so, that the third hour would disappear. She asked me if I wanted to meet her mother, and to see how she managed that moment that had not yet arrived. There she had me. Could I refuse to see myself? [*He stops.*] No. It did not happen that way.

SPALLA: What didn't happen?

FUADACH: A small, dark boy, dressed all in white, came running up the street. He got between me and Carmen; he drew her away from me, tried to hurry her steps. She seemed to respond to his urgency, and yet she turned her eyes toward me, asking me to follow, or to release her. So we ran together. I could see only one light on a darkened street. The silence of the street seemed to inhabit that light. Do you understand me? At that moment, I could not account for the bell that had followed us out of the plaza. I could not account for that ecstasy that had me by the hair.

POLSO: Let's mark this off the books.

[BACÁN *suddenly has* POLSO *by the throat.*]

BACÁN: No. Let's go back to that light.

GINOCCHIO: To the silence washing that street.

FUADACH: [*Exhilarated.*] Yes. Yes. Did I go in that house? Did I find the mother? Had Carmen led me astray, made me abandon an obligation in the plaza, for one for which I had no preparation?

SPALLA: What did you see?

FUADACH: A woman washing the body of a dead man. Carmen coiled at the foot of the bed. My own body embracing every wall of the house.

POLSO: So you had really not arrived, and Carmen had disappointed you.

FUADACH: Not at all. She had brought me home.

POLSO: That does it. The man could go on like this forever.

FUADACH: Yes, Polso, I would touch upon that infinity that grace might recognize. And Carmen should go with me, until we exhaust it.

SPALLA: Bravo. But you haven't convinced me that you have learned to dance.

[FUADACH *sings the Lydian scale.*]

FUADACH: Will that do?

SPALLA: How ridiculous. The man considers himself a note in a scale.

FUADACH: I have to give some shape to this composition, Spalla. You must sing along with the others, or lose this moment. [*To the others.*] Shall we get Spalla in the spirit?

[*The actors now repeat their first entrances—a single line, a series of differing positions with respect to each other, a new configuration, rest.*]

BACÁN/VOICE D: Night mare, "Her nests, when one comes across them in dreams, lodged in rock-clefts, or the branches of enormous hollow yews, are built of carefully chosen twigs, lined with white horse-hair and the plumage of prophetic birds and littered with the jawbones and entrails of poets."

POLSO/VOICE F: Every day begins with a silence that has earned its keep. This morning requires a translation.

SPALLA/VOICE E: It happened just about the time I thought I had a solution to the problem of identity. The identity of indiscernibles. Well, this doesn't concern you.

LORG/VOICE B: The geometer draws no conclusion from the existence of the particular line of which he speaks, but from what his diagrams represent. Furthermore, all hypotheses and postulates are either universal or particular, but a definition is neither.

BRICCO/VOICE C: Why, after all, should the earth fall? If the universe is symmetrical, there is no more reason for the earth to move down than up.

TIBIO/VOICE A: Death steps on the garden egg, and the garden egg drops suddenly.

[*The figures embrace, dance to exhaustion, sit heavily, laughing.*]

TIBIO: That ought to satisfy anyone.

POLSO: Even your wives.

TIBIO: I had no wives.

BACÁN: Exactly. But you left us halfway along the route to understanding. These contemplative, destructive moments only awaken a desire to see all love settled.

LORG: Yes, Tibio. [*Coaxing.*] Josefina…

BRICCO: We remain, of course, with that descant you composed in Buenos Aires.

TIBIO: You want me to put the lid on the pot.

SPALLA: Exactly.

TIBIO: Bricco came late to our convocation in the Tortoni. You think he saw everything because he thought he saw betrayal in Josefina's eyes. Who did the talking? Tell them, Bricco. I say another body, with another name, sat at our table. One that had traveled some distance, one that we protect in the place where this garment goes. You understand me.

SPALLA: I thought so. He wants to dress Carmen in that garment, and tell us a story that doesn't fit.

TIBIO: No, you will not do this to me.

BACÁN: Why, Tibio, should you take us from one altar to another, and pretend that love proposed it?

TIBIO: Because love did.

[*They turn away from him in disgust.*]

All right. I let the woman lead me into her imagination. She had this gift of creating theatres where we could play, she and I, with our affinities, with my jealousy.

GINOCCHIO: Do any of these theatres have names?

TIBIO: Of course they do. And we always have three tragedies and a satyr play to get through before nightfall. You can imagine the slow approach of the most significant death, and feel the rumpled benevolence of its presence. We have come to another form of measure, perhaps an evasion. I often stand at this point—Athens, Lagos, Berkeley—but I sometimes do not see the subtle shifts of landscape the light allows, or provokes. Josefina, or the woman you call Josefina, stands with me. She reminds me that we once saw a figure playing in our space. He wore a heavy cloak, radiant white knee boots and dark velvet trousers. He stood near the altar. But I had every reason to resent his implied piety. I knew the man. He didn't have the feet to stand in such a sacred precinct. For all his parading, he had no understanding of what it meant to stand under the theologian. He knew nothing other than violation. Not sacrifice and suffering. Not the gift of suffering and its radiant withdrawal. Bricco will tell you how this love shivered the air there in Buenos Aires. You know the way, along the *parodos* into the orchestra. We exist there upon this lower level...Time now to recall the procession of masks. I feel disfigured, a feeling I will disguise with my exhilaration.

[*A bell begins to sound in the distance.*]

BACÁN: We cannot enter *that* hour with you, Tibio.

POLSO: I think he never intended to take us along.

GINOCCHIO: Somewhere along the way he lost the purity of his intention.

SPALLA: Now he wants to persuade us that we caused this contamination of purpose.

BRICCO: Perhaps he thought that while we still had our masks we had nothing to fear.

TIBIO: I remind you of the alacrity with which you signed our antiphonal covenant. [*He groans.*] I should have known, I should have felt it right from the start. The pulse escapes you. Give me your hands. Let's write this one off.

BACÁN: Saints, I think we should bury this man.

TIBIO: Ah, the melody of such an assertion. Bacán wants to turn me into an ancestor. But go on with your redemptive insanity. [*He starts a grotesque dance.*] I'll give you a rhythm.

[*He tries to urge them into his dance. The others begin a menacing dance around him.*]

SPALLA: We know the rhythm, Tibio.

POLSO: We have eyes.

TIBIO: Nonsense.

GINOCCHIO: Dance, Tibio.

TIBIO: This won't work. You haven't paid any attention.

BACÁN: Look at him. He can no longer feel his body.

BRICCO: Where did *you* lose the rhythm, Tibio?

POLSO: In Elzbieta's bed, *por supuesto*.

GINOCCHIO: Do you think he even remembers Carmen?

SPALLA: Well, of course, this composition always seemed to court its own stillness.

BACÁN: Exactly.

TIBIO: Exactly.

SPALLA: [*To* TIBIO.] Whatever do you mean?

TIBIO: Pay attention.

GINOCCHIO: Do you think he remembers the knife?

BRICCO: What does he expect to find in the church?

BACÁN: That hour.

POLSO: That pulse that measures.

SPALLA: That expectation.

TIBIO: I resent the fact that you think you sat with me back there, in expectation.

BRICCO: [*Holding out his hand.*] I'll take that garment, if you don't mind.

TIBIO: [*Challenging.*] Take it.

BRICCO: I appeal to the others. You can offer us nothing but a certain discontinuity.

GINOCCHIO: *Calma*, Bricco. Tibio has brought us a new measure for our composition.

SPALLA: Can you play that for us, Lorg?

GINOCCHIO: I make no claims.

SPALLA: Yes. I thought so.

[TIBIO *throws the garment at* BRICCO. *The others rush to retrieve, protect and contest it.*]

TIBIO: Take it. Do whatever you want with it.

POLSO: We refuse to let you abandon us. Just when we might have come to understand these harmonies.

TIBIO: Don't try to bully me, Polso.

BACÁN: Tibio, you can't continue to use that third hour as a refuge. Forgive me, saints, I should have said sanctuary.

TIBIO: Delicate, Bacán.

[*The bell sounds again.*]

But I have to tell you. I had already left that third hour, a mile up the hill. I picked my way, on a burro's back, to that plaza, to wait for that inaccessible requirement of joy, a liberation, that the knife couldn't cut away, and the garment couldn't cover. You see that, don't you? I had learned, in spite of myself, the careful mastery of time.

[*A vigorous old man, dressed all in white, presents himself. He carries a small bell, which he uses to signal his office as a musician.*]

MUSICIAN: Carefully spoken, if not well sung. What should we call you: the *maestro* of isomorphic space? What about the reconstruction of these other pilgrims? Did you think about that before you started with your subtractions and distractions? No, you dance with your form for the sake of form. Don't worry, I have no designs upon this choir. I just came to repair Bricco's clock and his metronome. You others will have to find your own indirection. Maybe Fuadach will teach each of you a separate mode. Can we give it a try? [*He pulls everyone into a ragged configuration.*] There now. Put on your masks. No, leave them off for a moment. I want you to test your unadorned voices. [*Once he has them rearranged, he skips among them cajoling and assigning scales.*] From D to D octave, from E to E octave, from F to F octave, from G to G octave, from A to A octave, from C to C. You see that you can do this, can't you? Sure, you can. We all have our voices; we all have something a voice must address, or even tame. First, listen to yourself, each one. [*He points at each one for the assigned scale, then draws each one into singing a separate mode at the same time.*] How appealing you all seem to my thirsting spirit. Such glorious affinities. [*He faces* TIBIO *with* POLSO, LORG *with* BACÁN, BRICCO *with* SPALLA.]

All that remains, all that changes. Live with it, pilgrims.

[*He takes the white garment and dances away. The six figures continue to sing. A speaking voice sounds above them.*]

VOICE: There was a story that began with the usual drainage of certainties, but the tale was quickly delivered to the failing stars and propped upon inconceivable delight.

SYNTAX

[*A flat granite stone, large and wide enough to bear a body, lies stage center in the dark. Intermittent light appears as shooting stars, though nothing seems shaped or perceptible as a familiar light. We soon notice a figure lying on the stone. The figure's dress (a crimson robe, sandals) and movement do not tell us how to read it. The figure sits, stretches, turns away, looks toward the front.*]

FLANÍ: *Es el presagio. Solo el presagio.*

[*A figure dressed all in black suddenly appears in half-light to the left.*]

VIGILIUS: Give it up. This garbage. Speak up. Speak clearly. Or get down.

FLANÍ: So it's you again. Why have you come, if I so disturb you?

VIGILIUS: Lord, what arrogance. He thinks he disturbs me. I have a message.

FLANÍ: From?

VIGILIUS: What do you care who it's from? The message is impeccably honest.

FLANÍ: You and your redundancies.

VIGILIUS: Can we have light?

[*Light floods the area.* VIGILIUS *scrutinizes* FLANÍ.]

I see you're in scarlet again.

FLANÍ: You have no skill with color. Scarlet, red, burgundy, rose, or a tone in your imagination. What does it matter? Let's complete our correspondence.

[VIGILIUS *looks around at the space. Canvases in various stages of completion lie scattered about or stacked against any available surface.*]

VIGILIUS: Do you think you will ever get some order in this mess?

FLANÍ: Put? Or get?

VIGILIUS: Don't play with me.

FLANÍ: The message.

VIGILIUS: The committee would like your thoughts on the exposition. In addition, they would like to interview you about your response to my review of your work as it stands.

[*Flaní taps the stone.*]

FLANÍ: This is granite.

VIGILIUS: I know. It breathes. You've told me. And you've told me how perfectly in tune with the canvas it is.

FLANÍ: Did I say that? I only meant to call attention to its vitality.

VIGILIUS: The vitality of a stone?

FLANÍ: Stone!? Is that what you see?

VIGILIUS: I take it that this is your response to the committee.

FLANÍ: I have no response to the committee. I'm not a very good member of the party.

VIGILIUS: Clever. What party are you talking about? We're no party. How many times do we have to tell you? We're a gathering of aestheticians. Birds who gather on the same branch to sing their delight. Does that grab you, Flaní? Poetic enough for you?

FLANÍ: I didn't think you had it in you. A little passion. I'm impressed.

VIGILIUS: Do you want our support, or not?

FLANÍ: Oh, my. What happened to the subtle logician, the mathematician of the eye?

VIGILIUS: [*Touching the granite.*] It does feel a little like skin, doesn't it? Maybe I'm falling under your spell, Flaní. I was very taken with your talk. You know the one. The one you gave to the ladies, was it? An invitation that seemed so bizarre .

FLANÍ: Your point.

VIGILIUS: Yes, well, my point. You seemed very concerned to have everyone agree…forgive me, I meant, understand—that art grows as it will, a notion that seems to me a kind of deviant platonism.

FLANÍ: You missed the point. Nothing comes from nothing.

VIGILIUS: I have time, Flaní. Let me see you dance.

FLANÍ: Get out of my face.

VIGILIUS: You haven't realized yet. That you need me. Not to explain you. I have no interest in that. I'm only here to further your disengagement.

FLANÍ: [*Singing.*] Whose side are you on, boy, whose side are you on?

VIGILIUS: Don't pretend, Flaní. You don't care about alliances, shared worlds. I've already read you. So you see, you really didn't have to put on this crimson garment. I have to tell you that there are times when I feel paralyzed. [*He picks up a painting.*] I look at this, and I don't even think that there is a judgment to be made. Sure, you're flattered. The purity of this… instrument…has gone beyond me. Where is the nothing, Flaní?

FLANÍ: You're looking in the wrong place.

[VIGILIUS *thrusts the painting at* FLANÍ.]

VIGILIUS: Here. I have the instrument, Flaní. Show me where this nothing resides. Show me what I've missed. There's no one here.

FLANÍ: *Oh, no es nadie, señor, soy yo.* [FLANÍ *gently takes the painting from* VIGILIUS.] That one is not quite finished, Vigilius.

VIGILIUS: You won't betray me, will you?

FLANÍ: How could I? Do you know about granite?

VIGILIUS: We've had this conversation.

FLANÍ: Not this one. *Granito,* or *granum.* Latin tongues to speak about rocks. Common rocks, old rocks down along the earth's crust. You get these veins which run into surrounding rocks. Our friend, the granite, is an intrusive little scamp. He forces his way into things, splits the very bed upon which he lies. You might even accuse him of being a painter. The little devil changes himself by being crushed. Doesn't that sound familiar, Vigilius? What really interests me, apart from the uproarious processes that this angel suffers…Don't cringe, Vigilius, I know you have no interest in the preservation of feldspars. Where was I? Ah, yes, I was just getting to the rotted materials. Delicious when you have this consummation in the painter. *N'est-ce pas?* Somewhere along the line you get these wonderful things, these vapors and emanations, this shifting and reconstruction. Things that get left behind suddenly shine in their utility, and, by god, of a sudden you have food, and beauty. You might even have a painter named Flaní.

VIGILIUS: You're not listening to me.

FLANÍ: Speak.

VIGILIUS: I am on your side, Flaní. Don't disappoint me. It's cost me plenty garlic to account for your virtues, my man. The artist. Oh, yes, I get a cupful of that every morning, even when all I want is a cup of coffee. But I have to listen to a different Magus going on about his aesthetic vision, the angelic beatitudes he's learned from humping his own hand.

FLANÍ: Such chauvinism!

VIGILIUS: Spare me. You know what I mean.

FLANÍ: Am I what you mean?

VIGILIUS: What do you mean?

FLANÍ: Friends, you'd never know that this was improvised.

VIGILIUS: You won't stop me this time.

FLANÍ: From?

VIGILIUS: Pointing out that you and all your brothers and sisters are living on impure intentions. Don't cringe, Flaní, I know you have no interest in alienation. You take your solitude for the face of things.

FLANÍ: That is an impossible construction, Vigilius.

VIGILIUS: Oh, he's disturbed. [VIGILIUS *walks, feigning a search, among* FLANÍ's *paintings.*] Let me see if I can find an example here.

FLANÍ: Stop it.

VIGILIUS: He wants my renunciation.

FLANÍ: I want…

[FLANÍ *gestures toward the stone.* DARAG, *wearing a morning coat, green silk trousers, red shoes with spats, pops up on the stone.*]

Darag. One of your crowd, Vigilius. Aren't you happy to see him?

VIGILIUS: Enchanted.

DARAG: Shut up, Vigilius. Life is nasty, brutish and short.

VIGILIUS: They can never shake the mud of Cambridge off their boots.

DARAG: I could be insulted by that.

VIGILIUS: Then take offense.

DARAG: No, thank you.

FLANÍ: Welcome, Darag. But what's the occasion?

DARAG: I was on my way uptown to a show. I didn't want to be left out when the photographer for the *Times* came.

VIGILIUS: Ridiculous. This isn't New York.

DARAG: Oh, it isn't? Tell that to the young who have just cut their hair. But I feel I'm interrupting something.

VIGILIUS: You are.

FLANÍ: Not at all.

DARAG: I see. Why have you conjured me, Flaní? A good gnostic like you who can't sit still for his own heresies.

FLANÍ: Vigilius was complicating my life.

DARAG: With visions of the canon.

FLANÍ: We hadn't arrived.

DARAG: Then it's good that I came.

VIGILIUS: Darag always pretends an empathy he doesn't feel.

DARAG: He reads me.

VIGILIUS: Did you know that that is granite?

DARAG: I assumed it was.

VIGILIUS: Assumptions. Oh, god. We owe it to Flaní not to assume anything.

FLANÍ: I can speak for myself.

DARAG: Vigilius seems uneasy with the way you've treated his criticism, Flaní.

FLANÍ: He said you were.

DARAG: That's not nice. Vigilius is going to put himself forward as your only champion. I'm sure he's told you that I sprayed skunk oil over your painting of the beach, or was it the bitch? You see my malignancy has me confused. Straighten me out, Vigilius. Remind me of my last scurrilous report of Flaní.

VIGILIUS: I don't like getting into this game with you.

DARAG: *Certo.* The process tires me, too.

FLANÍ: *Is* there a committee?

DARAG: Who told you that?

FLANÍ: Vigilius.

DARAG: What kind of nonsense is that? I'm ashamed of you, Vigilius, though I am not surprised. What's our scribbler here trying to promote, Flaní?

FLANÍ: I was about to ask you.

DARAG: I think I'm going to have to lie down. [*He crawls onto the stone, and assumes a languid pose.*]

VIGILIUS: Get him up from there!

[DARAG *sits upright.*]

DARAG: *Basta,* Vigilius, your prancing has gone far enough. I'm sick of your flagging your political concerns.

VIGILIUS: Don't be vulgar.

DARAG: Don't you borrow a passion your eye doesn't justify.

VIGILIUS: What do you mean?

DARAG: This drawing us all into the ninth circle of your critical judgment. You came here simply to frighten Flaní.

VIGILIUS: You sent me.

DARAG: I sent you?

VIGILIUS: Because you never say what you mean.

DARAG: Oh, my. [*He resumes his languid pose.*] And what would I say, if I could say, or meant to say, what I mean? If you see what I mean.

[VIGILIUS *drops the painting, and turns to go.*]

Pay attention, Vigilius. Flaní is in limbo. Don't you see? That was my first thought when I saw you standing here. Good, I said, Vigilius has come to console Flaní. He's brought the news from our little delegation, our mission, as it were, that we will offer our services while he gathers his adolescent powers. *Calma*, Flaní. I'm not marking the wall. This committee, this gathering of aestheticians, as Vigilius frames it, recognizes your gift, and wants to protect you against your softness. "Precious in the sight of the Lord / is the death of his saints." Gloss that for me, Vigilius.

VIGILIUS: [*To* FLANÍ.] I leave him to you.

DARAG: Such blindness.

FLANÍ: Psalms 116, verse fifteen.

DARAG: Exactly. How did you know?

FLANÍ: All gnostics know scripture.

DARAG: There you go. That's what Vigilius holds against you.

VIGILIUS: Can I speak for myself?

DARAG: *Can* you speak for yourself? Look at him, Flaní. He's embarrassed by your softness. It's the Irishman in Vigilius. He spends too much time picking the poets' pockets, and talking about pride.

VIGILIUS: Haven't you been…?

DARAG: Haven't I been what? Haven't I exposed you? "You don't hold your head high enough, Yeats." Is that it, Vigilius? You resent this Buddhist cheeriness in Flaní.

FLANÍ: I thought I was in another hemisphere, Darag.

DARAG: Your filthy bottom perhaps, but I'm talking about your art.

VIGILIUS: Ha!

DARAG: Do you find that ridiculous, Vigilius?

FLANÍ: Give him time to parse this word, ridiculous, Darag.

DARAG: Let him parse his fucking emotions.

VIGILIUS: [Starting to remove his jacket.] Get off the stone.

DARAG: Well, now, this is an insightful career.

FLANÍ: Curious, the way you brought up Vigilius's feelings just at the point you were asking his benevolent judgment.

DARAG: Since when has judgment been benevolent?

FLANÍ: It's indisputable, Darag. You're the one who placed Vigilius among our Celtic singers.

DARAG: Are you taking his side?

VIGILIUS: Oh, marvelous. There is hope, there is hope. I could kiss you, Flaní.

FLANÍ: Pull on your jacket, Vigilius.

VIGILIUS: Of course. Of course. [He does.] You've nailed him to the stone, Flaní. The subtle Darag loses his subtlety when you ask him to sit up straight on his own bottom.

DARAG: I will get off this stone. [He starts.]

VIGILIUS: Your first ethical decision.

FLANÍ: Gentlemen, the sun has set, or maybe it has just arisen. I can never be sure when I'm lying here in the dark. What was my point? Ah, yes. Until Vigilius turned up, I seemed to be wandering. Not necessarily dreaming, not nightmares. But something closer to the bone. I'm sure you understand me.

DARAG: Should we?

FLANÍ: It's up to you.

DARAG: What do *you* say, Vigilius?

VIGILIUS: I'm not sure I want *you* to ask me.

DARAG: Well, that's a straightforward account. So it's evening, or it's morning, and we're here with Flaní who seems only to accommodate our presence.

VIGILIUS: My twin Darag. Never mind, it's just a gnostic joke.

DARAG: Well, Flaní sees that I am here. There must be something in that. Even you, Vigilius, recognize the fact that I am most decidedly here. Does it matter that I was summoned?

VIGILIUS: I didn't summon you.

DARAG: Of course, not. You're not an artist.

VIGILIUS: I'm waiting.

DARAG: For?

VIGILIUS: For the rest of that proposition.

DARAG: Nay, that was an expression. Complete. Finished. Leading nowhere. Not even a judgment buried within it.

VIGILIUS: Keep talking. Listen carefully, Flaní.

[FLANÍ *smiles, closes his eyes.*]

DARAG: Something I meant to ask you, Flaní. How can a gnostic like you be content with this chaos?

FLANÍ: What kind of gnostic am I, Darag?

DARAG: A fastidious hermit.

FLANÍ: Then I must be forgiven for having failed myself and my calling. Or perhaps, Darag, your eye has fallen on the wrong qualities.

DARAG: Now I know why these things look the way they do.

FLANÍ: What do you know about seeing?

DARAG: Listen to him, Vigilius. He wants to treat me like an innocent.

[VIGILIUS *snorts*.]

There. He's bought you.

VIGILIUS: Not likely.

DARAG: Yes, I see. It doesn't really matter that these instruments, as Vigilius calls them, are opaque, and that something is dreadfully missing. Strike that. Absent. Because it was there; or perhaps it is still there, and only available to that innocent eye.

VIGILIUS: Yours.

DARAG: Yes. Oh, thank you, Vigilius.

VIGILIUS: You're welcome back again, Darag.

FLANÍ: Did anyone see the cardinal in the birch?

DARAG: What was that all about?

FLANÍ: I just thought that things were being so imaginatively disposed that a furtive redness would be welcome.

DARAG: A hint of an invitation. Vigilius, are you with me? This gnostic revelry has given me an appetite.

FLANÍ: Hold. I seem to recall that I summoned, as you put it, you.

DARAG: So?

FLANÍ: So we haven't disposed of the question.

DARAG: What is the question?

FLANÍ: You're treating me like an accident, Darag. Go on. Get out of my yard. And take Vigilius. He seems to have lost his appetite.

VIGILIUS: Spin around, spin around, all you want, Flaní. Your trace will always be there. You understand me. [*He points arbitrarily at a painting.*] I don't like the woman in that canvas.

FLANÍ: There is no woman in that canvas.

VIGILIUS: You say. But you've already been compromised. Coming, Darag? The drinks, if not the dinner, are on me.

DARAG: Did I have to be dressed like this when you called?

FLANÍ: Decorum, Darag. Measured by imagination.

[DARAG *and* VIGILIUS *march off. A woman, dressed in white shirt and trousers, has placed herself above the stone on a white chair. She looks away from* FLANÍ, *showing shame and disgust for him.*]

Is there a problem?

[*The woman rises, gives* FLANÍ *a last contemptuous look, picks up her chair, and walks away.*]

Why do they come when there is nothing to refuse?

[*A woman, dressed in black, enters, carrying a small rectangular suitcase. Her dark hair and features give no clue as to her ethnic identity.*]

PECA: You have some nerve to talk about measure. You've just spent an hour lying to yourself. *Perdón.* That was almost a lie. You've been at this camouflage for most of your life. Nothing to refuse! Spare me.

FLANÍ: Were you invited?

PECA: Don't pretend you've forgotten. You anticipated this nightmare. It's just like you to turn taunting Vigilius into a *faena.* And the measure— yes, I said measure—of your arrogance was to call upon Darag before you called for me.

FLANÍ: I didn't call for you.

PECA: I know you didn't. Some moments are free for nothing, Flaní. I came on my own. Isn't that sweet?

FLANÍ: Delightful.

[*She holds up the suitcase.*]

PECA: Bearing gifts. [*She goes to the stone, opens the suitcase, takes out a white robe similar to the robe* FLANÍ *wears. She walks it toward him.*] I thought you might like to refuse the one you have on.

FLANÍ: Talk about arrogance.

PECA: Is there a problem?

FLANÍ: What an ear. You pick up a certain cadence, a certain form of words, but you lose the sense.

PECA: What a remarkable way of refusing a gift.

FLANÍ: I'm refusing your presence. Take your robe out of my face.

PECA: There you stand, with your crimson robe. Definition. Ah, yes, it's not red, the martyr's color. That would be just a tad too sentimental for you. And then there's that other dimension I'm sure your gnostic frenzy encompassed.

FLANÍ: And that is?

PECA: No, no, no. Let's not hop into that bed. I have enough to do keeping you focused on all your evasions. So keep your shirt on. That is, keep your robe on. What was the question put to Darag?

FLANÍ: This won't do. Your dancing around in a nightmare with me. Even if you convince me that it's necessary to go through this *huevada*, you will not have convinced me.

PECA: Another evasion.

[FLANÍ *takes a few dance steps, stops.*]

FLANÍ: Why is the robe white?

PECA: Another evasion.

FLANÍ: Mine, or yours?

PECA: *Epa!* The first indication that he sees me. Fantastic. It's too bad Darag isn't here to savor this. Or would you prefer having Vigilius capture your temper? Or terror? Or tone? Say when. What was the question put to Darag? Why the white robe? A perfect solution to that cardinal in the birch.

FLANÍ: Why are you all in black?

PECA: The color of purity.

FLANÍ: Where did you get that?

PECA: From your imagination.

FLANÍ: Such a sycophant. But it won't work.

PECA: Two plus two is not equal to five. Oh, don't worry, Flaní; it's just another gnostic joke.

FLANÍ: Well, you're here. Unfold your blessings. Show me some consideration. Give me a reason for your presence.

PECA: Would you be amenable to a glass of wine?

FLANÍ: I understand, I understand. You don't want to be found, located. It's my failing, certainly. I haven't even asked your name.

PECA: First, the convivial gesture. [*She spreads the white robe on the stone, takes two goblets from her suitcase, and busies herself with arranging the goblets on the robe.*] There. Ready, if ever. [*She points at the painting* VIGILIUS *criticized.*] A propósito, niño, there *was* a woman in this canvas. I remember her distinctly, as she had my features.

FLANÍ: There is nothing distinctive about your features.

[PECA *replaces the goblets, folds the robe.*]

PECA: You're a lost cause.

FLANÍ: I am not a cause.

PECA: True. That would imply that you had a memory. *Aspetta*, Flaní. I know you know your way home. But that doesn't have anything to do with your being here. Don't answer that question. Your answer would just convict you of being a dreamer.

[FLANÍ *stops to consider the painting in question.*]

FLANÍ: So you see the face, do you? Think about that.

PECA: I have, Flaní. I won't tell. I know you need time to repair your future. After all, there is enough ambiguity and ambivalence in your past.

FLANÍ: [*Begins to sing.*] "In a quaint caravan…"

PECA: Vigilius is the gypsy. He can write upon your soul. The little Roman Vigilius, out of Africa, with a soul to the left, a soul to the right. Why do you refuse his embrace, Flaní? Don't answer that. Your answer would tell me that you believe you have been alive, and that Vigilius has the instrument to make this insanity a true judgment. These paintings go nowhere. They're at war with themselves. And, of course, you lived them. Right, Flaní? There he is, in his own crimson robe, afraid of his own eyes. Do you want my advice?

FLANÍ: I want your eyes on a plate.

PECA: Bravo. The artist-assassin. Face to face with the restructured reality of his foolishness. Burn this shit.

FLANÍ: I might.

PECA: You won't.

FLANÍ: What do you suggest?

PECA: Enter another area of judgment. Go where no human can go, where none can speak.

FLANÍ: Ridiculous on the face of it.

PECA: You're the one who thinks about redemption. Gnostic he calls himself.

FLANÍ: Enough of that! I don't play games with names, nor with God.

PECA: You're obscene. I have to point out that your red is corrupt. Here [*She points at him.*] and there [*She points to the canvases.*]

FLANÍ: You have no authority...

PECA: Authority! This little ascetic talks to me about authority!?

FLANÍ: It's time to know who you are.

PECA: Peca, a rigid designator.

FLANÍ: Princeton, right?

PECA: Indefensible. Berkeley.

FLANÍ: I should have known. I could tell by the informal manner in which you went about arranging our formal occasion. I said nothing at the time. But I was offended. Wouldn't you agree that we should try that celebration again?

PECA: The offense was to me.

FLANÍ: Impossible. There was no personality in your behavior. You compounded this error by usurping Vigilius's soul on the left. Caught you, didn't I?

PECA: That, you understand, is the one that courses the world.

FLANÍ: *Tais-toi.* Don't play the village *maestro.*

PECA: All right. What have you decided?

FLANÍ: That you're a thief. You contributed to her disgust for me.

PECA: The woman in white.

FLANÍ: Damn straight, the woman in white.

PECA: There's no evidence of her compassion.

FLANÍ: What do you know about compassion?

PECA: You're disturbed that perhaps her recognition was mistaken.

FLANÍ: All right, you bitch. Let's make it possible for her to return. Give me the goblets. Spread your winding sheet.

PECA: I'll do no such thing. Winding sheet, indeed. I thought we were talking about a naming. Or a recognition. Or a resolution.

FLANÍ: Put the instruments on the stone.

PECA: Not under this temper.

FLANÍ: They belong to me.

PECA: Not now. Not yet.

FLANÍ: Ah, the treacherous Peca, promising.

PECA: I can tell you, she is not the absent woman in your canvas.

[FLANÍ *suddenly mounts the stone, and sits at its center.*]

FLANÍ: Tell me how to proceed.

PECA: I don't know.

FLANÍ: Then why have you come?

PECA: I don't know.

FLANÍ: Provoke me into sending you away.

[PECA *secures her suitcase, straightens, faces* FLANÍ.]

PECA: No provocation necessary. I follow the soul on the right. *Au revoir,* Flaní. We will celebrate our reunion. [*She walks away.*]

FLANÍ: Wake up! [*To himself.*] So she's not what she used to be. No one is. She tried to stir up injury, tried to make me feel ashamed. As though I couldn't remember the steps. *She* doesn't remember the steps. She thought that walking away would remind me of the debt I owe that other one. All right, I admit I have been inattentive. There's a certain slippage, an evangelical mistake that freezes me to this stone. Look at these bodies scattered about. They're mine. The shattering of a tonal framework. Let it go. Let it rest. Let it come again.

[DARAG *returns, pushing a wheelbarrow of paintings and artifacts.*]

DARAG: You thought you had shed me, did you? You counted on my being a little bit fragile, a little in awe of *art* or the artist, whichever is which. It wasn't your first mistake. You, of course, remember your first mistake. It doesn't matter. Look, get out of that womb, and take a look at these.

FLANÍ: I'm quite comfortable here in my womb, as you call it. And I can see from here that what you have in your cart doesn't concern me.

DARAG: Doesn't concern you. [*He pulls, and tosses some of the wheelbarrow's contents aside.*] Of course, these concern you. They're your competition. Wake up, yourself. Look what I can pull from any corner tavern. You see what I'm getting at?

FLANÍ: No, I don't see what you're getting at.

DARAG: Vigilius and I weren't in the bar twenty minutes. Didn't this shit, this bartering of the soul, go out of fashion decades ago? Who lives like this? [*He scatters more things.*] I had no idea why I brought you this gift, until just this moment. I suppose that it's the second time within hours that I have called you home.

FLANÍ: I remember you called me an accident.

DARAG: No, sir.

FLANÍ: I forgive you.

DARAG: He forgives me!

FLANÍ: Isn't that why you came back? I mean, when it's clear you're not wanted.

DARAG: I get it now. You know, I knew a trumpet player, marvelously gifted. Always insulted the audience, so they would be sure to despise his music. It struck me that he regretted that his music could sail on its own. Isn't that how you'd read it?

FLANÍ: I didn't know the man.

DARAG: I did, Flaní. In a certain sense, so did you. He's in the cart. Shall I find him?

FLANÍ: [*As though awakening.*] Darag, we've changed places. [*He comes off the stone.*] So, let's say you've just summoned me. Here you are with your work in hand. You're wearing your finest robes. Only one thing is missing. Vigilius.

DARAG: "Let me see thee caper."

FLANÍ: Ay, sir, "that's sides and hearts." You see we do speak to each other.

DARAG: Not now. Not yet.

FLANÍ: What did you say?

DARAG: Simple words.

FLANÍ: But those. Why did they choose you?

DARAG: What kind of talk is that?

[FLANÍ *scatters the rest of the goods in the wheelbarrow.*]

Vigilius was right. There's a knot you haven't managed to untie.

FLANÍ: What does Vigilius know about anything?

DARAG: Those words. Why did they choose you? Don't answer. It would just be your way of viewing a galaxy that has no light. Vigilius claims to know your perfection, but I know you have failed.

FLANÍ: Most certainly.

DARAG: Most certainly you have failed? Or most certainly you know that I know?

FLANÍ: I'm waiting.

DARAG: For?

FLANÍ: Syntax, Darag.

DARAG: You see. I've emptied the cart for you, Flaní.

FLANÍ: So?

DARAG: Put in what you want me to take on the streets.

FLANÍ: I thought you had given up on the mushrooms.

DARAG: Don't try to hide. This is a test. We'll put some of your things in here. You'll take off that robe. No, on second thought, fasten the robe to your person. It makes you you, Flaní. [*He starts to load some of* FLANÍ'S *paintings.*] I could use some help.

FLANÍ: Could you continue without hands? [FLANÍ *opens and shows a knife.*]

DARAG: Ah, we're getting serious.

FLANÍ: Put them back.

[DARAG *does.*]

DARAG: You wouldn't use that knife, would you, Flaní?

FLANÍ: I noticed it was a syllogism you didn't want to test.

DARAG: So much like you, my man. We have this moment when something strange could have happened.

FLANÍ: We have it, or it went past. Make up your mind.

DARAG: I mean, there you go. It was right upon us. And you, you little coward, let it slip through. If you've got no more regard for these things than that, then give me the fucking knife.

FLANÍ: Darag. That's the first time I've ever heard you swear.

DARAG: Then you haven't been listening. Swear!? Swear!? What's swear? Evasive Flaní. Admit it. You don't have the guts to use that knife.

[FLANÍ *picks up a painting, and cuts it to shreds.*]

Bravo. The artist-assassin.

FLANÍ: What did you say?

DARAG: I said you had awakened.

FLANÍ: No. Those words. The rhythm. The intonation. You can't leave it like that.

DARAG: Leave what like what?

FLANÍ: The moment. It did not happen.

DARAG: A proposition, *mein engel*. Put the canvas in the cart, and I'll dispose of it for you. No one will know that for one moment you had a true creative impulse. Call it a bargain, if you prefer.

FLANÍ: Get out of my yard.

DARAG: Friends, Flaní wants to chase me from the universe. I'm beginning to feel like an orphan. Between you and your twin Vigilius, I'll be run out of every corner of the village. *A propósito, niño...*

FLANÍ: Stop it!

DARAG: Stop what?

FLANÍ: This mimickry. Do you think I'm blind?

DARAG: Blind?

FLANÍ: Deaf. Insensitive. Choose any word you want. Darag wants to play with my light, to pretend he sees what I see. To call out! In the voice he thinks he hears inside him.

DARAG: That is Vigilius to the core.

FLANÍ: How would you know?

DARAG: Absolutely. How would I know? You have to believe in, and be susceptible to, a certain alienation. Until this evening, I wouldn't have thought you were capable of that.

FLANÍ: You do now, is that it?

DARAG: A minute of danger, and he begins to preen. I blame Vigilius for that. He bats you around a bit, talks tough, acts like a Fifth Circuit Appeals judge, then you and he make this pact to present you as an Olympian. Cozy. But it won't work. Your innocence is showing.

FLANÍ: My innocence.

DARAG: You doubt me? Look around you. Sweet things. [*He randomly chooses two or three paintings he lifts, gestures toward, and drops.*] Oh, you've learned the rough edge and crankiness of curving lines, the homely simplicity of broken things. They're all dressed in familiar garments, too familiar perhaps. Here we have it. Winter is summer, and fall is spring. It makes no difference what these ladies put on at any hour.

FLANÍ: You've just betrayed your eye, Darag. Why should I care what you think of my work?

DARAG: I don't give a damn about your work. I'm looking for the art in it. It seems to me you've betrayed that. Oh, give us a break, Flaní. Take your knife, and ravish these canvases. So we don't have to sit through another failure.

FLANÍ: Who the fuck are you?

DARAG: I thought I was your twin. But you're far too voluptuous to have anything to do with me.

FLANÍ: What do you want, Darag?

DARAG: I was about to ask you.

FLANÍ: I want her back.

DARAG: Who? What are you talking about?

FLANÍ: You think you saw her in the canvas. You were mistaken. That was another fiction. Mine, or yours, it doesn't matter now. She was never there; she was only here. Up there, in the light. And your avatar disrupted that light, to free me, you understand.

DARAG: You're babbling.

FLANÍ: You prefer my silence.

DARAG: God, no. That would be too revealing. You've hidden yourself very well with these. [*He indicates the paintings.*] That disturbs me.

FLANÍ: Abandon me, Darag. Give me up to this voluptuousness you've awarded me.

DARAG: I can stand here until you make sense, Flaní.

FLANÍ: And I will. Leave me. Let me sit here to contemplate the maladroit evil my aesthetician brothers have dreamed up to impose upon me.

DARAG: You don't understand them. They want you to be a success. That would be your most perfect failure.

FLANÍ: Ay, this Augustinian anguish doesn't suit you, Darag. If no one comes, if no one stands admiringly and silently before my "work," if, my god, they come, and walk away with their hands in their pockets, talking of Michelangelo, have I failed?

DARAG: I'm glad I came. You can forgive the cart's obsession. You can even forgive that I remind you of the things you've put away. *¿Verdad?* But I won't let you walk away from the one thing that will make your art true.

FLANÍ: And that is?

DARAG: Its offense. Its absolute imperfection.

FLANÍ: I'm talking to a fool.

DARAG: You seem preoccupied. Where was she, did you say? Up there, in the light? How far up? Let's be specific. My god, everything else around here is helter-skelter. So, if a man has a vision, we have to be damned exact about whether that vision occurred. *N'est-ce pas?* [*He positions* FLANÍ.] Stand here. I'll step it off. [*He begins to do so.*]

FLANÍ: Stop it!

DARAG: I'm trying to help.

FLANÍ: You never forget, do you, Darag? This flimsy cabaret turn is your way of getting even. All right. I conjured you. *Spérate.* I summoned you. Summon. Your Gaelic heart ought to rise to that. *Tais-toi.* Your Provençal bones. But you have been privily reminded, if not admonished in the very tongue of your Augustine. So, you will have to make sport of my dreaming, as you call it, and light of the light I have buried here. [*He points at his paintings.*] He looks astonished. Certainly, I understood your petition, Darag.

DARAG: You're very good. "What we cannot speak about we must pass over in silence."

FLANÍ: Ah, but Darag, everything happens as it does happen. And now you're asking me to forget that this sitting [*He nods toward the place where the woman sat.*] did happen.

DARAG: Oh, no, Flaní. I'm asking you to measure the time. And to tell me when these [*He indicates the paintings.*] infants came into being.

[*Small bells tinkle in the distance.*]

FLANÍ: What's that?

DARAG: A celebration somewhere. [*Pause.*] Then we are agreed.

[FLANÍ *laughs.*]

Then we ought to agree. You do see the necessity of replacing the women. For a start.

FLANÍ: Of course, Darag. I'll include your mother.

DARAG: *Miren, señores, me mentó la madre.*

FLANÍ: Your mother is the model for my work.

[DARAG *puts a hold on* FLANÍ.]

DARAG: We don't want to get too frisky now, do we, boy?

FLANÍ: I had no idea you were so itchy about your ma.

DARAG: Leave that. We were on our way to saying what we can do to spill some aestheticians' blood.

FLANÍ: You're one of them, Darag. Why do you want to involve me in this family business?

DARAG: Tell me I haven't made a mistake, Flaní. I read your power. I see what they want from you. Listen to me. They see your strength. They know you can't make up your mind. They will cradle you.

FLANÍ: You will cradle me.

DARAG: They.

FLANÍ: You're one of them.

DARAG: I am not. I have eyes.

FLANÍ: Why should you betray them for me? Give me a reason, Darag.

DARAG: Syntax, Flaní.

[FLANÍ *walks toward the stone, looks away.*]

FLANÍ: Are you going to wait here with me, Darag? I mean, for the reconciliation. Which was on the books before your Peca appeared.

DARAG: How do you know her name?

FLANÍ: You told me your name.

DARAG: I'm talking to a fool.

FLANÍ: Exactly. And you have persuaded me to set fire to the gallery, and to let it burn with everything in it.

DARAG: Logical Flaní. It's not what I had in mind.

FLANÍ: What did you have in mind?

DARAG: A reconciliation that would make you strange. I trust you will find that hidden canvas, and hang it.

FLANÍ: You almost managed it. You and Vigilius. These little ascetic pilgrimages. He turns up, begging me to give up my secrets, to him, if to no one else. So would I, or could I? Of course, I could, if I had a secret. It doesn't matter. He wants me to invent one, one that he has already divined. Well, I say to myself, what's the point? This secret would be better off inventing itself, and having nothing to do with me. So I refused, Darag. I tell you I refused. Vigilius rumbles into despair; he gives up his vigil. Appropriately, I tell you. Now here you are, begging me to conceal my secret by singing it in the streets.

DARAG: Berkeley. Right?

FLANÍ: You said your name was Peca. Or did I make a mistake?

DARAG: Get back in your womb. Go to sleep. I leave you to yourself. I must tell you, Flaní. I am often civilly disobedient. I sometimes can't trust my judgment. [*He throws the goods he brought into the wheelbarrow, and leaves in a quiet fury.*]

FLANÍ: [*Calling.*] Be careful of the celebration. [*Pause.*] He bragged about his perfect pitch. Why should his failures disturb me? I will get back in my womb. [*He climbs on the stone.*] What was that song? Or was it a prayer? Their bodies made everything too apparent. You can see that the light doesn't do much for these infants, as Darag calls them. Why does he think I sit here so much in the dark? Did he ask me that? Or is that a question I dreamed he asked? I remember now. I was the one asking the questions. Judgment. They're filled, all of them, with this absolutely irrelevant speech. They wake up with their clocks, their quartz, their crystal beads. Where is my imagination? I'm buried in my ignorance. Oh, you want to talk about an inharmonious body? Speak to me. Walk where the light is a skeleton of an irrecoverable body. That is my design.

[*Several men and women, dressed in various shades of disrepair and party dress, burst on the scene. Some have musical instruments, seemingly homemade; some play the bells we have heard. They have remnants of food and drink. They dance around the stone, and appear to ignore* FLANÍ.]

Marvelous. Did you get rid of him?

[*The celebrants carry on at a higher pitch.*]

I'm not asking for an invitation. I only want the answer to my question.

[*A man, wearing a shaggy ruana, signals a halt to the music and speech.*]

BRAUCH: We're not interested in your question.

FLANÍ: So, you *do* speak.

BRAUCH: What did you expect?

FLANÍ: I expected nothing. I like to be astonished.

BRAUCH: I hate the Gallic sound of that.

FLANÍ: Gallic? Or Gaelic? Or the complementary instant of a history you seem concerned to celebrate?

BRAUCH: Proud of your ingenuity, aren't you?

FLANÍ: Do you refer to the ingenuity, or the pride?

BRAUCH: I refer to the knot I'm going to put on your head in a minute.

FLANÍ: Whoa. A citizen of Cananea. I once played ball with a catcher from Cananea. Great one for blocking the plate. But you really don't understand that, do you?

BRAUCH: We're very much underwhelmed here, counselor. You're wasting your breath.

FLANÍ: I should have known. Well, you're only passing through, so it doesn't really matter, does it?

BRAUCH: We were thinking of settling for the night.

FLANÍ: Here?

BRAUCH: Why not? You've got space. You're very much alone. Unprotected.

FLANÍ: Do I need protection?

BRAUCH: It was just an observation. Look, we seem to have disturbed you. We beg your forgiveness, your indulgence, and permission to continue on our revels. If it so pleases you.

FLANÍ: You want, of course, to please me.

BRAUCH: I see you haven't forgiven me.

FLANÍ: What do these others say?

BRAUCH: Oh, they play as I play. You're looking at a world of experience, my man. What do you think? Just because you catch us on a night out, you think we're frivolous? You think we have no concern with what's going on out here? Sealed away from our own experience? Don't insult us.

FLANÍ: Oh, bravo.

BRAUCH: You need convincing. [*He gestures for two people from his group.*] Give him the Sprites from *Don Perlimplín.*

[*They begin to arrange themselves to do the scene.*]

FLANÍ: Just a minute. Do I look foolish?

BRAUCH: I'm talking to a fool.

FLANÍ: What did you say?

BRAUCH: What you heard. Now, can we go on? You will enjoy this. One of your own indigenous dramaturgs persistently copies the form. In countless variations, of course. But you're not going to sanction borrowing, even a little thievery. I trust my eye. What I see here [*Indicating the paintings.*] is thievery of a high order.

FLANÍ: No one accuses me of that.

BRAUCH: It was just an observation. Can we continue?

FLANÍ: What are you, then? A patchwork circus?

BRAUCH: Oh, my. I had no idea you were so itchy about your ma.

FLANÍ: Who are you?

BRAUCH: Brauch. [*Pointing indiscriminately at the others.*] Simeon, David, Asuo, Solange, Rafael, Pilar, etcetera, etcetera. I'm sorry it took us so long to make you comfortable. So. What can we do to compensate?

FLANÍ: Pack out.

BRAUCH: Impossible. The event has started. That's not too difficult for you, is it? That conception of rhythm? Ah, but then we're getting into microinstants, the presence of the past, and the ever-delayed arrival of the future. We can't have that. There is such a thing as form. Or should I say decorum? Even a physicist has to pay attention to his manners. We are ready, if you are.

[FLANÍ *grabs the bells.*]

FLANÍ: Wake up!

BRAUCH: I see that you're not ready to give up on Darag and Vigilius.

FLANÍ: What?

BRAUCH: Their demands…

FLANÍ: What do you know about their demands?

BRAUCH: God, counselor, you're wearing that form of inquiry pretty thin. What do you know? What does he know? What does anybody know? Questions like that make no sense. The answers always lie outside the form of the question. Certainly, an old gnostic like you understands that.

FLANÍ: You were addressing Darag's and Vigilius's demands.

BRAUCH: Ah, yes, he's intrigued.

[*The other people pair off, and disperse themselves around the area. The women sit, silently and still, in lotus position. The men revolve in place, alternately regarding and turning away from the women.* BRAUCH *approaches* FLANÍ, *becomes intimate.*]

Listen. They think you're incapable of anger. So one encourages you to submit your fragile soul to that river that never runs dry, and the other wants to take away the river, or take *you* away from the river, or dig a bed for a new river. What do you think, Flaní? Don't you have anything to do with this story?

FLANÍ: What are these people doing?

BRAUCH: Rehearsing. Do you mind?

FLANÍ: Get them up!

[BRAUCH *gestures. The others begin a frenzied dance upon and around the stone.*]

Get them away from the granite.

BRAUCH: Speak to them yourself. [*Pause.*] I know what disturbs you. She wasn't there. You took her out of the painting; she took you out of the story. Fair bargain. New form. Don't you agree?

[*A woman comes forward, babbling to* FLANÍ.]

FLANÍ: What is she saying?

BRAUCH: How do I know? This is your domain.

FLANÍ: She's one of yours.

BRAUCH: He! He gives her to me. He enslaves her. So you learned your lesson from Darag. Or was it Vigilius who taught you? Be that as it may. You're not the man who welcomed us.

FLANÍ: I haven't changed.

BRAUCH: Deny it all you might. I can feel the wind. Companions, we are no longer welcome. Our services are no longer required.

[*The people effect a slow dance of disdain around* FLANÍ.]

You see what you've done to yourself.

FLANÍ: Did I summon you?

BRAUCH: Please. Give no credit for grace. We heard your heart speaking. Forgive this medieval insistence, this romantic flare we've never been able to shed.

FLANÍ: What if you stayed? If you settled for the night, and we got to know each other?

BRAUCH: Such arrogance. You're proposing a mystery. Of course, we already know you. We do know the terms of inquiry, all that you have failed to decide.

[*The people clear a space. They place a blanket, food and a bottle of wine.* BRAUCH *speaks to* FLANÍ.]

Sit. A most favored audience.

[FLANÍ *is established.*]

Now, give us license for something rare. The unforgiving and true celebration of your art. We'll need one of your paintings. You choose.

FLANÍ: For what?

BRAUCH: So we can tell your story.

FLANÍ: That's not what art is.

BRAUCH: Did you say *my* art? Come on, enter into the spirit here. There's such playfulness in what I see about me. You're not ashamed, are you?

FLANÍ: Why should I be ashamed? *Flaní fecit.*

BRAUCH: Oh, that's good. Give yourself a little weight by turning to the Latin tongue. Then, it's settled. You'll play. Choose.

FLANÍ: There's a misunderstanding here. I have no evidence of your art. I mean to say I've never seen you and your colleagues perform. It doesn't matter, does it? I mean you do whatever it is you do, and then there's my art. And, I mean, even you can see that they do not marry.

BRAUCH: What nonsense. I thought you had more imagination.

FLANÍ: Well, if we're talking about imagination…

BRAUCH: Exactly.

[*Another woman sensuously approaches Flaní.*]

WIDOW TWO: *Lo que me duele…*

BRAUCH: Not yet.

WIDOW ONE: Let her go on.

BRAUCH: When we set the scene.

GAUCHO ONE: We have set the scene.

GAUCHO TWO: Let this pretender give us something to work with. Can he?

[*The first woman slaps a painting before* BRAUCH.]

WIDOW ONE: We'll start with this one.

ALL THE OTHERS: Imaginative.

WIDOW TWO: Does the painter approve?

FLANÍ: Of what?

BRAUCH: Our interpretation.

FLANÍ: You haven't even begun…

GAUCHO ONE: I sense a small taste of fear.

WIDOW TWO: Such timidity for one who's wearing his own robes.

WIDOW ONE: Perhaps the canvas isn't ready.

GAUCHO TWO: Exactly. Put up something with more flair.

GAUCHO ONE: It's not the quality of the painting. One can see that they're all fulsomely done. It's the nature of the spirit made manifest.

[*The second woman mockingly laughs.*]

WIDOW TWO: *Toma tu...*

BRAUCH: None of that. Respect for those who respect our resources.

FLANÍ: I knew you were frauds.

BRAUCH: That's one way out of the fix you've got yourself in.

FLANÍ: Go on, Brauch. Tell my story.

BRAUCH: Well, then, I will dispose my resources.

FLANÍ: You've already begun on the wrong foot. Dispose. Why should I trust you, when you don't know the difference between dispose and distribute?

BRAUCH: A *petit magister*! Very good. You quarrel with the disposition of your disingenuous flummery. What's your motive, my man? Or is your motive that there is no motive, and we have exposed you?

FLANÍ: You're the one responsible for this *choricera*.

BRAUCH: "That's sides and hearts."

FLANÍ: Clear this space.

[*The first woman faces* FLANÍ, *and rings a small bell in his face.*]

BRAUCH: I think this space will submit to a correction.

[*The woman again shakes the bell. Each of the others approaches* FLANÍ, *bows, and places an offering before or around him.*]

FLANÍ: What is this?

BRAUCH: What do you think? A teapot of coins to buy your way up the mountain. You wanted that, didn't you?

FLANÍ: [*Rising.*] This is ridiculous.

BRAUCH: Sit down, or I'll let these wolves devour you.

[FLANÍ *hesitates, then sits.*]

Teach this nigger the lotus position.

FLANÍ: That's about enough!

BRAUCH: First, you get itchy about your ma, and then you get upset over a simple linguistic designation. A rigid designator. Haven't you learned anything?

FLANÍ: Oh, you have no idea what I've learned, Brauch. Send these others away, and we can have a private session, unraveling certain physical problems.

BRAUCH: Lotus!

[GAUCHO ONE *roughly seats* FLANÍ, *and puts him in the lotus position.*]

I'm talking about peace. Balance. Depth. Silence. You have to understand this. Don't you, Flaní?

FLANÍ: I notice that the performance seems to have come to an end.

BRAUCH: Yes, yes. The evolving judgment. That small bit of empathy that had begun to surface. We thought of it as a rescue. *¿No es verdad?* He won't answer. All right. We continue.

[*The others begin a disjointed rhythm, at times embracing each other, at times standing rigidly apart from each other, walking clockwise and counterclockwise around* FLANÍ, *almost approaching a collective dance. They speak as they move. All speak at once.*]

GAUCHO ONE: He came out of the corner of existence. The property depends upon the point of departure. Leave it all there.

WIDOW ONE: *Exegeomai.* Do not repeat my song. All is conceivable. Construct me.

WIDOW TWO: Instruct me. The world remains. Rational. A dialogue as such. Nothing is felt. Faustus becomes felted.

GAUCHO TWO: "It is a property of this number that this process leads to it." The order of recitation. The consecration of the day. *Un pueblo caribeño.*

[BRAUCH *blows a whistle. The people repeat these phrases, each one taking over from someone else.* BRAUCH *blows the whistle.*]

WIDOW TWO: Why should I affirm the consequent? Prayer is invalid. Leave me here. Sign.

GAUCHO TWO: "The proof prescribes carrying out an operation until you reach the point at which it can no longer be performed." No is thunder. Trace.

GAUCHO ONE: *"El fandango es el fandango, / fiestón mestizo..."* What marks the constitution of thought? Sketch.

WIDOW ONE: "Being is unborn and indestructible." I am left-handed, and all things will return to their proper state. The realized design.

[*The people rise to a high pitch, subside, and come to rest.*]

BRAUCH: You're spitting in the wind. He will never understand.

[*The others display razors and knives.*]

WIDOW ONE: Of course, he understands this.

BRAUCH: Test him, then.

GAUCHO TWO: We have tested him.

BRAUCH: Ah, Cambridge. I recognize the manner. But I assure you that you have not examined our *fabbro*. The man is a gnostic, after all. He thinks he can illumine that instant of becoming.

WIDOW TWO: I thought we had agreed.

BRAUCH: Upon what?

WIDOW TWO: There is no becoming.

BRAUCH: Step away from that mysticism.

WIDOW ONE: Put away the instruments. I think we have misconstrued our *fabbro*. I remind you of what he was doing when we came upon him. Sitting on that rock, savoring the sugar of his own death. He doesn't want an exposition. Why should we liberate him?

WIDOW TWO: [*Approaching* FLANÍ.] Is that true, *liebchen*?

GAUCHO ONE: Brauch.

BRAUCH: Leave her be.

GAUCHO ONE: It's the intention.

BRAUCH: Intention. Invention. You speak to him then, *magister*. Probe him. Undress him.

GAUCHO TWO: I swear I think you think he's innocent.

BRAUCH: God, man, I know damned well that I am. I've given you time to make your case.

WIDOW ONE: [*Beginning to pack.*] The rooster done crowed. We've run out of fun.

GAUCHO ONE: Two of a kind. Unless the bitch wants to abandon him.

BRAUCH: We've gone through that.

GAUCHO ONE: Not yet.

GAUCHO TWO: Curious. One mystic wants to defend our *fabbro*.

WIDOW TWO: These gauchos are blind.

GAUCHO ONE: I resent this chorus of justification. The man is a thief. Look carefully. What do you see? Evidence of things he couldn't possibly have seen, things he couldn't possibly know.

FLANÍ: [*Crowing.*] Can I be excused from this witches' sabbath?

WIDOW ONE: You haven't answered the question.

FLANÍ: I didn't know there was a question.

GAUCHO TWO: Smart. You take what we've given you. You plaster it there. And then you parade around and flog it for a couple of crullers. I wouldn't mind, Jim. But look at what we have here. Is any of it true to me?

WIDOW ONE: Righteous. Ask me about him. Talk about being unfaithful.

WIDOW TWO: *Seguro.* Look at what he did to her.

FLANÍ: Who gets the final say here?

BRAUCH: What nonsense. Who gets the final say? Take away this nigger's card. Good god, man, don't you know that the only reason we let you go on disfiguring us is that we know you'll never finish.

FLANÍ: I will stand. I will get back in my womb, if that satisfies you. I never expected you to understand. But at least I thought there would be room for a perfect misunderstanding that would allow each of us to live.

BRAUCH: Quit begging, man.

GAUCHO ONE: [*Indicating the paintings.*] What do we do with these?

BRAUCH: Let them live.

WIDOW ONE: Only under our terms.

FLANÍ: So that's it. A rogue's game of intimidation. But it will never work with them. Your play. Burn them, if you dare.

GAUCHO TWO: Don't be brave.

WIDOW TWO: Shouldn't we offer him some compensation, some comfort?

WIDOW ONE: I protest. We have done better by him than Darag or Vigilius.

GAUCHO ONE: *Certo*, they had no life here.

BRAUCH: You see how it is, counselor. I brought them here in the spirit of inquiry. Prepared, nevertheless, to celebrate whatever was, or is, worth celebrating. But we find you depressed by your own liberation. How can we save you? No, no. Notice that I didn't ask how you could save us. So my colleagues have corrected me, and we have come to a still moment. Wouldn't you say?

FLANÍ: I would prefer silence.

BRAUCH: Don't. Don't. There's no place for that, now.

FLANÍ: Brauch, Brauch. We've created the space for an awakening. [*He approaches* BRAUCH *to whisper.*] Listen. They think you're incapable of beauty. But you, my pilgrim, have reminded me of perfection.

BRAUCH: As I say, proud of your ingenuity.

FLANÍ: So you refuse?

BRAUCH: Refuse what?

FLANÍ: To defend me.

BRAUCH: If you had asked me to defend that imperfection...

GAUCHO TWO: Are we going?

BRAUCH: [*To* FLANÍ.] You see the case.

[FLANÍ *suddenly raises his voice.*]

FLANÍ: My house is open! I forgive your blindness. You are welcome to stay here. I remind you that it is awfully dark out there to be starting off. Unless, of course, you know the way. And I sincerely doubt that you do.

WIDOW ONE: Look at him, posing and threatening.

WIDOW TWO: Was there a bargain on the books? I suggest we rescind our offer.

GAUCHO TWO: Are we going?

BRAUCH: [*To* GAUCHO ONE.] You, my gaucho, what do you say?

WIDOW ONE: Are we leaving it to him?

BRAUCH: A perfect balance, my widow. We don't want to give this pilgrim [*Pointing at* FLANÍ.] the idea that we have failed.

GAUCHO ONE: *Vamonós.* The man himself is blind.

BRAUCH: All right, Flaní. Remember, all goodbyes ain't gone. You might hear our footsteps, or see our shadows, around your house.

[BRAUCH *and his people gather their material, and go belling away.*]

FLANÍ: So the sprites from *Don Perlimplín* escaped, or never appeared. This would be a good time to recall them. A moment to reflect, if reflection is necessary. Take the line from that horizon to my right big toe. I breathe, and my clavicle understands. Take the line from this stone to the bell-sound in the valley. I breathe, and my liver awakens. Line following line along a boundary that disappears. Act upon act, an argument performed in isolation. I ask these sprites, where does the granite go? I wonder if that silly dramaturg can put me back in the womb, where I will wait, until I feather and flutter from the world I have made my own.

[*He climbs back on the stone. Pause.* VIGILIUS *and* DARAG *come creeping, looking around. They do not sense* FLANÍ; *he seems sometimes vaguely aware and sometimes unconscious of them.*]

DARAG: Under the best of circumstances this seems absurd.

VIGILIUS: You're the one says he has a secret.

DARAG: He's holding out, yes. I know he has a canvas to which he attaches a special importance. Will he show it? Oh, no. That is the one he has locked away. Now, why is that?

VIGILIUS: How do you know about this canvas?

DARAG: I keep my eyes and ears open.

VIGILIUS: Darag, you see this mistletoe…?

DARAG: Stop. I won't let you violate yourself by being so flamboyantly archaic. Intuition, Vigilius. There's a deep hurt in Flaní. Even you can feel it. Can't you?

VIGILIUS: Stop. I won't let you…

DARAG: I'm sorry, Vigilius. I realize that this talk about intuition, this *geistige* intimidation, offends you. You'd really like to be very much closer to Flaní than you are. Of course, you see the danger in that.

VIGILIUS: I sense an accusation.

DARAG: God, you'd think you were the one floating in this orbit. Too sensitive, Vigilius. What am I proposing, the cult of Flaní, with the high priest, Vigilius, sitting in state? You, or should I say, we, have been perhaps too close to that stifling orbit we call the circle of aestheticians.

VIGILIUS: Well, now. What is it about this stone, this granite? We come around it, and all of a sudden we're schoolboys at confession.

DARAG: Speak, Vigilius. So there is occasion for confession?

VIGILIUS: Such treachery. What is this?

DARAG: A delicious understanding of a power you didn't know they would give you.

VIGILIUS: Who is this they?

DARAG: Why, us.

VIGILIUS: Then you are part of that danger.

DARAG: Will you have me, Vigilius?

VIGILIUS: I don't have the patience for this.

DARAG: Exactly. And that's my point. Touch the air here, Vigilius. Feel it.

It's Flaní's breath, turbulent, almost blue with its desire. A nice touch, that? The tight apprehension of blue, or the white of that woman's dress. The one Flaní claims to have conjured.

VIGILIUS: He didn't make her up.

DARAG: Of course, he didn't. He needs her. And so, it seems, do you. And there's the danger. Your presence is just a small taste of contamination. This formal necessity escapes you. You have to see that your growing attachment to Flaní's limbo, if such there be, can only destroy the logic of his art.

VIGILIUS: This is ridiculous.

DARAG: Think about your own restlessness, Vigilius.

VIGILIUS: What about yours?

DARAG: I sense an accusation. I could have come here alone. I could find that secret canvas. I could remove it, and everything would remain just as it is, obscure. You would come along later, and you would find some way to take credit for this disaster.

VIGILIUS: Syntax, Darag.

DARAG: Was I talking about anything that you could measure?

VIGILIUS: Give me a minute, I'll come up with her name.

DARAG: Ah, my friend, I left her back there at the crossroads.

VIGILIUS: It won't work. Peca, wasn't it?

DARAG: Which fiction did you mean, Vigilius?

VIGILIUS: Peca. Yes, it was Peca, But you never spoke with her. She came too late to be considered a part of this domain. So you try to turn her into that fiction of a white dress that you have conjured, and cast upon the doorstep of our very own Flaní. And then you threaten me with some outrageous desert proposal—Disappear, Vigilius; consider the time, consider time dispensed, consider the lovely execution of time as the perfect reconciliation. They frighten you, don't they? The women. They have that way of lingering, the way that he does. Those folk are comfortable with each other. They understand the accidental pleasures of Flaní's existence.

DARAG: Lord, help us. A damned philosopher. Then riddle me this. Vigilius gives rise to Darag, and Darag gives rise to Vigilius, as Peca gives rise to the woman in white, and the woman in white gives rise to Peca. Then must Vigilius give rise to the woman in white, etcetera, and Peca give rise to Darag, etcetera? Where is the balance?

VIGILIUS: Darag would be a gnostic. Flaní, where are you at this hour?

DARAG: Flaní. Flaní. This is our world, Vigilius, not the world of some half-assed gnostic who can't make up his mind.

VIGILIUS: Oh, Darag, prove to me that you have intelligence of these women.

DARAG: It's quite obvious. You're the one, after all, who pointed out the absence.

VIGILIUS: I was looking for an explanation. Why did she disappear? There was the fact that she wasn't there. There was the fact that she was there. Did Flaní understand this? Why was he giving us this different world? You have to understand that, Darag.

DARAG: And Peca?

VIGILIUS: Peca is your concern. I've never touched her.

DARAG: There. I caught you. You won't play in Flaní's little mystery. You'd rather walk away from that silence, that prepared field. How can you ask for an explanation, when the only one Flaní can give is that Peca saw the woman sitting there?

VIGILIUS: Flaní never said that.

DARAG: What did he say?

VIGILIUS: Nothing. That's the damnable quality of it.

DARAG: There's no quality in silence.

VIGILIUS: Speak of contradiction!

DARAG: No. Let him speak.

VIGILIUS: I will! [*He walks about, scattering paintings.*]

DARAG: Finished?

VIGILIUS: What did we hope to find?

DARAG: Some imaginary proposition, a momentary agreement upon the size of Flaní's big toe. Coming?

VIGILIUS: You go. I'm ashamed of this mess.

DARAG: You want help?

VIGILIUS: No.

DARAG: *Ciao.*

[DARAG *goes.* VIGILIUS *begins to reorder the paintings. The woman in white is suddenly above him, silently and sternly observing him.*]

VIGILIUS: Let's not begin with magic. Right? This is a useful proposition. You turn up when I'm alone. No warning. Just there you are. What you hope to accomplish is beyond me, assuming that you could possibly care about purpose. Don't think I'm going to ask you to forgive me. Not yet. I have to be sure that I have the right body. I have to tell you that I'm only pretending to recognize you. You are not she. And it isn't that I'm confusing the space. It's most apparent that you do not fit. I trust my eye. I trust the sensation that tells me I'm in the presence of some one, or some thing familiar. So you see, there's really no connection here. And trust me, there will be no explanation for my presence. Oh, I seem to have gone on. Madame, the floor is yours.

[*The woman continues in her mute stillness.*]

Well, I have other things to do. I think I've done my penance here.

[FLANÍ *awakens.*]

FLANÍ: Vigilius? Is that you?

VIGILIUS: Say nothing about what you saw.

[*He rushes off.* FLANÍ *comes down, looks around, turns to see the woman.*]

FLANÍ: What happened to your seat?

WOMAN: You care.

FLANÍ: Well, that's at least a beginning, something between a question and contempt. Point of fact, I do care, and it's lovely to have you speak to me. She's breathless. She thinks I'm going to ask her for an explanation.

WOMAN: You disgust me.

FLANÍ: I wouldn't have thought you'd be so blunt.

WOMAN: Thank you for giving me a chance to come again. Disgust strikes me now as nothing more than a brothel anthem. I need something far more nefarious to do justice to your self-abuse. Help me out, *fabbro*.

FLANÍ: Good, good. My white woman, or the woman in white, has lost her seat. So, of course, there is no place, and, must we say it, no one there. But here is something, a figment, a figure, a fiction, with a voice, and a need to be in command of a moment that escaped it before.

WOMAN: Watch your language, blind man.

FLANÍ: Gor', she's so insensitive she thinks I'm blind.

WOMAN: I have a suggestion. In this interview, can we keep to I and you?

FLANÍ: Disastrous. Now you've lost your grammar.

WOMAN: Stop the pretense. You know that I'm talking about a logical domain.

FLANÍ: Point of order. You're talking about order, and I refuse.

WOMAN: I could have assaulted you in your sleep. But I waited until you awakened, so you could contest this self-pity you display. *Tais-toi.* I'm bringing you news from Buenos Aires.

FLANÍ: Now I know where we've met. In a raunchy little café in the Colonia Roma, near Salamanca. It was a political discussion with Tico and that Venezolano and, Beatriz, was it? You had nothing to say. Sat there in your white summer dress, and kept referring to some doctor in Cuernavaca.

WOMAN: Typical. You've got it all wrong.

FLANÍ: Correct me.

WOMAN: I was never in Mexico.

FLANÍ: I put you there.

WOMAN: Syntax, Flaní. You remember me there? Or you need me there, and have created a space for my body, as you have here?

FLANÍ: Why should I need you?

WOMAN: I thought perhaps you could tell me. Why don't you take off that robe? You're ridiculous. Undress. I won't look.

FLANÍ: You've broken your rule.

WOMAN: And how, *maestro*, have I done that?

FLANÍ: By dressing me.

WOMAN: Nay, sir, I have only introduced a form of *autenticité* into our interview.

FLANÍ: This isn't Buenos Aires, you know. You should be doing something about getting used to our vernacular.

WOMAN: *A propósito…*

FLANÍ: That woman is blind!

WOMAN: Our rule, Flaní.

FLANÍ: Our rule says pay attention to what you see before you, to what you see all around you. My art.

WOMAN: Ah, the music of it.

FLANÍ: You're being obscene.

WOMAN: I'm being exact. There's only this moment in which we can do that. [*Pause. She makes a move toward her breast.*] I have a *fleur-de-lys*.

FLANÍ: So?

WOMAN: It means I've always been in motion. Even at that moment in the Laurentians when you tried to kiss me. I say nothing about your doodling insipidities at the Dieu du Ciel in Montreal. Derrida had just inflamed UQAM, and had set his sights on McGill.

FLANÍ: I suppose I'm to applaud your deep well of experience. But I know you're lying. Peca put you up to this, didn't she? Where is your pride?

WOMAN: They will be back, you know. The ones who had the hard questions you refused to answer. They were astute enough not to go off on that rabbit hunt, looking for my absence. Think of it. Looking for an absence! Wait for it, they'll hammer you to the cross.

FLANÍ: Watch your language, you witch!

WOMAN: You have no cause. [*She walks to the stone, sits daintily upon it.*] This is granite. You did say, granite? Correct. I thought you had forgotten why we are here. You can see that I'm asking you to defend the evidence of my attention, or my attention, which is evidence enough for the attention you have paid…Well, I was telling you about my *fleur-de-lys*.

FLANÍ: She said there was no evidence for your compassion.

WOMAN: She might have been mistaken.

FLANÍ: She said that you were.

WOMAN: Who do you want to believe? One who just walked away, following the soul on the right? Or one who has the perfect temper for solitude? I'm asking you to recognize the difference.

FLANÍ: Why, that's Vigilius to the letter.

WOMAN: Such laziness. Do you refer to the texture of my voice?

FLANÍ: Not at all. There's only that quality of silence.

WOMAN: Evasiveness will not decorate this grave. Indulge me, *fabbro*. Show me the occasion for what I see all around me.

FLANÍ: Don't be silly. There's no occasion for this life. That's Vigilius. He can only see a little contraction that comes out of dead things, a small shift in the light's coursing. You tell me that you are all motion, a body surfacing from a music that never ceases. These others think that you belong to me.

WOMAN: Ridiculous!

FLANÍ: I argued with them. Look, I said, at her foot. Would I have made it so true to a snail's shell? Look at her head. Would I have made it so true to a hemlock? So I determined to insist that there is no occasion for this vision. Do you think that satisfies Vigilius, Darag? No. They have married your non-existence to my art.

[*The woman slowly and mockingly applauds.*]

WOMAN: What a performance! *A propósito*, I hear you're going around talking about the *performance* of your canvases.

FLANÍ: You wouldn't understand.

WOMAN: School me.

FLANÍ: I beg your forgiveness for the contrariety of that expression. But I have no intention of interrupting the performance, as you have so astonishingly noticed.

WOMAN: Fine. I notice that you have put…Oh, excuse me. Have we admitted that word into our theory? Silence. All right. Put. A yellow sun in a yellow sky.

FLANÍ: Sky is only an interpretation.

WOMAN: Forget that. Whatever happened to a white egg on a white background?

FLANÍ: You must have picked that up from some gigolo in Texas.

WOMAN: And here we have a black stairway; leading nowhere in particular, crowned by a brownish eruption we might call a light.

FLANÍ: Can we put a stop to this?

WOMAN: That word again.

FLANÍ: Are we talking about my painting, or holding a seminar in semantics?

WOMAN: I thought we were watching the performance of your canvases.

FLANÍ: Why, you're just Vigilius in drag.

WOMAN: Is that the case? The set of all confusions. Strike that. Call them permutations. Much better. And they would fit the radiant wave or particle flush of your canvases. Oh, *niño*, don't wrinkle so. *Ven.* [*She makes a place for him beside her on the stone.*] We can comfort each other.

FLANÍ: No, thank you.

WOMAN: I'll take off my dress, and lay it here on the stone. What's the problem? You were ready to do it for her. Down with the goblet, out with the wine. You were hot to trot, I'll tell you.

FLANÍ: I was doing it for you.

WOMAN: Good. Here I am.

FLANÍ: *Pas exactement.* Your semblance is there.

WOMAN: Shall I show you my leg?

FLANÍ: It wouldn't do any good.

WOMAN: My heart? My spirit? Is there anything that would engage you in this moment? Speak to me. Or better still, come here and touch me.

FLANÍ: I have a morning to address. Your touch would be an impediment to my speech.

WOMAN: My god, a Propertian painter! [*Calling.*] Peca! Peca!

FLANÍ: What are you doing?

WOMAN: I thought she had purged you. Oh, I'm sorry. I forget. You didn't lie with her. The aesthetics of this womb frightened you away. Silly me, I had unraveled my theory. There, that makes you feel better, doesn't it? But I would really like to have you come closer, and touch me.

FLANÍ: Another proof.

WOMAN: Exactly.

FLANÍ: You know I have no delicacy when it comes to my materials.

WOMAN: I've seen the evidence. [*Pause.*] Do you think I sit well here?

FLANÍ: Where?

WOMAN: On the stone, of course. I mean, do I belong? Or is there something out of phase? A line that has no color in it, a color without a curve. Oh, you know what I mean. After all, you conjured, me.

FLANÍ: Stop it.

WOMAN: I will not. I will not. I'm delirious with being you up here. Seeing with your eyes. And feeling the heart almost stop because the woman wants something from me I cannot give.

FLANÍ: Oh, what a masquerade.

WOMAN: Perfect. You caught me singing. So, as a reward, I will take off my mask. And you will design me on this stone just as my mother left me. Oh, I forgot. I'm talking with *il fabbro*. That scuttles any talk of mothers. *N'est-ce pas?* [*She climbs off the stone.*] Don't preen yourself. This was a detour. I was on my way to the river with Peca.

FLANÍ: *Que te vaya bien.*

WOMAN: Don't rub it in. [*Walking away, she chants.*]

> "That night a gazelle
> of a girl showed me the sun
> of her cheek and veil
> of auburn hair."

Oh, you will not win, sir, you will not win.

[FLANÍ *does not watch her go, but looks instead at the spot where he first saw her image.*]

FLANÍ: If only I could erase my footsteps. These people come with their promises. Every one a different promise. Each one plays with my skin, scrubs me, and then disappears. Why don't they bathe me in sesame oil? That ought to suit the case. You know, they say that cantankerous dramaturg would enjoy this *choricera*. But even he wouldn't have the guts to deal with this rhythm, arsis and thesis. So what would he do? He'd bring on his little angels, and start them singing. Ignoring, of course, that there is a person who wants to get out of this dancing incivility. Ah, look at it this way. You turn up in Veracruz. You sit still for a moment in the square, have a sandwich, a coffee, light your cigar. You wait for the music and the *danzón*. Old guys, too crippled to walk, display their elegance in the dance. Surely, this is a mistake. Surely, there is nothing they can hope to recover in the square, in the dance. That ought to tell you something. Look at this dancing density I've arranged, here, around this stone. Shouldn't that be breath enough to keep these pilgrims satisfied? No, we start all over, right from the start. The same pilgrims wearing the same red, or black, or white, as blind as ever to that granite. Did I tell you about that granite? It doesn't matter. Can I say that the rhythm has caught you? No, I might as well talk about the biblical Baca swimming in the muddy Rio Grande. Perhaps that's where the woman means to go. What am I waiting for? Nothing as tangible as compassion, humility, grace. You can see, I've made an acceptable existence from the smallest evasions.

[BRAUCH *returns, slightly disheveled.*]

BRAUCH: Do you know a piece of work named Peca? Of course, you do. She was part of that party stranded in Tunisia. Take some advice. Don't let her in the house. She has my widows in my face over some debt she claims I owe her from some gospel show in Newark. Do I look that crazy, to get caught with an office and a van in Newark?

FLANÍ: Why are you telling me this?

BRAUCH: Why shouldn't I tell you? Weren't we whispering consolation to each other the last time I was on the scene?

FLANÍ: Does everybody speak in some linguistic Euclidean geometry?

BRAUCH: That's what my widows say about you.

FLANÍ: What are they doing now, passing for Cantabrigians?

BRAUCH: Oh, it hurts, doesn't it?

FLANÍ: Nothing but make-believe and passing fancy. I don't give a damn what your widows think.

BRAUCH: I suppose you won't want to know what my gauchos say about you.

FLANÍ: I thought your gauchos were the widows, or your widows were your gauchos.

BRAUCH: I won't report that. But I must tell you what my number one gaucho says, sustained, of course, by the other members of our society. In fact, the gauchos agree that you lack *delicadeza*. You would have to adore the image that our principal aesthetician has drawn. You're like a cow, patiently doing her business after a full supper.

[FLANÍ *feigns throwing up.*]

Well, all right, delicacy does admit of degrees.

FLANÍ: And Peca?

BRAUCH: Yes, Peca. She had you in her book.

FLANÍ: Meaning?

BRAUCH: She spoke to me of your redemption.

FLANÍ: That's ridiculous. Why should she speak to you?

BRAUCH: I happened to be there.

FLANÍ: There? Where?

BRAUCH: That is a secret.

[FLANÍ *scoffs.*]

I resent, sir, that you're calling my delicacy into question.

FLANÍ: Not at all, sir. I honor every aesthetician. Certainly, I'm disposed to respect your purity. I see that convocation now. You, Peca, the gauchos, the widows.

BRAUCH: I said nothing about the gauchos and widows. Only Peca and I were there.

FLANÍ: To negotiate my redemption.

BRAUCH: A serious undertaking.

FLANÍ: Shouldn't I have been there?

BRAUCH: You were there?

FLANÍ: An abstract object.

BRAUCH: Nay, sir, you were more like a categorical sentence, like your art.

FLANÍ: Syntax, Brauch.

BRAUCH: You can't avoid me.

FLANÍ: I'm simply trying to avoid Simeon, David, Asuo, Rafael, Pilar, et-cetera, etcetera.

BRAUCH: I admire your recollection. Perhaps that sits as a problem with your art. This facility with recalling things. There. I'm digging my own hole, calling up facility to complicate things.

FLANí: I'm sure your gaucho has a *planc* about that, modulating, of course, into his own bereavement.

BRAUCH: *Tais-toi.* I won't have you playing with us. Do you thank us for our concern? Oh, no, not you. You start a quarrel with your own failings, and then post them in the air for our admiration. You can mock Brauch and Peca, but you cannot, no, you cannot despise our vocation.

FLANí: Leave me!

BRAUCH: Of course not. You need me. I betrayed my widows for you.

FLANí: Impossible.

BRAUCH: How would you know?

FLANí: Why, I was there.

BRAUCH: There? Where?

FLANí: At this convocation for my soul.

BRAUCH: Shouldn't you have said, with my soul? You could have persuaded me that there was a where there. And, most importantly, that you knew what was being saved. I assure you it wasn't this ill-dressed phenomenon I see before me.

FLANí: Why bother with me?

BRAUCH: Wake up. We wouldn't, if you were as inauspicious as you think you are. Ah, this night air curdles my brain. I should have said, autonomous.

FLANí: Don't apologize. The others never do.

BRAUCH: Exactly. So there you have it. We don't ask for anything special. Only the recognition that, if being is one thing and one is another…

FLANí: Proud of your ingenuity, aren't you?

BRAUCH: It's the falling, Yeats.

FLANÍ: Stop this playfulness.

BRAUCH: Damn me, I can't. You have intelligence of our ladies, our widows, Flaní. How would that sit, if I just walked away from their pleasure? You tricked me into betraying them once. But, oh, no, my pilgrim, this time I rest on the side of justice. So tell that to your dramaturg.

FLANÍ: I get it now. You and Peca want to rewrite me, to suit your widows.

BRAUCH: The man is a marvel at turning a handsaw…Go on, give me what I'm missing.

FLANÍ: Why, the whole world, Brauch.

BRAUCH: Strange. In her defense of you, that's what Peca said about you.

FLANÍ: Don't you have an opinion, Brauch?

BRAUCH: All that I can afford is judgment, Flaní.

FLANÍ: All right, then, Brauch. Lend me your eyes. Take a look at the devastation around me. Surely, you see a hand other than mine. Or could I have accomplished this without Vigilius, or Darag? Now, here you are. What' s your offer?

[*The bells start, and approach.*]

Is that Peca?

BRAUCH: Don't be silly.

[*The* WIDOWS *and* GAUCHOS *flow into the space. They carry a bloodied effigy of* FLANÍ, *dressed in filthy rags, and prop it against the stone.*]

WIDOW ONE: Face to face.

WIDOW TWO: Who is who?

GAUCHO ONE: Give him a chance to catch his breath.

GAUCHO TWO: Heaven, give him breath.

GAUCHO ONE: Leave that out of it.

[WIDOW ONE *claps her hands.*]

BRAUCH: *Certo.* This is among the living.

WIDOW TWO: Definition.

GAUCHO ONE: I thought we had decided…

WIDOW ONE: He will decide. Well, *fabbro*. [*Pointing to the effigy.*] Look what this one has made out of himself.

GAUCHO TWO: A terrible composition, if we had let him continue.

WIDOW ONE: That implies that this one is finished.

WIDOW TWO: Definition.

[BRAUCH *goes to* FLANÍ, *trying to pull him aside.*]

BRAUCH: Why didn't you put yourself in my hands? I understand. I understand. I have at times been wounded into silence. I only asked you for trust. Now, look what we have.

FLANÍ: Did you trust me?

BRAUCH: Only your eyes. I see now that was a mistake.

FLANÍ: Call them off.

BRAUCH: Never. We're just beginning to get cozy. Strike that. This is no time for trivial notions. I am one of them. We won't let you go. You hear me? We won't let you go.

[FLANÍ *turns to the others.*]

FLANÍ: What do you want from me?

GAUCHO ONE: Me. Me. He only thinks about himself.

WIDOW ONE: Soft, my gaucho. You can see our *fabbro* is in distress.

WIDOW TWO: And so close to escaping his loneliness.

GAUCHO TWO: His first mistake.

BRAUCH: Yes. Tell us, Flaní, what it's like to be so liberated.

FLANÍ: You can see what I've done.

WIDOW TWO: Put the question to him again.

GAUCHO TWO: We're wasting our time with this one.

GAUCHO ONE: Exactly. Let's burn him.

BRAUCH: Nothing so pure.

WIDOW ONE: He's trembling.

WIDOW TWO: For his art.

BRAUCH: Impossible. You can see he's got over that. He must have got over that. Speak up, Flaní.

FLANÍ: Well, I see that we finally understand each other. [*He gestures toward the effigy.*] Light him up. The stone won't mind. Then torch the rest of this detritus. Oh, my. You didn't come prepared for that, did you?

BRAUCH: Darag said you had a secret.

FLANÍ: Marvelous. The solidarity of Darag and his widows.

WIDOW ONE: I beg your bootlapping pardon.

FLANÍ: Pardon? I thought that was what you were offering me.

WIDOW ONE: No, *niño*. Don't let Brauch lead you astray. We do not…let me repeat that…we do not have to be concerned with you.

[FLANÍ *points at the effigy.*]

FLANÍ: And this one?

WIDOW ONE: Simply a part of the plot.

FLANÍ: Oh, neatly fashioned, that. My own possibility laid before me.

WIDOW ONE: *Maravilla.* I had no idea you were so imaginative. Brauch will tell you…

FLANÍ: Brauch will tell you nothing.

GAUCHO TWO: There you go, Brauch. You and your special narrative.

BRAUCH: Oh, ho. Oh, yes. How was I to know that Flaní could be so arbitrary?

GAUCHO ONE: You had evidence. We had been here before.

BRAUCH: I ask you for precision, my gaucho. When was that? And who were we then?

WIDOW TWO: I will not go on. No. This crucifixion doesn't suit me.

WIDOW ONE: Come to yourself. There is nothing here as grand as that. We have only this maker. And a history that, from the evidence, seems to suit no one. But go on, my widow, take yourself away from it. We don't need you.

WIDOW TWO: Well, I will. And those who care about self-respect and compassion will follow me.

[*The first widow applauds.*]

WIDOW ONE: Notice, she hasn't moved. She prefers this insecurity.

WIDOW TWO: Flaní, forgive me.

BRAUCH: Not now, my widow. We still haven't seen his face.

GAUCHO ONE: Exactly.

FLANÍ: Peca!

WIDOW ONE: Such a charlatan.

FLANÍ: Vigilius!

WIDOW ONE: Disastrous.

FLANÍ: Darag!

WIDOW ONE: Overbearing.

BRAUCH: *Calma*, Flaní. You've lost your angel.

FLANÍ: Leave me!

BRAUCH: But we are here. We must be here. If there is to be any light, we must be here. Give us this consolation, Flaní. Give us this consolation.

GAUCHO TWO: I told you we're wasting our time with this one.

WIDOW TWO: Let him talk.

WIDOW ONE: Defend himself.

FLANÍ: Why would I do that?

BRAUCH: Obviously we've reached a point in our pilgrimage.

[FLANÍ *laughs.*]

GAUCHO ONE: Forget that. I've got more pride than some. [*He goes up to* FLANÍ.] You do recognize my pride. Don't you?

FLANÍ: Why, of course, my gaucho. All pilgrimages start with an understanding of our pride.

GAUCHO ONE: There you go. I only ask you to assure me that your understanding owes nothing to your cowardice.

FLANÍ: Brauch, you're harboring a philosopher. A Pascalian. Oh, forgive me. You see I haven't come to terms with being abandoned, being left to my own dark.

BRAUCH: Don't go any further.

FLANÍ: Then what was the point?

WIDOW ONE: It's true. [*She indicates the paintings.*] They seem quite comfortable. Having no place to go. Having nothing to tell us about having been here. They don't need us, you see. I would declare, *mis hijos*, that they seem not to need *him*.

BRAUCH: *Tais-toi.*

WIDOW ONE: I will keep my silence. [*To* FLANÍ.] You didn't expect that, did you? You thought their reticence would sustain you, and that we would flutter about until our exuberance faded. And then you'd be left alone with a presence you could take or leave, or rearrange at your pleasure.

BRAUCH: Flaní, I apologize.

[*The others groan.*]

I am responsible.

GAUCHO TWO: For what? You didn't make this situation. He did.

GAUCHO ONE: I'm ready. [*Preparing to leave.*]

BRAUCH: For what? You came with me.

GAUCHO ONE: Did I?

WIDOW ONE: Yes, Brauch. Weren't we just answering a call?

WIDOW TWO: I came on my own.

WIDOW ONE: Such innocence.

GAUCHO ONE: Our *fabbro* has nothing to say.

GAUCHO TWO: And no place for us.

BRAUCH: Speak up, Flaní.

FLANÍ: I thank you for your courtesy.

GAUCHO ONE: You will observe the mistletoe on my coattail. I don't give a damn about your courtesy.

WIDOW TWO: I came on my own. Pay attention. There was a measure of exactness in our bodies. Someone came to us, you all agree, saying there was a story being written that concerned us. None of us was idle. None of us needed to explore this space we've found here. We didn't have to find Flaní here. We didn't have to bring our own abandonment here, and offer it to him as a gift. So he refuses our gift. Leaving him here alone might be our ultimate gift. Is that what your heart is telling us now, Flaní?

FLANÍ: Have I offended you?

BRAUCH: My widow believes too much in her saintliness.

FLANÍ: And I too much in your freedom.

GAUCHO TWO: Freedom he calls it.

FLANÍ: Absolutely.

WIDOW ONE: He talks about darkness. There is nothing here that reflects that dark. Take me out of this. I want nothing to do with this man.

BRAUCH: Impossible.

GAUCHO ONE: Nay, perfectly possible. Don't give us your reconciliation, Brauch. And don't think, *fabbro*, that you have won.

FLANÍ: You told me that on your last appearance. You used those very words.

GAUCHO ONE: What?

FLANÍ: Don't pretend to forget. I recognize your voice. I am not a sleeping log. I am not dead.

WIDOW ONE: This interview is over. There are too many voices speaking at the same time. And nothing to be said. Call us away, Brauch.

BRAUCH: I have an obligation...

FLANÍ: None to me!

BRAUCH: Is that what it's come to? Is that how you want it, my *fabbro*? All right, then. We accept this abandonment. We appreciate your exquisite solitude. Leave us to our own explorations. A blessing upon you and yours, such as they be. Pilgrims.

[*They gather everything, including the effigy, and go belling away.* FLANÍ *is alone.*]

FLANÍ: The measure of exactness in our bodies. A pride of darkness. The perfect understanding of a story I haven't written. What is my first thought? I must be growing crude. I let them get away before I gave them the history of granite.

[*He disappears behind the stone. Pause.* PECA *and* VIGILIUS *enter separately. Each seems to be searching for something, and unaware of the other, until they bump into each other.*]

PECA: What are you doing here?

VIGILIUS: Who are you?

PECA: Peca.

VIGILIUS: Just Peca?

PECA: You must be Vigilius.

VIGILIUS: What makes you say that?

PECA: A certain form of inquiry, that overlooks the obvious.

VIGILIUS: And what, in this case, might that be?

PECA: That I'm here. That I know where I am.

VIGILIUS: I don't doubt that you're there, but I'm not so sure that you know where here is.

PECA: This is delicious. I pictured a stubby little fellow, looking into his homburg and wondering where his head had gone. You haven't disappointed me. What was your question?

VIGILIUS: Why, you're a perfect danger.

PECA: My, my, a connoisseur of danger. You scribble this nonsense for some rag, I suppose. May I remind you that you have given no account of yourself.

VIGILIUS: Give an account of myself! I run into a strange woman stumbling in the dark, devilishly close to the recent production of a very important artist, and she asks me for an account of myself. Stand still, Lady. We need to get to the bottom of this.

PECA: Indeed, we do. Where is Flaní?

VIGILIUS: You know Flaní?

PECA: Of course, I know Flaní.

VIGILIUS: I mean in the flesh.

PECA: Well, is there another way?

VIGILIUS: You could be one of those who knows him in spirit. Or, god help us, one of those who claims to have done his work.

PECA: You find that ridiculous.

VIGILIUS: Don't you?

PECA: Should I?

VIGILIUS: You say we've never met.

PECA: Until this blissful moment.

VIGILIUS: Ah, but there's a trick in it. Your rambling juxtapositions get in the way of sense. You don't happen to know a certain dramaturg who does this sort of thing, do you? Or maybe it's just the way a gaggle of offended women have of getting even. Listen, I'm not Flaní.

PECA: *Certo.*

VIGILIUS: Say that again.

PECA: *Certo.*

VIGILIUS: Yes. Little things. Echoes. Intimations. It's in the voice. That was his first mistake, trying to capture the voice on a piece of stretched linen. Thank you, Peca. Mystery solved. He'll listen to me now.

PECA: Who will listen to you?

VIGILIUS: Himself, Flaní. Haven't you been listening?

PECA: I've been distracted.

VIGILIUS: Better distracted than disoriented. Better Vigilius than dead silence. I'm joking, of course. But you must acknowledge a certain presumption in your style. You see, I have a reason to be here, breathing the energy for another minute.

PECA: Getting into the spirit.

VIGILIUS: You might say.

PECA: Flaní manages that fairly well. Putting people into the spirit.

VIGILIUS: Well, of course. What would you expect? You make it sound like a failing.

PECA: *Pas de tout.* It might be the only gift he has.

VIGILIUS: You scribble this nonsense for some rag, I suppose.

PECA: What an ear.

VIGILIUS: I would prefer your admiration of my eye. And that you would pay some attention to my intuition. Which tells me, my lady, that I am fortunate to have stopped whatever devious design you had on this place.

PECA: Does everyone here speak in some linguistic Euclidean geometry?

VIGILIUS: Tell me about yourself.

PECA: Why, you're a perfect danger.

VIGILIUS: Not yet. Not until I absolve Flaní of these creative misunderstandings.

PECA: My god, the man has the smell of the Old Testament about him. Absolve? Stand still, let me touch you, master.

VIGILIUS: *Basta.* Unmask yourself.

PECA: I already have. I am part of these personages you see about you. Your eye should have told you that. You're good at seeing what is not there. Your own misconceptions give you a hint of possibility. I know your conspiracy, Vigilius. You thought you could hide it behind this enthusiasm for the flagellant master, Flaní. Don't pretend you mean to justify him.

VIGILIUS: What were you looking for?

PECA: Good. You admit you've been inattentive.

VIGILIUS: In what way?

PECA: You've read these paintings, and missed the very absence you've proposed.

VIGILIUS: We've been over this ground.

PECA: Blindness twice over. Nothing here concerns an absent woman, an erased line, a color gingered into another form. The absence, the one you have always proposed, is Flaní.

VIGILIUS: I despise this disingenuous dancing in brackish waters. I've noticed...

[She stops him with a slow look.]

Look, we're both out of line here. Neither of us can justify this intrusion. Call it by its name. So the author is not here, and we have become authorities, of a special sort, mind you, following perhaps an inadvisable intuition.

[She laughs.]

Let me finish! All right, I came here with the sense of being protective. Do you understand?

PECA: Of course, you needed protection.

VIGILIUS: Not me. Flaní.

PECA: The same.

VIGILIUS: Agh, you're flying. I don't have to explain myself to you. Don't you have anything to say? I don't expect a confession. But, goddammit, why are you here?

PECA: To protect myself against misconceptions.

VIGILIUS: She plays me. Vigilius, the aesthetician, the benevolent eye.

PECA: Bully for you. That's the one thing I could never give this Flaní. Let him choke himself with his mathematical disappearances.

VIGILIUS: So you came to present your resignation.

PECA: You might say.

VIGILIUS: I see. [*He looks around.*] What do you think is alive here?

[*She points at the tattered painting.*]

PECA: That.

VIGILIUS: He left it, didn't he?

PECA: *Equivocado.* He found its hidden energy, and took control.

VIGILIUS: A veritable *mãe-de-santo*, aren't you?

PECA: *De veras.*

VIGILIUS: I think you should revise your assessment of Flaní's gifts. Why don't we start with evasion?

PECA: Oh, I thought you would prefer abandonment.

VIGILIUS: Or your resignation. Tell me again about those misconceptions.

[FLANÍ *appears, wearing a different robe, one with an elaborate and strange cross.*]

PECA: Well, now, you look more like yourself.

FLANÍ: And how do you know when I am like myself? The robe? Some other appurtenance that escaped you in the past? There you go, Vigilius. Behold the unsheathed eye. [*To* PECA.] Where is your kit?

PECA: My kit?

FLANÍ: Your *juego.* The things you carry from place to place, in hopes of some ceremony. You haven't forgotten the glasses, have you? Or were they ceramic? I had them in my hand, but the touch was unfamiliar. I told myself later on that I was foolish to try to conjure a presence, when

I didn't even know what I had in my hand. I am in awe of your subtlety. You examined me without a proposition, nothing to indicate that the moment was serious. *N'est-ce pas?* A defining instance of passing over. So here you are to examine yourself. But you seem to have misplaced your instruments. Help her out, Vigilius. There. He's too astonished even to talk to me.

VIGILIUS: Speak of conspiracy. You two…Yes, I am, as you say, astonished. That cross is the one that the woman wore in the painting.

FLANÍ: The woman I removed.

VIGILIUS: Yes. You don't deny it now.

FLANÍ: Enlighten me, Vigilius. Are we talking about my faith? Or about some mysterious figure who supposedly inhabited one of my canvases? Or about some configuration of crosses that leads to an interrupted dream? What do you have to say, Peca?

PECA: I had a white robe, but I was all in black, the color of purity. Surely, you haven't forgotten that. And the goblets were neither glass, nor ceramic.

FLANÍ: Impossible.

PECA: What an embarrassment. Everything that would justify your vision was insubstantial, a form not even your hand, or your spirit, would recognize. This bullying because your senses failed you doesn't appeal to me, Flaní.

FLANÍ: Where was the woman?

PECA: An impossible question.

FLANÍ: Well, then, let us say it's a possible construction.

PECA: The white robe with a cross.

FLANÍ: And the life therein.

VIGILIUS: Stop it. Even if she is missing now, has been abandoned, she is part of that configuration. Let me finish! Even if she was never there, she is part of that conception. Oh, I know Peca will play with her misconceptions. But I am talking about coherence.

FLANÍ: All right, let's try that on.

VIGILIUS: Fuck you, Flaní. Any fool can see the imbalance in your art. You keep running away from solutions, from any solution. And what have you given us? [*He points at the paintings.*] Wingless birds, a bear in a trap, a wounded, fleeing doe. What's the point, if you don't intend to put them out of their misery? And what do you want from me?

PECA: Vigilius has made a mistake.

VIGILIUS: Forget you.

PECA: No, no, no. Was it something you lost somewhere, Vigilius? Oh, *gioia*, what a parade. We can help Vigilius find his mistake right here in Flaní's yard. [*She leaps ecstatically around the paintings.*] Come on, my angels. [*She stops.*] Well? What's the matter?

FLANÍ: I'm afraid your misconception escapes me. I would prefer that you hide your enthusiasm for my anxiety.

VIGILIUS: Leave it, Flaní.

PECA: Get back in your womb.

FLANÍ: It's too late for you to insist upon your freedom. I am here. Instruct her, Vigilius. Oh, I'm sorry. Your most astute and proper pupil wears a white robe with a cross.

[DARAG *enters with his cart, loaded with objects.*]

DARAG: I see the city never sleeps.

FLANÍ: Apparently, neither do you. What is this?

DARAG: A manifestation of my skill. Forget the garbage I had in the cart. I've been busy trading. If we were in private convocation, I'd show you what I turned up.

FLANÍ: You know Vigilius. [*Glancing at* PECA.] Oh, I see.

VIGILIUS: I love it. I knew I'd catch this nigger in a lie.

PECA: Do we have to have that kind of language?

VIGILIUS: Damned straight. Darag claims he knows you. You met upon a summit, and came to terms. You mean you don't remember? Sounds like something didn't quite come up.

FLANÍ: Let's not let things get out of hand. I want to see what's in the cart.

DARAG: Oh, yes, you're good at this mockery. No matter. I've done pretty good for myself.

VIGILIUS: Good.

DARAG: You caught that, did you?

[PECA *makes a move toward the cart.*]

Hold on there, baby. I'm the *dueño* here. And I will take my time to show you the touches of my genius. [*He draws out a clay pipe, some ceramic objects and a knife made from a cow's rib.*] A fine example of a pipe. Notice how well it's held up. Right? [*He hurries on.*] You wouldn't expect ceramics of such quality. Right? And the piece-de-resistance, a perfectly constructed knife made from a cow's rib.

FLANÍ: And the joke is...?

DARAG: Don't insult me. I traded for this art. Even an idiot like you can see the quality of it.

FLANÍ: Oh, I can see that there's great pretension in it. Where did you get it?

DARAG: At last, a curious notion. An Indian who had been in Argentina brought it back.

PECA: Impossible.

DARAG: Do you know the man?

PECA: You fell for this?

DARAG: Examine the material.

VIGILIUS: I will.

DARAG: Not you. Her.

VIGILIUS: Don't trust me, Darag?

DARAG: Not a question of trust. I want her to show you how to handle the lives embodied in these instruments. You must be Peca. Go on. What do you see? What's in the touch?

FLANÍ: That's enough of this.

PECA: No. We haven't finished.

DARAG: Exactly. [*As though recounting a story.*] And one thing led to another, and another thing led to something that was not there, and then to top it all, the thing that got expressed had no means of expression. You might say somewhat like the galimatias we have scattered all about us here.

VIGILIUS: There's no need...

DARAG: Yes!? Tell me about need, Vigilius.

PECA: Do I examine these bodies, or not?

[DARAG *gestures for her to proceed.*]

You're counting on my feeling age, a certain fragility, perhaps a little fear, an uncertainty. You know that these things were stolen from me.

DARAG: The woman is a liar. Get her away from the cart.

PECA: Don't worry, Darag. I'm not putting in a claim. I'm happy to see that these instruments, as you call them, are seeing the light. I would have given them their freedom myself. I can only assume that you will.

DARAG: Oh, very clever. I never would have thought...

PECA: Yes?

DARAG: No, I do see now that they might have thrived under your care. You see, Flaní, the delicacy of these institutions. Carry on, sister. Preach.

PECA: My, my, such theological understanding. [*She picks up a piece.*] Of course, you need me. Even though, without knowing it, you've done your best to scare me away.

VIGILIUS: No claims, she says!

FLANÍ: I notice the way you handle that. A bit of memory in that, isn't there? Memory is a bitch, isn't it? It leads to a certain disorientation. Our last conversation was about home. You strung me out over some winding sheet. I had to suffer your accusations. Don't ask, Darag. She knows what I mean.

PECA: *Attento!* No more of your tricks!

VIGILIUS: Wasn't she going to give us a reading of these things?

FLANÍ: Ridiculous.

DARAG: All things in order, Flaní. I come back, and find all this confusion. So I say to myself, slow, slow. You can't help him, if you don't do things decently and in order. First, I open your eyes. Then your ears. Then your heart. Then I could tell you why I brought these things to you. Don't you want to know?

FLANÍ: Ah, yes, what a spring of ambrosial verses he found, being a guest. Tell me about myself, Darag.

DARAG: Cut it. I'm not a judge. But take a careful look at these fragile instruments. Did you think they had disappeared? Nay, Flaní, I brought them back to you. You have a second chance, or a third, or a fourth, I don't know. But here they are. They've lost their innocence, and so have you. All right, you say, who am I to be their messenger, to place myself between their bodies and your eye? I don't appeal to your eye, but to the sight you seem to have lost, or to have never defined. [*He vigorously arranges some of the objects into a small still life on the stone.*] Have you been here before?

FLANÍ: What do you want from me?

[DARAG *points at the scattered paintings.*]

DARAG: Look at the shadows there.

VIGILIUS: Everything seems painted over.

FLANÍ: Impossible.

PECA: Oh, but I've noticed that some things seem uninvited.

DARAG: [*Pointing at his still life.*] Like these.

FLANÍ: These things have nothing to do with me.

PECA: That's not what they say.

FLANÍ: Well, then, they lie.

VIGILIUS: To whom, Flaní?

FLANÍ: To themselves.

[*The others mock this.*]

DARAG: Ah, yes. To themselves. He speaks for them now.

VIGILIUS: Of course. He's their historian.

PECA: What do we call such a chronicler, who can't even get the figure straight?

DARAG: One?

VIGILIUS: No. The whole society of the living.

DARAG: I refer to the shadows.

PECA: I call your attention to an unfigurable presence.

DARAG: Why don't we leave Flaní to his contemplation?

PECA: *A ver.* But can we trust him?

DARAG: What about it, Flaní, can we trust you?

VIGILIUS: I don't see the point.

DARAG: Well, look at it your damned self, Vigilius. You started us on this road.

PECA: *Certo.* What are you doing, Vigilius, backing off? Open the house again, Darag. Maybe we should sit Vigilius down before his belly button. He persuades himself not to be persuaded by the very notion he has persuaded us to entertain. What is it, Vigilius? Can't you see that these bodies have been proposed as opposition to the things they show?

DARAG: Exactly. This Flaní is a subversive little mite. Strike that, strike that. But, god almighty, we have this prophet of the brush, who shows up here now pretending he doesn't believe in what he's done. Or who does believe in what he's done, but doesn't care to have it in the house.

PECA: I won't forgive you, Flaní.

FLANÍ: Don't laugh, Vigilius. She really wants to burn you.

DARAG: Look at them. They have this beggar's covenant between them. It won't work, *pochos.*

FLANÍ: A covenant! I feel almost biblical, Vigilius.

VIGILIUS: Perhaps you should, Flaní.

FLANÍ: What does that mean?

PECA: Syntax, Flaní.

VIGILIUS: Put the woman back in the canvas. Give us the old law.

DARAG: Exactly.

PECA: Ah, yes, let him rescue himself by dangling this invisible body before our eyes.

DARAG: The very condition.

PECA: We won't even ask for a first philosophy, that original face you saw when you first put your question.

VIGILIUS: She thinks the face is mine.

FLANÍ: That's obscene.

VIGILIUS: Prove it isn't.

FLANÍ: Prove it!? I didn't need your faces. Forgive me. I didn't.

> *"Remedio de alegre vida*
> *no lo hay por ningún medio,*
> *porque mi grave herida*
> *es de tal parte venida*
> *que eres tu sola remedio."*

DARAG: Another puzzle he proposes to himself.

PECA: Scandalous. He refuses to account for these erasures.

VIGILIUS: [*To* FLANÍ.] The verses you just sang for us never saw light before the singer died. Curious that you should sing them now. Darag and Peca resent the attempt to find some significance in what they consider a trivial loss. They don't know *"como se viene la muerte / tan callando."* What was I trying to tell them? Where's my dramaturg, the band director, now that I need him? [*Noticing* PECA's *impatience.*] Surely, Peca, I'm piggish. But set down this, my lady, Flaní has never made the mistake of considering death inessential. I salute you, Flaní. You understand how light is the ultimate loss.

FLANÍ: Are you leaving, Vigilius?

VIGILIUS: Not yet.

[*The woman appears as a distant figure, wearing a cross similar to* FLANÍ'*s, and smoking a pipe.*]

There she is.

DARAG: She is? What she is? Who is? Damn it, what are you talking about?

PECA: It will not work, Vigilius. You have no right...

VIGILIUS: Notice, Flaní, how they skate.

FLANÍ: Look at her. She doesn't look anything like what I've done.

VIGILIUS: Will you insist on giving in to these cretins? You take another look.

PECA: To see what? Something has got lost here. Shouldn't we at least see why she's come back?

FLANÍ: She's never been away.

DARAG: What an impossible expression.

PECA: There's a woman there.

VIGILIUS: Exactly.

PECA: I mean no one has greeted her. No one has made sure that she has come to the right place. *Schweigen.* I'm talking about respect. No one? Then I will go. [*She starts toward the woman.*]

DARAG: She seems so out of place.

[FLANÍ *moves to stop* PECA.]

FLANÍ: Nay, Darag, you are the one out of place. I admire your passion, Peca. But you will observe the woman's stillness. [*To the others.*] You notice she doesn't speak. Does she see us? Does she acknowledge us? Does she have a message? *Pace*, Peca, is she even there? Isn't it reasonable that she and I should be left alone?

DARAG: I resent these tricks.

VIGILIUS: Why are you crying, Darag? Look what you've uncovered.

PECA: You make it seem as though we'd just dug up a body.

FLANÍ: I tell you she was never dead.

DARAG: [*To the woman.*] Do you hear me!?

PECA: *Tais-toi.* Peace. Let's wait upon her.

VIGILIUS: We have no choice.

DARAG: What will we do?

PECA: Who are we?

[*The woman turns, and slowly walks away.*]

FLANÍ: Just that image. The perfect thought. The one we all had. And now it has escaped us.

PECA: I hold you responsible.

DARAG: I will bury you, Flaní.

VIGILIUS: Pay it no mind, Flaní. I love you more than ever.

FLANÍ: Get out of my yard. [*He points to the still life.*] Can't you see I was doing a still life? I need these hours. Disappear.

[*The others scurry away, quarreling, and finally separating.* FLANÍ *sits on his granite.*]

They were only curious. They came searching something they didn't intend to find. They chose the darkness, perhaps thinking there was something discretional in that, some propriety that elevated them. They pretended to be one, or at least that smallest unit of meaning that could only inhabit this place. Or perhaps they were arguing a changed life. One thing I know: they were never pilgrims.

[BRAUCH *comes, limping and cursing. The* GAUCHOS *and* WIDOWS *steal forward, and disperse themselves around the area.*]

BRAUCH: Couldn't you get your people to show some courtesy? They practically ran us off the road coming up.

FLANÍ: You mean my critics.

BRAUCH: [*To the* GAUCHOS *and* WIDOWS.] You see the kind of garlic it costs me to deal with this angel. Will somebody mark the first crow of the cock? [*To* FLANÍ.] We forgive you. From the look of things, it seems we've done more than they have for you. Speak up.

FLANÍ: I did.

BRAUCH: We didn't hear you. You let us go. Don't pretend we had a choice. But no, we will not rehearse that failure. Ask us why we're here.

FLANÍ: Why are you here?

BRAUCH: Good.

[*He gestures to the others who move to surround* FLANÍ.]

You can see I've kept them together. Did I promise them things, accomplishments you couldn't conceive? Did I play upon their resentment, of you, of this little paradise of forms you think you've created? Not at all. They walk with me because they have determined to ransom you.

FLANÍ: The road seems to have disoriented you, Brauch. I hadn't thought so much time had passed. Or, really, I had thought it would take some time before you reached this stage of madness.

BRAUCH: You're not talking to Darag, now. Look at him. I thought we had done away with such innocence. We don't insist upon our suffering. But, damn it, man, there comes a time for accounting. I don't want to hear your Peca and Darag. Listen, I have to tell you: we saw her, too, that image, that perfect thought. We heard you singing.

FLANÍ: No, I don't fall for it.

BRAUCH: Don't insult us.

FLANÍ: You were not invited. You weren't here. You didn't hear me then. Why should I believe you hear me now?

BRAUCH: Syntax, Flaní.

[FLANÍ *tumbles the still life.*]

Look what you've done. If it goes on like this, your granite will have nothing on it but the blood of old canvases and old constructions from the past.

GAUCHO ONE: What was the phrase that Darag used?

FLANÍ: Choose one.

GAUCHO ONE: No. He tied you again to Vigilius.

WIDOW ONE: I think he thought he was fading in your regard.

WIDOW TWO: Exactly. There's this strange proposition of a disciple who needs a covenant.

GAUCHO TWO: Yes, some manifestation of faith.

WIDOW TWO: The conjunction of Peca and Darag. Your critics.

WIDOW ONE: Impossible. They have no voices.

BRAUCH: Isn't that how you see it, Flaní? They have no church.

GAUCHO ONE: Let's not confuse our *fabbro*. One doesn't need a church for that exemplary covenant.

WIDOW TWO: We haven't determined whether Flaní cares about that covenant. He sent Vigilius away with the others.

GAUCHO ONE: A disguise.

WIDOW TWO: Never. We had reached the point where there was no need for a mask.

BRAUCH: Good. We've unmasked Flaní.

[*The* WIDOWS *and* GAUCHOS *start to arrange their seating and materials.*]

   What are you doing?

WIDOW ONE: What you proposed.

BRAUCH: I spoke of possibility.

GAUCHO ONE: You used the wrong word.

BRAUCH: Forgive me. I'm weak.

GAUCHO TWO: Redemption would have been better.

BRAUCH: Is that what you think? Notice, Flaní, this dimensionless companion wants to preserve a dimension in your…existence…you seem to have abandoned.

WIDOW TWO: I protest. There is no reason to humiliate another pilgrim.

BRAUCH: *Seguro.* I apologize. I admit I was treading water until Flaní came to his senses. Or, that is to say, he came into this space with us. We didn't return to be scorned. There is a divinity among us, whether your eyes are capable of it.

WIDOW ONE: *Peut-etre, enfin, tu vas un peu loin.*

GAUCHO TWO: Not far enough.

GAUCHO ONE: Why don't we simply burn Flaní?

WIDOW TWO: *¡Bárbaro!*

BRAUCH: Yes. Don't confuse us with Peca and Darag. [*To* FLANÍ.] Do you know they've started a pamphlet war on you?

FLANÍ: Too late. [*He gestures.*] Words won't outweigh these bodies.

BRAUCH: No one needs the bodies.

[WIDOW ONE *does a brief dance.*]

WIDOW ONE: Let it go, Flaní. You have us.

GAUCHO ONE: That's what frightens him. The night has transpired, and what is he left with?

GAUCHO TWO: [*Holding up a dagger.*] With us, phantasms and figurations, mystifications he thought he had under control. He doesn't know what to do with us.

GAUCHO ONE: [*Holding up an axe.*] Time for instruction.

WIDOW TWO: I heard he was a gnostic.

WIDOW ONE: Nay, he long ago abandoned that church.

BRAUCH: Stop it. This is a serious moment, not the time for your heresy. Put away the cutting instruments. Let's go forward with our judgment.

[*The* WIDOWS *and* GAUCHOS *close in on* FLANÍ.]

WIDOW ONE: Will he testify?

GAUCHO ONE: Let's not contaminate this act.

BRAUCH: Righteous.

[WIDOW ONE *starts her interrupted dance.*]

All things decently and in order.

FLANÍ: *Maravilla*, Darag, I hadn't noticed your disguise.

[*He picks up a broken object, tries to hand it to* BRAUCH. GAUCHO TWO *knocks it from his hand.*]

GAUCHO TWO: We don't need that now. We need you.

BRAUCH: Pilgrims. *Ya.*

[*The others begin to touch* FLANÍ.]

WIDOW ONE: Gnostic, or not, he is so thoroughly there. Flesh, fragile bones. We ought to be able to care for him.

GAUCHO ONE: *Basta.* Where's the evidence of his concern for us?

WIDOW TWO: He needs a covering. [*She produces a rough blanket, spreads it.*] There. Sit him down.

[BRAUCH *claps his hands.*]

BRAUCH: You're going too fast.

FLANÍ: I'm sorry, Darag. I sold you to Vigilius.

BRAUCH: [*To the others.*] Pick it up. He's lost his reason. We have nothing to do here. [*To* FLANÍ.] You want us to go, do you? This time we won't come back.

WIDOW ONE: We haven't finished. Lie down, Flaní.

[FLANÍ *tries to move away. The* GAUCHOS *restrain him.* WIDOW TWO *goes through her travel bag, tossing garments aside, until she comes to a diaphanous veil which she holds up to* FLANÍ.]

WIDOW TWO: Not quite like hers. But something we've carried remembering this moment.

FLANÍ: Darag...

[*The* WIDOWS *and* GAUCHOS *force* FLANÍ *onto the blanket; the* GAUCHOS *hold him down.*]

I am Flaní, you idiots! I am Flaní!

WIDOW ONE: Of course.

WIDOW TWO: [*To* FLANÍ.] You disgust me. Take off that cross.

WIDOW ONE: *Schweigen!*

BRAUCH: Let her speak. Our *fabbro*'s contradictions burn the heart.

GAUCHO ONE: I ask you to consider that our *fabbro*'s contradictions have paralyzed our hearts. Think of it. He's taken away our solitude. And now he pretends that he can't use us. Let him remember his promise to us. We have come back, even when there was no perfect thought of us. And what do we have? Let him answer for that. I have my axe.

BRAUCH: Use it then.

WIDOW TWO: Give it to me!

[BRAUCH *holds her off.* FLANÍ *appears to calm himself.*]

FLANÍ: Judgment?

[GAUCHO TWO *steps forward, raises the dagger, prepared to strike. The* WOMAN IN WHITE *suddenly appears. Pause. The woman walks to* FLANÍ, *stands him up, looks slowly in his eyes, blows smoke upon him.*]

WIDOW ONE: Don't you have a voice for her, Flaní?

WIDOW TWO: Not now, my widow, he needs their special silence.

BRAUCH: Judgment?

[*The woman rips the cross from* FLANÍ*'s neck.*]

GAUCHO TWO: ¡*Eso!* And off with this blood loving robe.

[*The woman restrains the* GAUCHO.]

You're not the only one.

WIDOW TWO: We're doing this for her.

WIDOW ONE: We don't even know her.

BRAUCH: That makes no difference. Logically, that is.

GAUCHO ONE: Talk to *him* about logic.

BRAUCH: There's no need for that. She's here.

WIDOW TWO: Certainly.

WIDOW ONE: I don't like the way our widow has changed sides.

WIDOW TWO: I didn't know there were sides.

GAUCHO ONE: I think we should leave them alone. We've done our part.

BRAUCH: A cathouse, is it? You disappoint me, my gaucho.

WIDOW ONE: [*Circling* FLANÍ *and the woman.*] Notice the way that they have closed us out. I remind you all that I did prepare. Imagine my going into the bush to retrieve the proper colors. The hours given to transforming nature so it would fit the tone of this occasion. Imagine the rehearsal of my body, whirling around the room with my whisk, coordinating every movement of spirit. I followed you here in good faith. I set aside my disappointment and despair to come again to meet this initiate on his own ground. Did I do this for her voice, or for my own? I ask you.

BRAUCH: You promised me that you would be empty when we arrived. All of you did. Pull yourselves together. Judgment!

WIDOW ONE: Impossible. She's taken his cross.

[*The others howl.*]

GAUCHO ONE: So it leaves a hole.

GAUCHO TWO: Solid, brother. That's the first thing you've said that shows you're awake. We don't have to decide that. Leave that for Darag, for Vigilius, the aestheticians. We know our limits.

GAUCHO ONE: Copacetic. Who's the *fabbro* here?

[*The* GAUCHOS *bump their dagger and axe.*]

Brauch, will you give me leave to address the lady of the choir here?

[BRAUCH *shows his annoyance.*]

No, don't get angry. Only one of us can walk away. Who will it be, now that we have restructured our desires?

FLANÍ: Syntax, Brauch.

[*The woman touches* FLANÍ's *face, folds his cross with her sleeve, and walks away.* FLANÍ *seems to awaken.*]

The morning feels fresh. You've sat with me throughout the night. I've been inhospitable. But that has nothing to do with my art.

BRAUCH: Pilgrims, am I a spirit, or ain't I a spirit? I've given this initiate here a yard full of *choricera*. You think he's about to thank me. No, he's going to sit here on his granite, trying to think of some way to get his hand in a cloud's pocket, and won't even realize that his first failure was his first and only success. I'm ready to ride.

WIDOW TWO: Shouldn't we at least tidy up?

BRAUCH: It takes a widow to misunderstand.

GAUCHO ONE: Watch it, Brauch. I won't travel with a cruel man.

BRAUCH: Begging your pardon, sah.

WIDOW ONE: Ask this place for forgiveness.

BRAUCH: Not yet. [*He nods toward* FLANÍ.] *C'est à lui.*

[BRAUCH, *the widows and the gauchos gather what they want, and go singing away. Flaní begins to settle admiringly among his detritus.*]

FLANÍ: Did they really expect her to speak to me? If they had been following the movement of my soul, they would have seen that that moment had passed. They have this strange idea of necessity, and then they close their eyes to the terms of experience, and overlook the body I have worked into existence. The widow left me thinking about forgiveness. Listen to them down there, banging their bells, jollying themselves, as though they had put me in my place. I have news for them: their voices will die. Count on it.

[DARAG *and* PECA *enter, pushing a cart loaded with paintings and objects.* PECA *has a large bag filled with rolled canvases. They make what they consider a 'joyful noise'.*]

DARAG: Here you have it, my man. I hope you trust me to have accounted for everything. They didn't give me a lot of time. Thank god, I had Peca with me.

FLANÍ: What is this?

DARAG: As you can see, your exposition. That is to say, what would have been your exposition.

PECA: There, by the grace...

[FLANÍ *tears into the material.*]

FLANÍ: You dangling cow turd! You crippled mosquito prick! Is this your idea of a joke!? [*He grabs* DARAG.]

DARAG: *Basta*, you cadaver! I could have burnt this shit.

PECA: I recommended a quiet burial in the river. Would that have pleased you, *maestro*?

DARAG: We will spare you the judgment of the aestheticians. Here you have your consummation. What else do you want? Think about me. About Peca. We're not cowards.

FLANÍ: What is happening to me?

PECA: Why, nothing. To you.

DARAG: I find your response most interesting.

PECA: I would say slightly laden with awe.

DARAG: Here we are, Peca and Darag, companions of this renunciation.

PECA: Definition, Darag. Whose renunciation do we attend here?

[FLANÍ *begins a sightless, whimpering exploration of what he sees before him.*]

DARAG: There is a message. Do you want it?

PECA: Of course, he will have it. This is his night.

DARAG: The aestheticians say that there is no more to wait for. They say that they have been sublimely patient, but they have grown tired of your fraudulence and evasion. So, under cover of night, they removed this empty excursion into nothingness. Surely, *fabbro*, we don't agree, but it's a question of control.

[FLANÍ *starts to unload the cart.*]

FLANÍ: Help me. Let's just scatter it about.

DARAG: It?

FLANÍ: The work, the work. What did you think I meant?

PECA: Well, no. What did you intend?

FLANÍ: Perhaps a fifth element. I'll know when everything is in place.

[*As they begin,* VIGILIUS *appears.*]

VIGILIUS: *Maestro.*

FLANÍ: Have you ever called me that before, Vigilius?

VIGILIUS: I've always been respectful.

FLANÍ: *Seguro.* Did they give you a vote, the aestheticians?

VIGILIUS: There was no vote. The event just happened.

FLANÍ: The event. How lovely. That kind of spontaneity embarrasses me. So, you seem to have come upon another event. A book burning, as it were.

[PECA *drops what she holds.*]

PECA: I'm out.

DARAG: A manner of speaking. Look at it this way: our aestheticians have given us a chance to start all over.

PECA: I remind you...

DARAG: That I was one of them. Of course. Flaní understands that. There was no reason to be an ascetic. Am I right or wrong, Vigilius? I'm talking about a certain assurance. We couldn't have had that if we had all acted like Flaní.

PECA: No, of course not.

DARAG: I will not be judged.

FLANÍ: I have a question for Vigilius. What is the difference between a *fabbro* and a *maestro*?

[PECA *begins to pack certain broken objects into her bag.*]

PECA: You don't mind? I have a long journey ahead, through hostile territory as you might suspect. I need something to trade. Did I phrase that properly? No. I need something to prove that I was here.

FLANÍ: You flatter me, Peca. But you would please me if you saw me through the rest of this night.

PECA: It's the absent one who makes me unprepared, Flaní. I told you, I follow the soul on the right.

FLANÍ: There you go, Vigilius. Trapped again.

VIGILIUS: I'll play. I'm good at exposition. There was an exposition that grew from the heads of the aestheticians. Then there was the exposition of my soul on the left. Oh, how did he know that?, you ask. Vigilius has exposed Flaní. Peca wants to leave us. And Flaní does not want the answer to his question.

FLANÍ: You see, Darag, you have been forgiven.

DARAG: Ah, yes, Parmenides, if the one is not, then nothing is. Should we be right? I hate to point this out to you, *fabbro*, but your granite begins to look a bit shaggy. Rumor has it that the widows abandoned you, and that the one you most counted upon grew destructive. Imagine my delight in delivering the evidence of this devastation.

[PECA *laughs deliriously.*]

PECA: That is absolutely rich. And now he expects that Peca in her dark robes will come flowing out of the darkness, and go down on her knees, and pretend to lament the demise of Flaní, the *fabbro*, or the *maestro*, whichever designation appeals. Will Flaní dress himself again?

VIGILIUS: That's not the question now.

PECA: He pretends to know.

FLANÍ: Why shouldn't he? [*Pause.*] My granite does look a little shaggy. But that's to be expected. I'm sure you've noticed. There is no star in your unruly heaven moving as swiftly as this stone. Oh? You didn't notice that? Well, take my word for it. Hold it! Listen. You hear it, don't you? Soft steps on sand, or in water, but most definite. Put it out of mind. Anyone who belongs is here. And all the uninvited have their own concerns. I have only one question, *compañeros*. Why are you here? Why haven't you abandoned me?

DARAG: That sounds like two questions to me.

FLANÍ: Indulge me, Darag.

PECA: Darag has no answer. He's given himself over to the inadmissible.

DARAG: My lord, that sounds like some mariolatry.

VIGILIUS: No need for insult.

DARAG: So he enters defending himself, our critic, always having "got it right." Tell us, Vigilius, why is it that this disengagement does not depend on getting it right?

VIGILIUS: Let go, Darag. She will not come back.

DARAG: Is there a name to this person who has miraculously disappeared?

PECA: Pay attention, Flaní. We are being written by one who disappeared, or who never appeared. But you settled with me long ago. I gave you my judgment. You refused it.

DARAG: This is no time for such judgment.

VIGILIUS: Flaní, my twin, tell me I am forgiven.

DARAG: And we are?

PECA: Blind within this light.

VIGILIUS: Flaní!

FLANÍ: Flaní is here, perfectly in tune with his own absence.

[*The woman appears, wearing a crimson robe and carrying* FLANÍ'*s crimson robe. She sets* FLANÍ'*s robe aflame, struggles to ascend the granite, where she majestically sits.*]

VIGILIUS: *Es el presagio. Solo el presagio.*

[FLANÍ *begins to scream.* PECA, DARAG *and* VIGILIUS *drop one by one to their knees, and join* FLANÍ *in his screaming. The lights leave all of them in a circle, and leave all the art in darkness.*]

ARIA

PROLOGUE

[*A plumed angel, smoking a cigar, enters. The figure bows left, bows right; stands as though it might fly; begins an awkward dance; stops.*]

ANGEL: Dawn slides into significance. I have awakened disoriented, without the slightest desire for comfort. I would go to Spain for my birthday, but the ocean intervenes.

[*Two women, dressed in white jackets and striped pants, come forward. They carry, and beat upon brass pans covered with silk handkerchiefs.*]

ALEA: [*To the angel.*] What are you doing out of your seat?

ANGEL: And what are you doing out of your place?

MADRIGAL: We made scales for the porcupine.

ALEA
ANGEL } Today all is well and we may say so, say so, say so.
MADRIGAL

ANGEL: Then you must understand that the tops of the beech tree have sprouted of late.

ALEA: Say that they come late.

ANGEL: Don't disorient me.

MADRIGAL: Why, this person lies.

ANGEL: I know that weeds grow behind the water pot.

ALEA: Scandalous.

ANGEL: Ho. I see, I see. You can't take that rhythm.

MADRIGAL: *Caterina asentada…*

ANGEL: What do you think of me?

MADRIGAL: *¡Desvistase!*

ANGEL: Only when we have arrived.

[CHISPAZO *enters, under a garland of flowers, and ringing a bell.*]

CHISPAZO: I would say that I have arrived just in time. Or should we say, just on time. You will note that the bell marks its own beneficence. Greetings to all assembled here, though much seems missing.

ANGEL: Did I ask for you?

CHISPAZO: What constitutes this "ask"?

ANGEL: What happened to the white powder you promised me?

CHISPAZO: We can live on promises.

ANGEL: [*To the women.*] Would you remove this plangent number.

ALEA: Why, no, he seems an exact messenger. He comes and goes like the wind.

MADRIGAL: *Y las campanas de la iglesia ya no quieren repicar.*

ANGEL: Nothing but a phantom, a withered state.

CHISPAZO: You say. But let's leave it to them.

ANGEL: They have nothing to do with my weaving. I sit here, alone.

ALEA: Ah, your discretion, your patrimony. I commend you, my angel.

ANGEL: I sense a little of the cosmic in your disdain.

ALEA: I have had my say.

ANGEL: Such antiphonal practice. She started to dance. She started to rejoice.

ALEA: Disturbs you.

ANGEL: Not at all.

> "*Cuando yo nací*
> *en una noche escura,*
> *ni gallo cantaba*
> *ni perro ladraba…*"

MADRIGAL: Go on. You left something out.

ANGEL: How would you know?

CHISPAZO: Exactly.

MADRIGAL: *Tacete.*

[PACATO *appears, wearing the tall boots of a fisherman, and carrying a bag of what appear to be flopping fish.*]

PACATO: So he came late to the party, but the revelers welcomed him with hymns and pastourelles. Chispazo, what happened to the dolls?

ALEA: There you have it.

ANGEL: Have what?

ALEA: You won't get me to tell them your true name.

ANGEL: Don't pretend you have the cowry tied to the bone.

MADRIGAL: [*Pointing at* PACATO.] I want to know this man's name.

PACATO: *Philomathes gar eimi.*

MADRIGAL: *Kà bàrà bà kí.*

ALEA: *Kà bàrà bà ké.*

ANGEL: I insist upon a thermal silence.

CHISPAZO: Then relieve me of him.

ANGEL: I refuse the offices of judge and jury.

ALEA: How quaintly you speak of being invested.

CHISPAZO: Shall I put her in the other room?

ANGEL: Yes, and sing her to sleep.

ALEA: Don't you put your hands on me.

MADRIGAL: [*Pointing at* PACATO.] I want to know this man's name.

PACATO: Oh, Cyprian mother, don't you remember me?

MADRIGAL: I can't say that I do, though you have the smell of deep water.

PACATO: And there you have it. We have all met before.

ALEA: Look how he argues for his existence.

PACATO: Stop it right there, with this existence scheme.

ALEA: *Kà bàrà bà kí.*

MADRIGAL: *Kà bàrà bà ké.*

PACATO: I felt once the enchantment of Gwydion.

ANGEL: You will not bring that into this council.

CHISPAZO: Exactly.

PACATO: Then I suppose we should all just stand here, and melt away.

ALEA: Well, I refuse.

MADRIGAL: And so do I.

ANGEL: I will tell you when to refuse.

[*The women howl, and sing in concert.*]

ALEA
MADRIGAL } *"Mais on m'offrit un petit plat de fonio bien salé."*

ANGEL: *Oh, la nueva luna / que brilla en su profunda oscuridad.*

CHISPAZO: Careful.

MADRIGAL: [*Pointing at* PACATO.] So no one will tell me that one's true name?

ANGEL: I think he lost it.

MADRIGAL: He smells of deep water.

ANGEL: Did I tell you about those fabulous moments we spent with Kafka in San Pedro?

CHISPAZO: Not San Pedro Tlaquepaque!

ANGEL: San Pedro by the Sea. Get out of my narrative.

ALEA: Well, go on with it.

ANGEL: She thinks I can't. That I have no imagination.

PACATO: *A dia fún.*

[CHISPAZO *rings his bell.*]

CHISPAZO: *Lo díá.*

ANGEL: I return to the conviviality of a white shirt and a wine stain.

ALEA: I thought that he had refused that judicial assault upon this design.

ANGEL: She wants me to feel foolish in trying to justify the accomplished face of the narrative.

MADRIGAL: I asked you for the brass spoon for the child.

ANGEL: Chispazo, ring your bell.

PACATO: That won't save you, my angel.

ANGEL: The day dawned for me at San Pedro.

CHISPAZO: Not San Pedro Tlaquepaque!

[MADRIGAL *edges up to* PACATO.]

MADRIGAL: They left something insistent out of your derivation.

PACATO: Don't disturb me with your Minoan chastity.

MADRIGAL: I charge this man…!

PACATO: [*To the others.*] Pay no attention.

MADRIGAL: You won't, you can't, put me off.

[PACATO *prepares for a peroration.*]

PACATO: Who but myself knows where the sun shall set?

ANGEL: *Basta,* brother. Step back, son.

MADRIGAL: So there we have it.

PACATO: Who foretells the ages of the moon?

[CHISPAZO *furiously rings his bell.*]

ALEA: *Àkèré pète ìyé.*

PACATO: Poetry does not inhabit this house.

ANGEL: Alea, he wants to betray me.

CHISPAZO: Sing again.

ALEA: Sloth for the shapeless neck. Eighty minstrels and only one drum.

PACATO: Listen. *Una luna llena en perfección, rodeada por una noche de abundosos cabellos negros…*

MADRIGAL: Fraudulent, and disoriented. Why have you done away with the rhythm of my hair?

PACATO: I have nothing to do with you.

MADRIGAL: Oh, of course, not now.

ANGEL: Speak up, son.

ALEA: Such a chromatic aberration always surprises. Speak of the binary star.

CHISPAZO: We dance in three and four. Such articulation. Sing, Pacato.

[SCACCO, *dressed as a 19th century aristocrat, enters, carrying a riding crop.*]

SCACCO: I thought I had sent an advocate, but look what I find on my arrival. Disgraceful.

ANGEL: You sent an advocate to me?

ALEA: Perhaps he means to specify you as the advocate.

PACATO: Certainly. That makes more sense.

ANGEL: Wait a minute, now.

CHISPAZO: Yes. Let's not get carried away.

MADRIGAL: Count on you to speak out of turn.

CHISPAZO: I speak as my voice directs me. [*He giggles at that.*]

SCACCO: *Miren no más,* he's lost the feel of his tongue.

ALEA: What in the world could someone so arrayed advocate?

[SCACCO *prepares for a peroration.*]

SCACCO: Thank you for the invitation…

MADRIGAL: Stop it right there.

PACATO: Let him proceed. Maybe he will lose that smell of the *disparatero.*

CHISPAZO: That never happens.

SCACCO: *"Quando mi diparti' da Circe…"*

ALEA
MADRIGAL } *Di nkra.*

SCACCO: *"Quando mi diparti' da Circe…"*

ALEA
MADRIGAL } *A dia fún.*

CHISPAZO: Don't pretend to understand this idiot. Can't you see the trick of it?

ANGEL: Well, go on, Chispazo. Uncover the trick.

ALEA: I didn't know you knew his name.

ANGEL: And why not? Just because I never said it, doesn't mean I didn't have command of it.

MADRIGAL: Oh, well, get to that. We have a magical angel before us.

ANGEL: I resent your blasphemies against this house.

PACATO: Careful, my angel. You can't just walk away from all of us.

CHISPAZO: Yes. I sense a Roman tuning of the fire.

ALEA: Scandalous.

MADRIGAL: We ought to organize a second coming.

ALEA: A second occasion for the dance.

ANGEL: Of course. Haven't I taught you to count?

SCACCO: [*Pointing at* CHISPAZO.] I don't trust this little warrior here. You can't count on him to carry his share of the load. He would turn up on some island, and swear he had never seen, or even heard, of any of us. I suspect he'll pull his cape over his scrawny body, and keep his mouth shut.

PACATO: Tell me again your name. Then you must advise me as to why I should pay any attention to you.

SCACCO: [*To the angel.*] What a scandalous proposition. He thinks he can avoid what happens to all of us.

PACATO: No. I simply call attention to how you came out here improperly dressed, whirling around, singing at the top of your voice, as though you had the hymn and the steps.

SCACCO: Maybe we should sort notions that have appeared in our garden.

ALEA: Not until you get your ass up on the proper sticks. My. Did I say that?

MADRIGAL: You did.

ALEA: [*Pointing at* ANGEL.] And he heard me?

MADRIGAL: He did.

ALEA: Should I ask his forgiveness?

MADRIGAL: No.

CHISPAZO: Let's not get carried away.

SCACCO: I refuse.

ANGEL: Refuse what?

SCACCO: The drumming of a different day that has come without my knowledge.

ANGEL: Make up your mind.

SCACCO: I have made up my mind. I see nothing perishable here, even though I note some degree of contamination and compromise.

CHISPAZO: Speech, speech.

MADRIGAL: No time for that now.

ANGEL: Speech, speech.

MADRIGAL: Oh. He calls for pity.

PACATO: Or piety.

ALEA: He doesn't see his face in the mirror.

MADRIGAL: Look at him. He has his mirror buckled on his shoe.

ANGEL: You think you've captured me, don't you? You think you see my face.

MADRIGAL: I have seen it.

[*The angel turns his back to her, speaks to the others.*]

ANGEL: Remove this.

PACATO: Not now. We expect more than what you have given us.

ALEA: *Certo.*

[*The women beat upon their pans.*]

ANGEL: Out of order.

CHISPAZO: No, my angel, the music serves. It takes a suppressed agility to command this dance.

ANGEL: He tries to speak in my voice.

MADRIGAL: We all do, my angel. Come. Step up. Dance with us.

[*They all step away in a graceful dance. A pulsing light grows from darkness; it runs an empty space from left to right, shuts off. The light again grows from darkness, but now runs from right to left, shuts off. During the first event this movement repeats itself several times. A figure, clothed in red, appears, and begins a spiralling dance. Suddenly, the dancer disappears. A figure, clothed in yellow, appears and repeats the spiralling dance. Suddenly, the figure disappears. A figure, clothed in blue, appears, and does the same spiralling dance. Three solemn bells. A wind sound. The grainy sound of water. The figures now seem to be aware of each other, each exploiting a series of movements, relational intervals with respect to the others. Torches flare at various points around the space. The torch light reflects and reveals the scallop shells hanging from the dancers' necks. The figures swirl to a clock ticking and the castanet clicking of their emblems. They raise this movement to a high pitch. Abrupt, unfocussed stillness. A flute in the distance sounds four notes, stops; then sounds five notes, and again stops. We hear a distant humming, hymnlike and dense, that contests the flute's softness. The figure in red moves as if to place the source of the music. The figure in yellow moves as if to restrain the figure in red's investigation. The figure in blue emits a solitary, grotesque note that gradually grows into a bird's trilling sound. The figures now move with respect to the intervallic light. They seem to attune their movements and voices to the flute and hymnlike voice. A melody seems to surface. The figures move closer to each other, each playing upon the bone sound of the scallop shells. The figure in red breaks left to sing into the distance. The figure in blue breaks right to sing into the distance. The figure in yellow stands erect in the center, arms elevated and whirling from left to right, from right to left. The flute and hymnlike voice become a counterpoint to the movements we see and hear before us. The figure in yellow begins an elaborate disrobing, momentarily showing what appears a green side to the yellow robe. The other figures seem repulsed and attracted by this play upon the robe. The figure in blue pulls away toward the sound of the flute. The figure in red makes a silent appeal to arrest that movement. The yellow figure erupts in roguish laughter. The flute and distant voice stop, begin again with an agitated rhythm. The blue figure sings a laughing scale. The red figure becomes agitated, erupts in a laughing scale. The flute and distant voice stop, begin that harmonious contest with the figures' scales. The figures fall into line, dancing carefully as though they would avoid erasing the line. The dance becomes a movement in which they rearrange themselves, the colors appearing in changing relationships. Each figure adopts an individual tone which rises and falls with respect to the other tones, as they step along the line. They stop, rest. They move again. Words surface quietly, repeated and proposed by different voices among the figures. We hear "no star," "no space." Rest. "No rhythm," "no number." Rest. "No memory," "no body." One prolonged scream from all three figures, "I do not sing. Remember the voice you will now choose." They improvise individual dances, come together and whirl away. A moment of stillness, no light, no sound. A young black woman, handsomely dressed and carrying an elegant leather satchel enters.* GARBH, *sturdy, soberly dressed and carrying a large suitcase, follows her into the light.*]

SÁNÚ: Garbh, what have you done? How in heaven did we end up here?

GARBH: I didn't draw the map.

SÁNÚ: Thank god you didn't.

GARBH: Do you always have to invoke him?

[SÁNÚ *turns, approaches* GARBH.]

SÁNÚ: Say that again.

GARBH: You heard me.

SÁNÚ: I did. Something about a him, or a hymn. Notice my syntax, Garbh.

GARBH: I never fail, even though you never acknowledge it.

SÁNÚ: [*Discounting this.*] Never acknowledge it. I hear you, Garbh. I see you, Garbh. I have you around me, Garbh. Could I do any more?

GARBH: Let's not have that argument again.

[SÁNÚ *puts down her satchel.*]

SÁNÚ: No. Let's. I feel up for a little analytical satisfaction this morning, or this evening, whatever we seem to have touched here.

GARBH: There we go again, slipping off into that mystery.

SÁNÚ: Don't. Don't lose your place in the composition.

GARBH: I won't. I've learned not to count on your understanding.

SÁNÚ: Now, what the fuck does that mean?

GARBH: There. You see. This swimming right out into the muck of a filthy stream. After…

SÁNÚ: After…?

GARBH: Forget it. [*He busies himself opening the suitcase. He fumbles with its contents: clothes, fragments of fabrics, useful tools, small cards cut into various shapes, lengths of variously colored string, small round balls.*]

SÁNÚ: You never give up, do you?

GARBH: Why should I? What, you see the card shapes, the string, the balls? All right. *Dyibi.*

SÁNÚ: Don't dress it up. I just think it a strange way to handle a geometrical intuition.

[*He holds up some of the card shapes.*]

GARBH: You can see how these fit, can't you? Anybody with an eye for patterns won't ever get lost. I could show the simplicity of these…things.

SÁNÚ: [*Questioning statement.*] The string, and the little balls?

GARBH: I don't have much experience with those.

SÁNÚ: Ah, experience.

GARBH: These propositions have lived a long time, Sánú, and I have a young, untutored brain.

SÁNÚ: Of course.

GARBH: [*Suddenly.*] You know I've told you that I love you.

[*She approaches* GARBH, *touches his cheek. He brushes her off.*]

I don't need your pity.

SÁNÚ: Well, you won't have it. What shall we do about this situation?

GARBH: Think of it as two versions of the heart, a story that might get told.

SÁNÚ: Yes. [*She turns away.*] What have we here?

[MUSO, *an older woman, dressed in a kaftan and carrying a large walking stick, appears.*]

MUSO: Why do you have to make so much noise? I suppose you have no idea of how the day comes to an end here. You don't care, do you? It doesn't matter to you that the fawn might not come back to that spot by the stream. I assume you have your own notion of trust and your own interpretation of what beauty the dying light brings.

SÁNÚ: I suppose we should take this as a meaningful welcome.

MUSO: You ought to take it as an invitation to dance away from here. You seem lost, and wanderers on an undefined journey scare me.

SÁNÚ: You have most questionable, if not questioning, eyes.

MUSO: Don't you think you should account for yourself? [*She points at* GARBH.] Him, I know. His capacity sits around his ears.

GARBH: I don't appreciate being treated as a specimen.

MUSO: *¡Eso!* He has a voice.

SÁNÚ: This encounter seems to me a gift. I'd like to know your name. Perhaps we've met before.

MUSO: Never. I wouldn't forget.

SÁNÚ: Nor would I. I shouldn't have closed that circle before we had fully opened it.

MUSO: Yes. You see that now. [*She goes toward* GARBH.] But I see I've insulted this gentleman.

GARBH: As you intended.

[MUSO *sizes him up.*]

MUSO: I'll leave you to Scaltro.

SÁNÚ: Ah, Scaltro, yes, the empiricist.

MUSO: Don't pretend to know him. He wouldn't stand for these repetitions you seem to have stumbled into.

SÁNÚ: Another way of establishing the requisite distance, madame.

MUSO: Well, since you won't give any shape to your presence, I'll leave you to your darkness.

GARBH: This Scaltro, where did he serve?

[MUSO *laughs.*]

MUSO: Such a Roman way of declaring a connection.

SÁNÚ: A relation.

MUSO: Too clever. [*She walks away, bent but majestically.*]

SÁNÚ: [*Coaxingly to* GARBH.] You say you love me.

GARBH: Why do you do this?

SÁNÚ: Then why didn't you recognize me?

GARBH: When?

SÁNÚ: A few minutes ago. You spoke to me. Don't you remember? [*She sadly shakes her head.*] I don't know what to do with you. Anyhow, Garbh, we seem to have taken the wrong path. We have to turn around. Put everything away.

[*She starts down the path from which they have come. He scrambles to close the suitcase, and hurries to follow her. They disappear.* MUSO *comes to look toward their departure.*]

MUSO: Why does this woman keep bouncing about, looking for God? Why doesn't she just stay at home? Doesn't she realize that the presence sustains her? *Calma,* Muso. Sometimes you judge yourself too harshly. Or so I say, when my intuition tells me that I step beyond the line.

[SCALTRO, *a young man dressed to disguise himself, enters. He observes* MUSO *for a moment before he speaks.*]

SCALTRO: No tears? They didn't seem too willing to hang on here. Wouldn't you say?

MUSO: I could count on you to say it for me.

SCALTRO: You have to keep up your strength, Muso.

MUSO: "Grieving in her heart, she sat by the well..."

SCALTRO: Stop it. You tire me out, having to defend you against yourself and every other idiot out here who has eyes in his head.

MUSO: [*Mockingly.*] Eyes in his head.

SCALTRO: You know what I mean. Listen, we have to come to some understanding.

MUSO: [*Questioningly.*] Yes?

SCALTRO: I have debts that won't wait.

MUSO: Your debts mean nothing to me.

SCALTRO: Oh, I see. They, or I, or perhaps our twin-like existence doesn't fit in the scheme.

MUSO: Would you like to start that sentence again?

SCALTRO: You sound like my mother, one of those "commensurable" agents. You know I could have disrupted everything by just stepping out here, while you walked your mask around those innocents.

MUSO: You give yourself too much credit, Scaltro.

SCALTRO: You threatened them with my presence. I heard you.

MUSO: Then you heard a voice that hadn't really sounded.

SCALTRO: Too clever.

MUSO: You know, I have considered the possibility of your mother. Hear me out, Scaltro. You brought it up. This complexity of inequalities, this floating beyond the body, this discontinuous behavior, that takes you nowhere. Your mother, my sister...

SCALTRO: When did that occur?

MUSO: Don't interrupt.

[SCALTRO *points toward* SÁNÚ's *and* GARBH's *departure.*]

SCALTRO: I thought your spirit had eyes for the golden one.

MUSO: My spirit has eyes for a space beyond your imagination, Scaltro.

SCALTRO: You like my name, don't you? It has the right feel of wayward-
ness and distemper.

MUSO: I didn't name you. She did.

SCALTRO: [*Mockingly.*] The golden one. The one who just walked away
from your fervent embrace. My mother. What more can I tell you, Muso?
This situation won't sing.

MUSO: Then I will have to sacrifice you, won't I, Scaltro? Sacrifice you.

SCALTRO: You offered me to them, without even introducing me. How
indelicate.

MUSO: Which do you prefer, Scaltro? Singing in the choir, in stillness? Or
following the golden one, who already has your number?

SCALTRO: You think you'll catch me standing still, a small variable without
a soul. That will never happen. [*He starts to walk away.*]

MUSO: Wait. Don't you want to learn the steps that give you a body? But
go away. I suspect you have already killed your mother, another of your
propositional mistakes.

SCALTRO: No one has ever accused me of that.

MUSO: [*Matter-of-fact.*] Not one of your debts.

SCALTRO: No, Muso, not one of yours.

[MUSO *begins to howl.* SCALTRO *runs away.* MUSO's *howl modulates into a soft,
rhythmic chant which slowly stops.* MUSO *goes up left, and rests there, watching*
SÁNÚ *and* GARBH *enter, going from left to right.*]

SÁNÚ: We should get some rest.

GARBH: I don't think...

SÁNÚ: Don't make more of it than we need, Garbh.

[GARBH *starts a small unpacking.*]

I know I give you a hard time. But you chose to follow me.

GARBH: Follow you? You make it sound like a pilgrimage.

SÁNÚ: Yes.

GARBH: I didn't mean it that way.

SÁNÚ: What way?

GARBH: Oh, good, good, good. Here we go again with the examination.

SÁNÚ: Shall I examine you, Garbh?

GARBH: You know nothing about the reason my mother bundled me and sent me away.

SÁNÚ: An orphan.

GARBH: No. Something hidden in me, in her.

SÁNÚ: A mystery.

GARBH: We should rest.

SÁNÚ: I will. [*He prepares a place for her to lie. She tentatively approaches it, slowly gives in to it.*] Thank you. What about you?

GARBH: Don't worry about me. I don't need sleep.

SÁNÚ: Yes.

[*She closes her eyes, becomes still.* MUSO *turns and walks away.* GARBH *turns to us.*]

GARBH: Make of this what you will. I don't ask for anything. I go at my own pace. I know it seems I move in a small chamber, buckled in by a light that I can't even see, or at least one to which I give little of my attention. [*He points at* SÁNÚ.] The woman there approves this disembodied fearlessness, or thinks she does. She goes along with me because she thinks I go along with her. That ruthless appeal to a simple ethic makes us twins, doesn't it? You might ask, where did that come from? Or you might even believe that we have just tossed the dice, and set off to establish a new category where we all turn up with our own disguises. Did I say I knew her father? You see I thrive on disguise and omissions. And yet I like to measure things, and she likes that limbo of love that makes danger imperative and desirable. Shall we wake her, or shall we draw a circle around this night, and forget the shadows that give it a depth of insistence.

[*The light slowly fades on them. Lights on* SCALTRO *who remains agitated.*]

SCALTRO: I need this disturbance. Right? I need this constant kick in the gonads, a certain repetition of pain. The little one—you've met her—likes to throw these moods in your face. [*He catches himself.*] I said that badly, didn't I? It doesn't matter. We'll all learn to sing somehow. I'll tell you something that disturbs me more than this confusion of evangelists. These women have no modesty, the two of them. They've created a fragile state of ups and downs. Get to that. Does Muso want me in her world? Do I want her in mine? Her body escapes purity, even though she brings these loud recitatives with Sánú. I won't convict her just yet. But I will keep my eyes open, and my voice clear.

[*He moves away.* MUSO *appears, poking the ground with her walking stick.*]

MUSO: Ah, my Scaltro, talk about contradiction. The little angel pretends to sing in another choir, swears he has nothing to do with the rest of us suffering through this moment. He thinks he can reinvent himself, start this composition all over again. I have news for him. No one here will submit her body to Scaltro's baton. Leave that. I have to correct myself. No, I did not misjudge Sánú. I made the mistake of thinking that we...I...would reach a point of ultimate quality. I spoke as though we had reached that point. And what would God have to do with it? Why, you people come across as cunning as Scaltro, or as the music that makes me geometrical and real. I won't stand for it. I won't sing for you. I, after all, have seen another light entangled in our flesh. I like to challenge our angel with a new event. Sánú. She ought to know my name.

[*She walks away, going the way from which she came.* SÁNÚ *awakens, looks with astonishment at* GARBH.]

SÁNÚ: You. Someone came around while I slept.

GARBH: Did that disturb you?

SÁNÚ: I knew you hadn't gone away.

GARBH: What if I had? Gone away?

SÁNÚ: I would think that I had made a grand and incorrigible mistake.

GARBH: Something, of course, unlike you, Sánú.

SÁNÚ: At times, I think you know too much about my possibilities.

GARBH: A metaphysician.

SÁNÚ: Oh, you go straight to the heart.

GARBH: Nay, nay. The heart scares me. Look what it has got me here.

SÁNÚ: Assuming you have invested it here.

[*He turns away.*]

My god, Garbh. Take the garments out. We will rest here.

GARBH: You seem so sure of this place.

SÁNÚ: Does that disturb you?

[GARBH *fumbles among the suitcase's contents.*]

GARBH: What did you do with it?

SÁNÚ: With what? I haven't touched the baggage. I left that to you. Don't charge me with your oversight.

GARBH: Oversight she calls it. I wrapped the ankh in a velvet cloth. You pushed me aside. You placed it in the case.

SÁNÚ: And now you can't find it. This ankh that belongs to my father. Forgive me, Garbh, I know I shouldn't mention this at this time, since you've lost the connection…the relation you claim to have had with my father.

GARBH: I had no connection.

SÁNÚ: I heard you praying. Come clean, Garbh. We won't find the voice if we lose the liturgy.

GARBH: Do you want me here?

SÁNÚ: Certainly, if only to listen to my dreams.

[GARBH *starts to repack the case.*]

Calma, Garbh. Look at him, he thinks he can run away. [*She edges up to*

GARBH, *becomes threateningly coquettish.*] Tell me what you know about this exodus, this *gatuperio* we've discovered. [*She caresses him.*] Come on, Juan, speak up, sing to yourself. Well, then, shall I tell you some of my dreams? Which you should remember, since you claim to have known my father.

GARBH: Stop it. I made no such claims.

SÁNÚ: Contradiction.

GARBH: Go on with your story.

SÁNÚ: You remember…

GARBH: Stop it. You can't make me responsible for this ingenious way of avoiding yourself.

SÁNÚ: Garbh, the mathematician. [*Narrative tone.*] We stepped down, you and I, into an arroyo.

GARBH: Oh, boy. You will. How did we come to that?

SÁNÚ: *Tacete.* I'll tell you how we got to that, as though it would matter.

GARBH: I thought so, a story without a point.

SÁNÚ: [*Continuing.*] We had spent the dry season repairing our gardens, the terraces you remember. We came into the village, you, I, and this third entity you now refuse to acknowledge. What do you call that circle where we sat? You know the one, where the coffee came in sugared glasses and the tea in pots of rose and gold. You took us there. You must know its name.

GARBH: At this rate, we'll never get out of this story.

SÁNÚ: You have a funny idea of what belongs. Shall we just throw away everything that tells us how the heart felt at that moment? Shall I go on, or will you give it up the way you did then?

GARBH: What did I give up?

SÁNÚ: At last. Come here, Garbh, let me embrace you.

[*He goes dreamily to her embrace.*]

There. So the man selling the cattle knew why we had come.

GARBH: He had scoped us out.

SÁNÚ: Vulgarity! He welcomed us.

GARBH: Yes, he knew we had packets of silver in our pockets. I felt the chill of him.

SÁNÚ: Of course you did. He took your soul with the money. He made everything he did public. You stepped in the water with him, you never came back. But we wanted to return, and we wanted our silver, and we wanted this place. We determined to fight him, within that circle. He came to our table, sat with us, counting "one, two, three." You must remember. You stood up, and screamed, "I will not go there"!

GARBH: What happened then?

SÁNÚ: You tell me.

[*The sound of Sosu Njako, singing Tǫba music suddenly arises.* LUTTUOSO, *dressed in a patchy tuxedo, and* SÚRÚKÚ, *wrapped in a seedy monk's robe, approach* SÁNÚ *and* GARBH.]

LUTTUOSO: What have we here? Lovers at this altitude? *Orgullo.* Did no one instruct you how to behave in such an environment? I see. You have taken our measure, and you will take us over. But not quite yet, *meine frau.* The place still answers for itself. Don't you agree? [*He turns to his companion.*] Súrúkú. Tongue-tied pilgrims. If, in fact, this represents a pilgrimage.

SÁNÚ: What did you do with the cattle, *monsieur*?

LUTTUOSO: [*Pointing at* GARBH.] Can he speak?

SÁNÚ: I speak for him.

LUTTUOSO: Get to that. [*To* GARBH.] Does she?

GARBH: You will never know.

LUTTUOSO: Yes, of course. I just have to discount the evidence of my eyes and ears. Give me some credick, brother. It really doesn't matter. I just want someone, you or her, to tell me how you got here, and why you think you belong.

SÁNÚ: Who speaks for you?

LUTTUOSO: [*To* GARBH.] I salute you, brother. You'd have to go a long way before you could find another like her. But some things we cannot avoid. [*Duro Ladipo, or Kubik, sounds* Mori keke kan. LUTTUOSO *and* SÚRÚKÚ *sing the phrase, gradually rising in pitch.*] I admit we started on the wrong foot.

SÁNÚ: The wrong note.

LUTTUOSO: Trust you to notice our mistakes. Anyhow, you must know us now. [*He gestures.*] Luttuoso. Súrúkú.

SÁNÚ: The obscure suggestion of a living light has lost his memory. [*To* LUTTUOSO.] I remind you of that road to Madrid, *monsieur*. You will recall, surely, how you crawled on that desert floor, begging for water.

LUTTUOSO: Hey, don't get nasty with me.

SÁNÚ: Nasty!? I picked you up. I came along in an old Ford, on my way to Santa Fe. How could I miss a dead body in the road?

LUTTUOSO: Can't get it straight, can you? Dead body? Or suffering beggar?

SÁNÚ: Both. I took it as a mark of my excursion.

LUTTUOSO: Excursion! Richer still. You don't lie very well, do you? But go on. You have us fascinated. You picked me up...And what did you do?

SÁNÚ: I carried you until I saw your eyes stand still in your head, and then I buried you.

LUTTUOSO: In Santa Fe?

SÁNÚ: No, of course not. That village wouldn't have you. We had to make do with a ditch along the road.

LUTTUOSO: We? I suppose you mean this entity here.

SÁNÚ: No, I mean the saintly woman who brought us through that unpleasantness. You wouldn't understand.

LUTTUOSO: Such unruliness. And all of it laid out altar fashion. What of this do you expect us to believe? This purification of your own desires. But you missed your mark, my lady. You left out the suffering.

SÁNÚ: How would I know how much you suffered before you left us?

LUTTUOSO: There you go. I haven't gone anywhere. Say, you say I misled you. And now you want to conjure your charity, to put your stamp on this little harmony we've got going here. Don't make me embarrass you.

SÁNÚ: Oh, no, *monsieur*, you can never disrupt my return. I don't need memories of your failure.

LUTTUOSO: Failure?

SÁNÚ: You never arrived. You had no public business in Santa Fe. You would have had to give up your dancing because you knew no one with the proper touch for your desiccated music. Does that surprise you, my dead one, to realize that you had no ear for what awaited you in Santa Fe?

LUTTUOSO: This convocation seems to have taken a scrawny turn. Let's leave it there.

SÁNÚ: Where? I suggest that you pack up and keep going.

LUTTUOSO: A threat! A palpable invitation to a grimy war. Move me, you witch.

[SÁNÚ *grips her bag, puts her hand in it, becomes very still.*]

SÁNÚ: We seem to have come to an impasse.

LUTTUOSO: I'd call it a cleansing. Nothing you and your companion seem to understand. Here you stand in a darkness you didn't intend, and you want me to recall something that never happened, and remember people who had nothing to do with me.

[*He spreads his hands in questioning fashion.* SÚRÚKÚ *takes a step toward the center.*]

SÚRÚKÚ: Not finished. [*He points at* GARBH.] I want to see the threads, paper figures, the carefully coordinated little balls that dance in our imagination. You do want to show them to us. Don't you, brother?

GARBH: This doesn't concern you.

SÚRÚKÚ: Then why should she...concern me?

GARBH: What I have concerns only me.

SÚRÚKÚ: How do we know that, unless we see the instruments in the bag.

GARBH: Why do you call them instruments?

SÚRÚKÚ: What do you call them? You do want to show them. Of course, if we have reached some limit, a boundary that keeps us on this side of understanding, you will have to say.

LUTTUOSO: *Ánima*, Garbh.

GARBH: Did I give you my name?

LUTTUOSO: The air carries your name, Garbh. Even if you withhold your magic, we know your importance.

GARBH: Ridiculous. I don't appreciate your assault.

LUTTUOSO: Nonsense. We speak out of sincere regard.

GARBH: Leave me alone.

LUTTUOSO: Oh, he subscribes to the ancient: *bene vixit qui bene latuit*. Perfect.

SÚRÚKÚ: But let's not forget our need, Garbh. You have these instruments, these forces where events can live. Help me out, irregular little people who know nothing, who want instruction. Don't you agree?

GARBH: I have no reason to agree to such a proposition.

SÚRÚKÚ: What, then, do you propose, my mathematician, Garbh?

GARBH: Sánú!

SÚRÚKÚ: Leave her out of it. You talk to me.

GARBH: Follow me, Súrúkú. [*He begins a tutorial.*] "A graph has an Euler walk precisely when it connects…"

SÚRÚKÚ: Go on, *maestro*, repeat your lessons.

GARBH: Perhaps you would prefer that I talk about the property of a topological space, a property of every space related to the given space by a homeomorphism.

SÚRÚKÚ: Yes…?

GARBH: The concept homeomorphism dangles you, doesn't it?

SÚRÚKÚ: No more than the walk you seem to have abandoned.

GARBH: Shall I draw you a picture?

SÚRÚKÚ: Go on, *maestro*, repeat your lessons.

GARBH: [*Continuing.*] "zero or two vertices of odd degree…"

SÚRÚKÚ: Yes…?

GARBH: "then the walk must start at one of these vertices; otherwise the walk may begin anywhere."

[SÚRÚKÚ *applauds.*]

SÚRÚKÚ: There, you see. You did manage to speak to me. But that doesn't explain the absence of the ankh.

LUTTUOSO: Exactly. Maybe we do need Sánú's voice here. She might explain this absence, or at least tell us why it matters so.

GARBH: Sánú, I told you.

SÚRÚKÚ: What did you tell her?

LUTTUOSO: Your confused antiquity won't help her now, not after such deliberate carelessness. ¿*Verdad, matrona?* Let's go back to that road to Madrid. Why did you choose to travel that road? You found me. You buried me, you say. Tell me, what did you want to kill?

SÁNÚ: Oh my, a soothsayer, a prophet.

LUTTUOSO: No, not at all. I just want to disentangle this ceremony of absences, and do away with this dancing around altars that have no place. This business with the ankh gives me an uneasy feeling. And you haven't answered my question.

SÁNÚ: Luttuoso. Such an inquisition doesn't appeal to my spirit.

[LUTTUOSO *breaks into loud laughter.*]

LUTTUOSO: Súrúkú, see what he had in that bag.

SÁNÚ: I wouldn't go there.

LUTTUOSO: *Matrona.* The ditch with the buried body we left back there. Go on, Súrúkú.

[SÚRÚKÚ *tears at* GARBH's *bag, spilling its contents.*]

SÁNÚ: Feel better?

LUTTUOSO: Disappointed. Did I tell you? I never knew your father.

SÁNÚ: Of course you didn't.

LUTTUOSO: You don't seem too surprised by these easy losses. We might even suspect that you orchestrate these miseries. Why don't you come clean? [*He grabs* SÁNÚ's *bag, and spills its contents at her feet.*] There, I've saved you a long walk.

SÁNÚ: Garbh! Do you see this!

LUTTUOSO: You think he cares about what you have at your feet? Let's see what we have here. [*He roughly examines several items, dropping them without any real regard for them.*] I thought so. Nothing here. You have disappeared the ankh.

[SÁNÚ *tries to gather and arrange her bag.*]

Leave it. Trash. What you've hidden left you without your noticing. ¿Verdad?

SÁNÚ: I'll have to burn everything here. Nothing can live with that filthy touch on it.

[LUTTUOSO *laughs.*]

LUTTUOSO: Sure. And of course go back to that road, find the ditch, and dig up the body.

SÁNÚ: Garbh, I need your help. [*He hesitates.*] I need your help! I need your help! [LUTTUOSO *gingerly kicks at what has been spilled.*]

LUTTUOSO: Come on, Súrúkú. Our angel has hidden her piety. Let's leave this danger.

[*He and* SÚRÚKÚ *stomp away, laughing.* SÁNÚ *howls.* GARBH *comes forward to comfort her. She beats him away.*]

SÁNÚ: No, not you. Not now. Get out of my face. You abandoned me. I suppose you agree with that bandit. You heard him, how he accused me of missing my mark. I'll tell you who missed the mark. That idiot lay in that grave, dead, yes, I said dead. The answer had already passed him, and he knew nothing about me, nothing about the road, nothing that would tell him why I had no patience with finding his insignificant body scattered on a road I needed to travel. Get out of my face, Don Federico. Look at you. You want me to take your sentimentalities to heart, and open a door to mine. What do you want? Why did I go to Santa Fe, Luttuoso? You will never understand that I had there to meet Don Estrafalario, who had a question for me and an answer that not even God could give.

[GARBH *takes a tentative step toward her.*]

Oh, you have found your courage. We live in diminished air, but you believe that we will go on. Together. Of course. No, don't touch me. We can't share this secret abandonment. I don't like your dancing. Go!

[GARBH *stands astonished, then hurriedly gathers his disordered bag, and limps away.* SÁNÚ *gathers her bag.*]

He took what didn't belong to him. No matter. I could never now sort it out.

[MUSO *appears, carrying a lighted lantern and a few sticks.*]

MUSO: But you must. Sort it out. Or should I ask, who got buried on that road to Madrid?

SÁNÚ: Why should you think to take advantage of me now, Muso?

MUSO: My, my, what aptitude. You recognize yourself. And what did happen to Don Estrafalario? Did he ever turn up, or should I ask, did he ever put himself in your way?

SÁNÚ: You know the answer.

MUSO: Don't play with me. I know, you didn't like my first approach. Anyone could see that you hadn't properly measured the distance between you and God.

SÁNÚ: ¡Maravilla! You've changed your story.

MUSO: No, my angel, I've never told you my story.

[SÁNÚ *turns away.*]

Ah, here we go, with that impatience I thought you had lost.

SÁNÚ: You've misread me.

MUSO: [*Questioning statement.*] A text that has hardly appeared?

SÁNÚ: Perhaps.

[MUSO *puts down her lantern and sticks. She unstraps a small cloth bag fastened to her side. She sits, as though she would sit near a fire she would light.*]

MUSO: Sit down. Let me tell you a story.

SÁNÚ: Just what I need, a story.

MUSO: As a matter of fact, you do, to help you to understand this emotion that has you so enthralled. Sit.

SÁNÚ: I prefer to stand.

MUSO: I can wait.

[SÁNÚ *cautiously sits opposite* MUSO.]

There. We have the right temper for my tale. [*She begins her narrative.*] "You will pass granite for a length of days you will refuse to measure." Her first words to me. "You will find comfort in scruffy spruces, white pine, alders and a rambunctious crew of lightning-scorched maples. But, as you turn, you will realize your error. You will have to see white pine, hemlock, blue spruce, paper birch, a living sheath around a divided heart, a layer of growing and dividing cells." You might guess my impatience with someone I thought felt a need to instruct me. Where did she come from? Did I ask for her presence? Can you picture her? A young woman in a white dress, mistakenly turned out it seemed to me. Her eyes appeared gems closed upon themselves, a light turned inward, no light for me. Sit, Sánú. You have to understand my discomfort, Or should I say, our discomfort.

SÁNÚ: I don't have time for this.

MUSO: Oh? Tell me about your time.

SÁNÚ: You entered it when you came upon us back then.

MUSO: When?

SÁNÚ: I resent this flagellation, Muso. My apologies. But, *ya*. [*She starts to stand.*]

MUSO: [*Quickly.*] She said to me, "I have it that some power has carefully installed the heart, to function until the elastic flare of artery grows small with age and stress. I have it that my mother's story writes itself in the manner of leaves' sugar, soil minerals, and water, an intricate chemistry that endangers my spirit." I wanted to stop this litany. I wanted her to go away. I held up my hand in surrender. But no, not yet. She said, "My mother died. I live like a rat, nibbling at grain, excessively in motion. An old, defrocked professor gave me the word for my peripatetic intensity, called me a *flâneuse.*" I did not want her there, you see, a body constructed from the means at its disposal, that unpredictable complexity of activated depth. Why did the woman fiddle with me? Why did I gravely solicit such systemic assault? Perhaps I relied upon a collateral vessel structured by another and simple desire.

SÁNÚ: I understand now. You conjure this fictive embrace to arrange your own disappearance. What happened to that elixir of sensations you felt. You will lie, and preen yourself with this flow of molecular loss and acquisition. No, Muso, the loss disturbs you. Tell me what she said about your mother.

MUSO: It won't work, Sánú, turning this necessary flaw into a necessary acquisition. You and I. [MUSO *lights the fire.*] I won't let you go until you tell me what you intend to do with those threads, that cloth, you have hidden in your bag.

SÁNÚ: Not your story. You don't intend to continue, do you?

MUSO: We don't need that orphan you sent away, do we? You guessed, I assume. I stole the woman in the white garment, stole her benevolent heartache, from you. Where have we arrived, except at that point where our harmonies overwhelm us.

[*The sudden eruption of Carlo Gesualdo's* Tristis est anima mea, *brief and gone.*]

SÁNÚ: Goodbye, Muso. Take care of your lantern. [SÁNÚ *gathers her possessions, and runs away.*]

MUSO: I won't disappear, and you won't invent me.

[*She gathers her possessions, and goes in the opposite direction.* SÁNÚ *reappears, standing above, alone.*]

SÁNÚ: She bled me twice. She neglected me, and bled me twice. What did she have fastened to her body? She tried to frighten me with her lantern, her torchlight. But I will tell her, nothing will make me sing in a choir where the voices have lost their edge, No, not now.

[*She stumbles off. We find* GARBH, *on his knees, tearing at his clothes, his material, himself.*]

GARBH: What does she want from me? I put my faith in her. No, no. Let's not speak of faith. That takes you back to an emptiness I felt all along. Yes, in her. Oh, you say, if you knew this, why did you continue? [*Accusingly.*] I don't know. I saw a reasonable composition of virtues, something that would let me go on, go on, find myself. We...I...had to wait for some thought, some feeling, something other than what I held, to astonish me. Why not wait at her side? Why not give in to the appeal of her voice when she first spoke to me? Blame it on my youth. How a certain clarity in that sound determined what I had chosen to hear.

[SCALTRO *is suddenly there.*]

SCALTRO: What did you choose to hear?

GARBH: Do I know you?

SCALTRO: My mama says you do. She sent me to look for you. She said that, even though she hadn't heard much of it, she liked your voice. She thought you might could use some help.

GARBH: You'll have to forgive me. I've found myself, as you can see, in a difficult position, a moment that should pass, briefly.

SCALTRO: You can't get it straight, can you? What do I have to see here? A man praying? Or a man scratching at the earth, trying to bury his humiliation?

GARBH: I notice a lot of talk about burials. What made you think that I had chosen this place...for another one?

SCALTRO: Peace, brother. I have only come to give light to those who sit in darkness.

GARBH: *Orgullo.*

SCALTRO: Don't pretend. Anybody can see your scars.

GARBH: What about yours?

SCALTRO: I don't make all that public.

GARBH: Yes, I see. You, too, must belong to her.

SCALTRO: You know, you remind me of a guy who stole a knife from me, and then called me a thief, denounced me to the Colima police and awaited my execution. I don't think I could recognize that man now. I don't even think I can recognize you. Muso told me that you have something to do with figures, or with their placement.

GARBH: Don't pretend.

SCALTRO: What, not to see this blind passage you seem to have come upon. Not to see that your story can't go much further because it has no place. You like these little ceremonies, this choirboy singing, so you went tripping with her in order to hear yourself. Or so you say. Right?

GARBH: Put it like that.

SCALTRO: No, Garbh. I have no interest in watching this flagellant possibility of return. Return to what? Can you tell me? You got caught in a cleansing. You got caught helping her remove all passion from this act you thought you had to perform. You need a desert, my man, somewhere where every heartache echoes in a body you want to hide. You didn't choose very well. I found you. Muso didn't give me a map.

GARBH: Bully for you. A genius.

SCALTRO: You might say so. Well, where do we stand? You have all these instruments, as you call them, that make me feel like a beggar on a street corner. Give me something. I could have taken another route, and left you out here to fiddle with your design, until you fell apart and gave it up. Why don't you give me some credit, brother?

GARBH: I don't need you here.

SCALTRO: Of course you don't need me. No one needs me. I make quite a bit of change masquerading as an improbability. Get to that. You can't dress that up, and burn it. Look here, let's start from square one. Tell me my name. Give me an identity you can handle, Jimmy.

GARBH: She sent you, didn't she?

SCALTRO: I said so.

GARBH: No, not her. The other one. She couldn't let go. She played with my power, and then she released me.

SCALTRO: Maybe she loves you. Uh oh, that little engine done got started. I can see it in your eyes. [*Mockingly.*] She loves me.

GARBH: Shut your mouth!

SCALTRO: Whoa. That sounds like something got shaken loose because of certain mistaken, and perhaps fanciful, declarations. *¿Verdad?*

GARBH: You have a minute to disappear.

SCALTRO: Hey, my man, the minute came with me. Did you consider that I might know how the ankh escaped the case? [GARBH *becomes very still.*] Speak up. These little factuals, artifacts, whatever you want to call them, always have minds of their own, and you might not understand what they intend. Think of this. You're thinking a certain freedom, and that freedom finds its place in a little emblem that hangs from your neck. And suddenly, your hand can't find it, and your heart won't let it go. So Garbh loves Sánú.

GARBH: Forget that name. You don't know her, you bandit.

SCALTRO: You once accused me of stealing a knife. You haven't gone very far in your understanding, have you?

[GARBH *searches his possessions.*]

Looking for the knife? Or looking for my name?

GARBH: For the God who made you a burden to this world!

SCALTRO: You've come up with a heavy proposition, one that I might resent. And that would make me unfaithful to Muso. Don't do that, pilgrim. We might have to revisit that road to Santa Fe. Haven't you learned anything with your sketches?

[*A chanting starts in the distance. Women's voices that grow more distinct as they approach. Several young women, draped in brilliant clothes, proceed carrying small pouches, a basket, and one bowl.*]

WOMEN: [*Singing.*] *Mori keke kan.* [*They ignore* GARBH *and* SCALTRO. *They circle, stop, place the basket and bowl on the ground. Looking scornfully at the men, they retreat, singing.*] *Mori keke kan.*

SCALTRO: So they must blame me. I will straighten this out with Luttuoso and Súrúkú. This doesn't concern you.

GARBH: Oh, Scaltro the judge. You have no right to tell me about my life.

SCALTRO: Oh? Then, of course, you saw the young woman bleeding by the side of the road. The wounded one.

GARBH: Stop it!

SCALTRO: I mean to stop you from fading away. Come away. We have no place here.

GARBH: I can go on my own.

SCALTRO: Then why did you let me find you? Come away. You carry an unnecessary burden for such a fragile body. Come away. I will go with you.

[*They gather* GARBH*'s possessions, and limp off. Pause.* SÁNÚ *and* MUSO *appear together.*]

SÁNÚ: What did I expect to find?

MUSO: Only what I have brought with me. [*She opens the bag she has fastened to her body, removes a brightly colored cloth and small, buttonlike, polished stones.*]

SÁNÚ: What will you do with those?

MUSO: Such a question. [*She drops the cloth in the basket, the stones in the bowl.*] I prepared.

SÁNÚ: You hold that against me, or shall I say, against yourself.

MUSO: Watch your syntax.

SÁNÚ: Why didn't you say, watch your measure?

MUSO: That would imply a singing, of which you seem most incapable.

SÁNÚ: Judgment.

MUSO: Prove me wrong.

SÁNÚ: You saw the young woman at the side of the road?

MUSO: *Basta!* Get on with your story. Have you no feel for the construction of this beautiful line?

SÁNÚ: No. Unless I start again.

MUSO: Impossible.

SÁNÚ: You say. I have my scarab. [*In a narrative voice.*] Someone sent the Galisteo Public Library an annotated copy of Horace's Fourth Book of Odes. No one quite understood the point. After all, the two, perhaps three, troubadours active in the whole life of Galisteo had composed *rancheras,* wedding songs, *boleros, plenas, guajiras* and *sones de mariachi,* nothing remotely like those Roman artifices. At any rate, the book disappeared, to turn up in a Central Avenue pawnshop in Albuquerque, where it chummily sat festooned with ribbons and an exorbitant price. Leroy Baca offered an evening of authentic cockfighting in exchange for the text.

MUSO: *Basta!* Don't play with my spirit.

SÁNÚ: You saw me wounded.

MUSO: I saw Luttuoso.

SÁNÚ: Yes?

MUSO: Súrúkú.

SÁNÚ: Of course.

MUSO: I heard them singing.

SÁNÚ: You heard me singing. Someone who dared to walk that narrow Turquoise Trail toward Don Estrafalario.

MUSO: Oh, my. I thought we had done away with his substance.

[SÁNÚ *acts this part of her narrative.*]

SÁNÚ: First, put the cardboard suitcase in the trunk of the car, and do not forget the picnic basket. I trust you packed the blankets on the top. Everyone knows the chill of the trail. Aunt Tidy calls it angel's breath, says it cleanses the soul—assuming one has a soul to cleanse. Well, now, that gets us close to a categorical syllogism, and there we go fishing after propositions and sentences and getting tangled in logical form. How do we begin that argument that tells us about that spirit-burdened predicate we found wandering that road?

[*The eruption of the chorus of Sirene from the Florentine wedding first intermedio.*]

MUSO: That road has washed out. Hear me!? Washed out!

SÁNÚ: Impossible. [SÁNÚ *picks up the cloth and the stones, lets them flow through her fingers.*]

MUSO: We knew her, you know. You tried to avoid her by giving all your attention to Luttuoso, or this quest for the indigenous Estrafalario.

SÁNÚ: Back off, my soul, you don't understand.

MUSO: Oh, but I do. Blindness doesn't suit my nature. We came out of that canyon. [*She considers for a moment.*] Canyon. The spiritually impaired hear the word as *kanon*, a Byzantine embarrassment expunged from Old Town. No one makes a point of that church anymore. We have only those caroling contingencies that come only on Saturday, when every *joven vaquero* must wed and feed upon the glazed cakes that have made their way from Chihuahua across a desert with an ambiguous claim. You might encounter a quarrel over the purple prickly pear or apache plum, and might have to sing a verse of *La Cigarra*, but those who have no ear for the resonant indifference gathered on this valley's floor won't bother you. Perhaps this Don Estrafalario knows that book, and knows the *musica sapientis* that constantly disturbs.

SÁNÚ: I don't like this habit of discounting suffering.

MUSO: Scandalous! Where did you get that? What can I say? You must remember the white dress. Of course you do.

SÁNÚ: Stop it.

MUSO: I can't.

[SÁNÚ *begins to unravel a length of bright fabric she takes from her bag.*]

SÁNÚ: What do you think about that? Shall we drop it in the basket? [*She does.*]

MUSO: Clever. Sing me something, give it the proper measure.

[*The eruption of Sosu Njako's Ṭọba music.*]

SÁNÚ: I don't think we should linger here.

MUSO: No. Our voices seem not to belong.

[SÁNÚ *tries to gather the basket and bowl.*]

Leave them. The others will have need of them.

[*They go off.* LUTTUOSO *comes into the light.*]

LUTTUOSO: Who will identify me as the witness to my own birth? I sense a betrayal. Too many questions lie dead upon me. Say, listen, this Súrúkú hangs on, gets in my way, tries to answer for me. You'd think he'd given me my solitude as a gift. Maybe I give him too much credit. The coyote followed me all the way up to Vermont. I tell you, Sylvester, Vermont does not believe in gray days. But as a courtesy to serve the rest of us, it gives temporary visas to a delegation from Québec province who will provide a melancholic gallimaufry that will endanger the happiness of everyone on the eastern seaboard. When you think of it, you have to acknowledge that blissful attribute and gift, this choreographing of *la nausée*, their perfect attention to a redeeming severity. Our Québecois neighbors have dedicated themselves to a task that few would undertake, and have asked for no compensation, no reward, no citation, no monument. They haven't even asked for per diem, preferring to make their way through the land picking berries and drinking from clear streams. My old buddy, Anthony Tipich, who likes to piss on everything, has introduced a little doubt into this story. He says the delegation consists not of people but of wind, rain, blizzards, frozen water, and a veiled sun. You will, of course, say that Anthony doesn't always hit the bucket. Leave it at that. I've got enough to deal with with this Sánú and this Muso. Take this Muso, for example, a field in periodic motion, full of energy, full of tales. And this Sánú, a half-assed geographer, can't get the trail straight, doesn't know a rock from a bleeding body. So there you have it. Say, I admit I sometimes can't tell them apart. They turn up in the same silence; they cuddle this lost objective possibility. And now they want to take this situation as an event. Get to that. I have died, and have become an event.

[SÚRÚKÚ *enters, tapping his walking stick.*]

SÚRÚKÚ: There you go again. You think all light just flows through your skin.

LUTTUOSO: What a composition. Syntax, Súrúkú. You have done it again, bending things out of shape.

SÚRÚKÚ: Don't hand me your disorder, Luttuoso. I remind you, my saint, of the generosity of this landscape. Look around you. I remind you of your geometrical failures, sir. Look at what we have here—a bowl, a basket. You can touch them. [SÚRÚKÚ *goes to do that. He pulls a cloth from the basket.*] Mercy, someone has left a bountiful exhibit of sun.

[*He goes with it toward* LUTTUOSO, *who withdraws.*]

LUTTUOSO: Get away from me!

SÚRÚKÚ: Yes. We did leave that there, didn't we? In the ditch?

LUTTUOSO: Don't presume.

SÚRÚKÚ: Absolutely correct. I should put this back, and keep my hands off these tokens until someone who can appreciate them, or has need of them, comes along. Their lying here on this ground might only nurture your lies.

LUTTUOSO: I don't lie.

SÚRÚKÚ: Ah, Luttuoso, how do you think we encouraged that periodic motion?

LUTTUOSO: Sánú!

SÚRÚKÚ: Why, the saint has again found his face. Oh, oh, oh, sing with me, Luttuoso. [SÚRÚKÚ *begins a tuneless fragment of a song.*] *Maa kọrọbá salē ká sáráká yé...*

LUTTUOSO: Wait a minute. You didn't sing that when she first came upon us. Listen to yourself, the last phrase.

SÚRÚKÚ: How would you know?

LUTTUOSO: Oh, yes, he wants to take me over, help to dig my grave.

SÚRÚKÚ: A service to myself, if you wish. A service to Sánú, if you wish.

[LUTTUOSO *confronts* SÚRÚKÚ.]

LUTTUOSO: Put these emblems back in their places. I have never violated the spirit.

[SÚRÚKÚ *disdainfully replaces the material.*]

SÚRÚKÚ: Satisfied?

[LUTTUOSO *nods.*]

LUTTUOSO: If you want to continue with me, pay attention to what your landscape tells you. We have a lot of ground to cover. We can't step out here naked.

[SÚRÚKÚ *nods.*]

Alright, then. I told you I would go with you.

SÚRÚKÚ: And I will go with you, Luttuoso, even if you sometimes mistake the music.

[*They move off.* GARBH *returns, empty-handed, and alone.*]

GARBH: Scaltro? I thought so. Well, I can wait. Three days into yesterday can make anyone breathless. Listen. There lie fifteen measures where I would now walk. I have no vision, only a sightful confusion. I have to go forward now, with this measure and an accounting of this place within this world. You won't believe me, but the body moves backward in time. I don't understand this labyrinth, the density of walking through space. Someone wakes me to a distance that will fit; someone invokes the name for distance. Think of it, this accounting for measure or for place. Why should measure so concern the body, so ensnare the mind? I have to account for distance, or movement, the borrowed words that no one saw fit to teach me. I can't get out of this labyrinth. Take this under advisement: I have not mentioned the light, or called my inner voice for that fable of discovery. You see me awkward about light. I cannot begin again before measure, the movement, and now I would say Sun, Sunday, Moon, Monday, nowhere apparent in spring or summer. How can I persuade myself of this fable of birth? Certain qualities undo me. I recall the attribute of lying still. I insist I have anticipated nothing. I swear by lying still.

[*He catches a movement, turns, and walks rapidly away.* SCALTRO *appears, looking off after* GARBH.]

SCALTRO: I have my music at my fingertips. I make no use of these harmonies that everybody knows, melodies that anyone can sing without a score. Sánú doesn't fool me. She keeps trying to find a transposition that will open a grave. I suppose she would put me in it, and do away with that aria that makes no sense. I leave you with one thought: which one of us will grasp the bird, and feel the fluttering blood that hums through it?

[He walks away. Pause. SÁNÚ and MUSO enter upon a clamor of bells that suddenly stops. MUSO carries a rolled parchment.]

SÁNÚ: [Referring to the parchment.] Why do you have that?

MUSO: You saw me gather it. I certainly thought you would understand that this belongs to the ceremony.

SÁNÚ: [Questioning statement.] The ceremony.

MUSO: A record of it.

SÁNÚ: Begin again, stepping across these borders. The bourrée of existence under siege, a different measure that speaks of accomplishment, plays over its own silence. Learning this difficult dance, must I consider my body as the active principle of the universe?

MUSO: I thought you left that reasoning there.

SÁNÚ: Where?

MUSO: Along the road where I found you. And now you come to me with these questions.

SÁNÚ: These questions get worked out in places redemptively abandoned by water.

MUSO: Oh, I love this, the way you account for your presence here.

SÁNÚ: What else can I do?

MUSO: Sánú, you haven't gone far enough. Imagine a theatre shorn of its ankle bells. Imagine its flamboyant solidity, its egregious color. What would you then have? Why, a perfect home to put the spirit on trial.

SÁNÚ: I assume you mean yours.

MUSO: I sense that you accuse me of a deliberate misconception, of constructing a figured box from which I will pull a parchment of the familiar dead.

SÁNÚ: Familiar?

MUSO: Do you deny me this?

SÁNÚ: Your theatre seems to have an athletic temper. Its dimensions overwhelm the body, and yet the body remains the summation of its existence. Your young woman in white.

MUSO: Well, given your skepticism, perhaps we could use a day in Athens. Three tragedies and a satyr play, all before nightfall. One could imagine the slow approach of the most significant death, and feel the rumpled benevolence of its presence. So we would come to another form of measure.

SÁNÚ: Of death? I admire your theatre, Muso. But the most intrepid actors avoid it. Its crumbling stone sits under an unforgiving sun or a docile moon, and the place has an air of abandonment and a flagrant smell of disaster and danger.

[MUSO *quietly goes to the basket and bowl with her parchment.*]

You don't mean to leave it there?

MUSO: And why not?

[SÁNÚ *moves to take the parchment from* MUSO.]

SÁNÚ: Give it to me.

MUSO: Sánú, don't you think we have reached a comfortable silence? You and I? *Calma*, Sánú. I ran into Cecil Napoleon.

SÁNÚ: When?

MUSO: Oh, say a moment ago.

SÁNÚ: And?

MUSO: Cecil wants to dismantle Lead Avenue. He will do it out of pique. Someone has given him a bit of obsidian, and Cecil says he handles it until his fingers bleed. The donor said something about Indians and cutting. Cecil knows that price. Morning after morning, he watches the Navajo pass the First National Bank on the corner of Central and North Fourth, and press their instrument against the bank's marble façade.

SÁNÚ: Cecil has told you this?

MUSO: Yes, of course. [*She continues her story.*] That secular vision makes him will the destruction of a street that has grown much too narrow.

SÁNÚ: Muso, the street no longer exists.

MUSO: You must understand that Cecil can never grasp the geometrical distance from Albuquerque to Gallup, or to the Canyon de Chelly. Think how he feels about this hard-edged instrument that has never served his heart.

SÁNÚ: Ah, metaphorical bliss.

MUSO: Don't abuse yourself, sister. And Cecil, this moment, belongs to me.

SÁNÚ: *Calma*, my soul. I have no designs on your dream.

MUSO: Good. [*She fiddles with an arrangement of the parchment, basket and bowl.*]

SÁNÚ: *Aspetta*, Muso. Something seems off here.

MUSO: Let's see. [*She starts to pull the cloth from the basket.*] Devilment, dishevelment. Sad. Well, at least we can repair things. [*She dumps the basket's contents, and starts to rummage among them. She finds an ankh.*] I suppose this belongs to you.

[SÁNÚ *tries to take it;* MUSO *holds it away from her.*]

I never want to believe such malignity.

SÁNÚ: Give it to me.

MUSO: Nay. Why did you leave it here? When did you leave it here? Oh, my princess conjures her own purity, and cuts me away. Then she disguises herself. What do you want from me?

SÁNÚ: You...

MUSO: Say it.

SÁNÚ: Luttuoso.

MUSO: What?

SÁNÚ: Súrúkú.

[LUTTUOSO *enters, amid a sound of bells, and leading two youthful drummers who circle and challenge* MUSO *and* SÁNÚ.]

LUTTUOSO: You need a judgment? Eyes that still can see what the light reveals. You want to give me that spiritual token, Muso? Since the thing itself has refused your bodies. Or should I say, your body?

SÁNÚ: Luttuoso, we don't want you...

LUTTUOSO: Yes? What? You buried me, and you think I will just disappear. Nay. Come to yourself. Why should I go away without what sustains me? Tell me that.

SÁNÚ: I told you...

LUTTUOSO: Ah, she told me.

[*He gestures. The drummers go away, drumming as they go.*]

Now. Who put the ankh in the basket? And who left payment in the bowl for lives that hadn't reached fulfillment? Speak up.

SÁNÚ: I will. I refuse the life I buried with you.

MUSO: What did you do with me?

SÁNÚ: But you know sharp-edged instruments that serve no purpose.

MUSO: *Bruto!* [*She holds up the ankh.*] Shall I give this spirit the key?

SÁNÚ: No. It will never open anything again. Luttuoso. Your shadow no longer serves me. Come, Muso. He won't follow us. He doesn't have the courage to carry this little emblem with no thought of reward.

LUTTUOSO: Don't you move. You have given no account of yourself.

SÁNÚ: Impossible.

[MUSO *and* SÁNÚ *walk away.*]

LUTTUOSO: What will those responsible here say!? You hear me, I know. You won't find another body to bury. Understand that. Hear me!?

[*He tears through the cloth on the ground, overturns the bowl, runs away. Pause. The light catches* GARBH, *alone.*]

GARBH: Something awakens me now. You might ask for evidence, some reliable measure of an unreliable state. I take nothing for granted, not even the argument you refuse to make. Years ago, I involved myself with a student, who insisted, day by day, upon taking me into the court he had established for the science of existence as existence. Some of those among the crusty offices and rancid cafés we frequented knew, or claimed to know, the fraudulence of his persistent occupation, knew it as something he had knocked up to titillate himself with my discomfort, even though I had no idea of the rationalization for an internal urge I could never see. A defenseless naïveté? I will say only that I trusted the exuberant anguish of the student, who led me through the wayward boustrophedon of the text he wanted to write. We would often meet in the most prominent coffee houses along the central avenue near the university, and would spend hours, crammed around an overflowing table, in the company of folk whose intellectual seriousness seemed suspect. So I have done nothing about addressing this unreliable state. I seem only to have reconfigured it, and have led you to distrust me.

[SÚRÚKÚ *comes cautiously upon him.*]

SÚRÚKÚ: Why, Garbh, I thought you had designed this event. Why else would you have given up your little figures, to swim around this desert of misunderstanding? All alone. You left us in a hurry. Such disregard. I will say nothing about certain propositions you made along the way, a certain mapping of sensibilities that seem not to disturb you at the moment. But consider those who had already awakened, and thought of you as a kindred spirit.

GARBH: Have I met you? I don't recognize you.

SÚRÚKÚ: [*Dismissively.*] Recognition. Here we stand. And I have attended to your hymnal pleading. [*He comes forward, as though they had settled a point.*] What will we do with Sánú, now that you have uncovered her? You know that she has taken another turn, away from me, of course. Now, here I come upon you, lamenting something that shouldn't even concern you.

GARBH: What do you know about my concern?

SÚRÚKÚ: Well, I trust my ears.

GARBH: Listen. I have found this place. You will notice that I have everything my spirit needs. I don't need your conjuration.

SÚRÚKÚ: My man, I do not conjure.

GARBH: That sounds so much like Luttuoso.

SÚRÚKÚ: Luttuoso.

GARBH: A dead body.

SÚRÚKÚ: You remember that, do you?

GARBH: Your point?

SÚRÚKÚ: Nay, *maestro*, I have no point to establish.

GARBH: My, he runs away from his own conception, and expects me to follow.

SÚRÚKÚ: Ah, I see. Your design requires an absence. I salute your bravery. I must have heard the wrong voice. You will forgive me. *Ciao, maestro.* [*He starts off.*]

GARBH: Wait a minute. She sent you, didn't she?

SÚRÚKÚ: That tells me that I made two mistakes.

GARBH: You won't get away with it, this flashing about in an emptiness you create.

SÚRÚKÚ: I meant to ask you. Do you remember, along the way, seeing an old Baptist church crumbling quietly away? Or somewhere around Madrid, seeing a cook's hat, abandoned, tumbling from door to unvisited door?

GARBH: I don't like this equation.

SÚRÚKÚ: Keep this in mind when you hear the cottonwood near the ditch begin its whispering vespers. [*He bows, and walks away.*]

GARBH: Come back here! We haven't finished.

SÚRÚKÚ: Impossible.

GARBH: You love her, don't you? You love her!

[SÚRÚKÚ *turns, and walks back guardedly but belligerently.*]

SÚRÚKÚ: What did you say?

GARBH: Something you know, and try to avoid. How do you put it, something about the nose? This little charade you worked up to test me.

SÚRÚKÚ: You really believe that? That I need to debase myself…

GARBH: Yes? Go on. This floating from feeling to feeling, that seems such a part of your nature, fascinates me.

[SÚRÚKÚ *laughs.*]

Jealousy.

SÚRÚKÚ: This gets more ridiculous.

GARBH: Not at all. Súrúkú. You have no edges. Anything that surfaces gives you an opportunity to test your shape. Look at you. You follow Luttuoso until those lines disappear. Muso grabs you, and you flow from point to point. Then you turn up here, asking me to read this new shape, this new you. And, of course, you can't admit that you need me, can you?

SÚRÚKÚ: I thought I needed Sánú.

GARBH: Your body has compromised you. There you stand. Heavier than air, certainly, but no more substantial than the thought of you.

SÚRÚKÚ: I noticed that you haven't asked me what Muso asked me to do when I found you.

GARBH: [*Mockingly.*] Oh? She sent a message? Why would she send someone so incomplete? There you go, think about it, Súrúkú. And get out of my face.

SÚRÚKÚ: No, no, no, Garbh. You can't just design another evasion.

GARBH: Go away, Súrúkú.

[SÚRÚKÚ *slowly draws tightly against* GARBH.]

SÚRÚKÚ: I do not love Sánú.

GARBH: Of course not.

SÚRÚKÚ: I will tell Muso that I lost you, that I never found a trace of you. I will do that for you, Garbh. [*He starts to walk away.*] I leave you with the one thing you cannot deny.

GARBH: *Dígame, patroncito.*

SÚRÚKÚ: You will never find the voice to sing a proper motion. *Ciao, maestro.*

[*He goes without looking back.* GARBH *howls, and runs away. Pause. The light catches* SCALTRO, *isolated, standing in shadow.*]

SCALTRO: Clever man, that Súrúkú, capable of the cut, even though he might go over the same ground, trying to uncover these discontinuities, trying to find something commensurable. Should I care? Listen, take what you have seen, this instrumental inattention to my person. No one asks about that debt. Wonderful. What should we call it? A phenomenon of a hidden economy, something that just moves against my body, and then suddenly disappears. But I must assure you here of the irrelevance of money. Certainly, I have learned to count upon a physical need of coinage, palpable stock. Muso might think that I embrace a pilgrim theology. The others who know my situation, or think that they do, dance around me with their fraudulent sympathy, palpating my belly, if you know what I mean. What can I tell you? I've always had to frame my debt in some kind of innocence. *Apátheia*, a beautiful word, and they all refuse it to me. So they charm themselves with their woundings and deaths. They pretend that Scaltro lives in a rhythm that will never return, and lets his appetites and failings rest in a loaded back pocket. Let me ask you, who put the ankh in the basket? Oh, ho ho, a rich harmony I have learned to sing, and perhaps I can tutor the choir. [*He replaces the basket and bowl, steps aside.*] Here we will watch for light to come again.

[SÁNÚ *and* MUSO *appear, their entrance having the appearance of a pilgrimage. A moment's stillness.*]

MUSO: You know, somewhere, there must surely exist a logicality of desire. *Ach*, the phrase seems wrong. Surely, we should speak of a logicality *in* desire. Maybe I will begin again, and escape this propositional arrogance. Say something, Sánú. Let me remind myself of how I stand here. You did recognize me from the first, didn't you? Yes, of course. How could you not? Sánú. Sánú. I would argue now from a certainty that we need to propose a theory of failure. All right. I remind you that, at that moment, which confronts us even now, you had only recently escaped a water burial in an arroyo. We ought to forget this Luttuoso who ignored the cold air drainage and the perils of winter in that valley.

SÁNÚ: Ah, Muso, you downgrade the dangers we found in that valley. Don't mishandle the point, *madre*. You came upon me when I thought I could speak about belief and command. *Et voilà*, my other self spoke to me.

MUSO: Yes, you like to confuse this external world of measure. You don't like these quarrels between *nomos* and *physis*.

SÁNÚ: Stop it with this language.

MUSO: I will. But I resent your having raised your marginal state into nobility. So there for your pilgrimage, Sánú.

SÁNÚ: But I have made fine use of my reason, Muso, to establish two domains. I thought Garbh, with his instruments and graphs, might help me establish the rule and function of these domains.

[MUSO *moves toward the basket and bowl, seemingly unaware of them.*]

MUSO: Watch your language, Sánú.

SÁNÚ: [*Adopting* MUSO's *tone.*] Watch your language, Muso.

MUSO: You do remember my initiate body.

SÁNÚ: Oh, look at me now, another assumption, another frame. No, I can only see myself embraced by those instruments that sustained me when I abandoned Garbh.

MUSO: You see now that this story begins with a calculation, a miscalculation, engendered by other voices.

SÁNÚ: You will forgive the triviality I displayed when we met.

MUSO: Of course. I have developed a distrust of self-revelation and confessions.

SÁNÚ: I hid away. I let familiar assertions carry me along a narrative path, until I grew tired of my own deception.

[*The young women enter, singing "Mori keke kan."*]

Stop it, Muso. Stop your singing.

MUSO: [*Grabbing* SÁNÚ *to steady her.*] *Calma*, Sánú. Consider that I sit on this tertiary crust with you, and I have no evidence that I have survived.

SÁNÚ: I have survived.

MUSO: [*Pointing to the singing women.*] Only if they say so.

[*The women suddenly disappear.*]

Why, they've gone. [*Calling.*] Come back here! You have nowhere to go without my body!

SÁNÚ: Don't make me embarrass you, Muso. You keep turning the earth around us. You call upon me to betray myself. You handle your divinity with such discretion. I refuse this playing with numbers.

MUSO: Scaltro…

SÁNÚ: Leave him out of it.

MUSO: Oh, I see. Such a manner of forgetfulness.

SÁNÚ: I learned from you, Muso. Or from the depth of my mind, or from the instance of my body.

MUSO: No. No, Sánú, don't give in. Pay no attention to me.

SÁNÚ: How can I do that?

MUSO: Search your domains.

[SÁNÚ *searches herself and her possessions, trying to uncover something.*]

Shall I help you?

SÁNÚ: What did you do with it? The ankh. [*She looks around.*] You lost the parchment. [*Pause.*] Yes, I get it now. A purification that Sánú will have nothing to do with.

MUSO: Watch your language, Sánú.

SÁNÚ: Oh, I do, Muso. I have really tuned my voice to your temper.

MUSO: Temper, no. Temper left with Luttuoso and Garbh.

SÁNÚ: Muso, Muso, I know they don't need me, the women. Yes. Yes. I tell myself I admire their singing. I stand under this great halo of the most celestial music. They will only remember that I walked away, and will reward my impatience by cutting me out of their lives. Save me, Muso. I have nothing left to discover in Santa Fe.

MUSO: Tell me, then, Sánú, about my losses.

SÁNÚ: [*False brightness.*] Look what I found. This cowry that seems displaced, or seems to have displaced me. Muso, I need your devastation now.

MUSO: Oh, Sánú, the weave of our singing confounds the place. Here, give me that voice that now belongs to me.

SÁNÚ: Shall we wait upon that music's return?

MUSO: We have no choice.

[SCALTRO *now comes down to them.*]

SCALTRO: Impossible. The universe remains yours to choose. I learned that from servicing the debt that lies upon me. Sánú. You know I love you. You and this angel who rides beside you. Does that surprise you, Muso? Say, your singers didn't fall for the fiction of Don Estrafalario, did they? I know you capable of negotiating an emblematic necessity that rises with that parallel singing, that dance of spirit that Luttuoso and Garbh desire, but seem willing to live without its accomplishment.

[*A movement starts in the distance.*]

Let's stand here quietly.

MUSO: Sánú, I suspect that Scaltro has hidden the ankh.

SCALTRO: Nay. But I have seen its wings fluttering about this harmony of persons that now approaches us.

[*The movement is now upon us. The young drummers lead the women,* LUTTU-OSO, SÚRÚKÚ *and* GARBH *in procession.*]

Speak to me, Sánú.

SÁNÚ: I think that we have found that bird of healing.

[*The others continue into darkness. One soft tone sounds.* SÁNÚ, MUSO *and* SCALTRO *are bathed in light.*]

The plays in this volume were selected by Jay Wright.

Not being in the habit of dating his compositions, Jay Wright's plays are difficult to fit neatly onto a timeline. The plays in this volume date mostly from recent years. A version of *The Hunt and Double Night of the Wood* was finished in 1983 but extensively revised in 2003. *Passage* was written the following year. *The Playing Space, Lemma, Syntax,* and *Aria* were each completed by 2015. All of the plays reproduced here have never before been published.

All inquiries concerning rights for the plays in this volume should be addressed to:

Jay Wright
PO Box 361
Bradford, VT 05033

(802)222-5286

SELECTED BACKLIST

Juana I, by Ana Arzoumanian, translated by Gabriel Amor

The Kenning Anthology of Poets Theater: 1945-1985,
   edited by David Brazil and Kevin Killian

PQRS: A Poets Theater Script, by Patrick Durgin

Hieroglyphs of the Inverted World, by Rob Halpern

The Chilean Flag, by Elvira Hernández, translated by Alec Schumacher

título / title, by Legna Rodríguez Iglesias, translated by
   Katherine M. Hedeen

Stage Fright: Plays from San Francisco Poets Theater, by Kevin Killian

There Three, by Devin King

Dream of Europe: Selected Seminars and Interviews: 1984-1992,
   by Audre Lorde, edited by Mayra Rodriguez Castro

Tomatoes, by Nathalie Quintane, translated by Marty Hiatt

Festivals of Patience: The Verse Poems of Arthur Rimbaud,
   translated by Brian Kim Stefans

The Dirty Text, by Soleida Ríos, translated by
   Barbara Jamison and Olivia Lott

Several Rotations, by Jesse Seldess

Hannah Weiner's Open House, by Hannah Weiner,
   edited by Patrick Durgin

Coronavirus Haiku, by Worker Writers School, edited by Mark Nowak